Sir Isaac Pitman.
Memorial Portrait by A. S. Cope, A.R.A.

THE LIFE OF
SIR ISAAC PITMAN

(INVENTOR OF PHONOGRAPHY)

BY

ALFRED BAKER, F.J.I.

CENTENARY EDITION

LONDON: SIR ISAAC PITMAN & SONS, LTD.
No. 1 AMEN CORNER, E.C. ❧ ❧ ❧ 1913

First Published 1908
Second (Centenary) Edition 1913
Republished 1980, being a near facsimile
of the second edition

PRINTED BY SIR ISAAC PITMAN
& SONS, LTD., LONDON, BATH,
MELBOURNE AND NEW YORK

ISBN 0 273 01587 7

Text of introduction set in Monotype Old Style.
Printed by photolithography and bound in
Great Britain at The Pitman Press, Bath

HO (s.2035:26)

TO

THE RIGHT HON. THE EARL OF ROSEBERY

K.G., K.T.,

PRESIDENT OF THE

FIRST INTERNATIONAL SHORTHAND CONGRESS

HELD IN LONDON IN 1887

THIS VOLUME

IS INSCRIBED WITH HIS LORDSHIP'S

KIND PERMISSION

PREFACE

In the illustrious roll of inventors who have in our own age conferred great and varied benefits on their country, the name of Sir Isaac Pitman occupies a unique position, as the originator of a method of brief writing as widely used as the language in which it is written. His bold experiment of giving to the world a system of shorthand having an absolutely phonetic basis was an immediate success, and for over seventy years it has proved of inestimable service for every purpose for which a written record is desired, and has become the standard method of English shorthand. He did not live to see success attend his proposals for a drastic reform of English spelling on a strictly phonetic basis. But it is only just to his memory to point out that, to his work as a pioneer, is to a large extent due the revived interest in simplified spelling manifested in our own time.

The life story of Sir Isaac Pitman has been related in many forms, but not hitherto with the completeness which has been attempted in the present volume. The author's thanks are due to Sir Isaac's family for placing at his disposal all the personal records in their possession. Mr. Henry Pitman, younger brother of the Inventor of Phonography, gave valuable information on many points. From the writings of Mr.

Benn Pitman assistance was derived in relation to his early reminiscences of his brother. The " Biography of Isaac Pitman," written by Mr. T. A. Reed in 1890, comprises a large amount of information which would not have been recorded at all but for his industrious pen, and this work has of necessity been freely drawn on.

Thanks are tendered to the proprietors of *Punch* for permission to reproduce the cartoon on page 219 ; to Mr. George Lansdown, of the *Wiltshire Times*, Trowbridge, for permission to reproduce a rare drawing of the school attended by Sir Isaac Pitman ; to Mr. F. H. Fisher (editor of the *Literary World*) for permission to quote the " In Memoriam " sonnet ; and to Mr. A. T. Donald, for assistance with the bibliography.

A. B.

Dec., 1908.

PREFACE TO CENTENARY EDITION

ADVANTAGE has been taken of the issue of the present second, or Centenary Edition, to make a few additions and corrections. It is hoped that these will add to the value of the " Life " to all interested in the Pitman Centenary of 1913.

A. B.

Jan., 1913.

CONTENTS

vii

PLATES

ILLUSTRATIONS

INTRODUCTION
BY SIR JAMES PITMAN
K.B.E.

I HAVE written an introduction to this reissue of
Alfred Baker's *Life of Sir Isaac Pitman* because it
has been one of three very important books in my
life and, as I know too, in the lives of many others
who have been inspired from reading about Isaac
Pitman and all he did and stood for.

I was once asked by the late George Bernard
Shaw to tea at his house at Ayot St Laurence. He
referred throughout the whole afternoon to "the
great Sir Isaac".

I cannot do better in providing an introduction
than to draw upon some parts of a speech I made in
the centenary year of 1937.

In Bath Abbey, England, there is a lovely
memorial to my grandfather in the form of a tablet
upon which the inscription reads –

IN MEMORY OF
SIR ISAAC PITMAN KT
1813–1897
INVENTOR OF PITMAN'S SHORTHAND

His aims were steadfast, his mind
original, his work prodigious, the achievement
world-wide. His life was ordered in
service to God and duty to man.

xiii

The Lord is good . . .
His truth endureth to all generations.

Isaac Pitman made his mark in that all *his aims were steadfast*. I suggest that he had two main aims.

Firstly it was education, and secondly, as an important part of education, reading and writing; because communication is the essence of human behaviour.

My grandfather was devoted to education. He believed that the Kingdom of God on Earth would come about only by the development of education, and that education was dependent upon communication, which in turn was speech in language, and literacy in reading and writing. In the course of his work he devoted his interest first of all to writing, and in 1837 at the age of 24 – a very young age indeed – he invented Pitman's Shorthand.

His mind was original. He saw what an appalling waste of time longhand was. He asked the fundamental question why need there be such a great disparity in speed between speech and writing? Written communication did not need to be six times as slow as speech. He also appreciated, with that original mind of his, that writing had been fixed for over 2,000 years; moreover it had been Latin, not English, as the language around which the alphabet had been designed; and that writing had become fixed in the Roman form. He appreciated, too, that longhand was longhand because it had been designed by those Romans for the purpose of carving in stone and not for writing quickly on paper.

The second point of his originality of mind was that he realized that we needed to have enough characters for the sounds of the English language. Isaac's concept was absolutely brilliant in that if we were to have a quicker system of writing then we would need to devise appropriate characters to match the 40 sounds of the English language.

The third point of his originality was that he realized that there was a value in what I call "syllabic" writing; that it was not necessary to restrict writing to the writing of only one letter at a time, one sound at a time; and that you could write a sign for a number of sounds which together made a syllable. This brilliant economy in writing makes possible the daily "miracles" which are seen to happen in the Law Courts and in Parliaments throughout the world, in which the record of what the human voice has spoken is placed on paper as fast as it is uttered. All that is needed is a pencil and a piece of paper and a personal accomplishment, and this fundamental disparity can be overcome. The persistence of the desire to learn shorthand and the joy in practising it, spring, and will continue to spring, from this new capacity to write quickly.

The challenge of Sir Isaac's life is still: Will mankind permanently accept this ratio of only one-sixth of the speed of speech? Roughly we write in longhand at 20 to 30 words a minute and speak at 120 to 180 words a minute. Pitman's shorthand is easily capable of that latter speed.

I have dealt with writing. Now might I deal shortly with reading longhand? Here again, his original mind grasped the real issues. He saw that there was a fundamental untruth. If we were to retain our longhand alphabet for the purpose of reading alphabetically, he appreciated that to spell OUGHT with an OU, to spell ONCE with an ON and to spell ANY with an AN, and SWAN with the same AN, was a disruptive violation of the alphabetic system. With over 2,000 differing spellings for only 40 sounds our spelling is clearly full of lies. He saw that the Roman alphabet, if it were to begin to tell the truth, would need at least 17 augmentations, in order to make the existing 26 characters (or 23 if the superfluous letters c q x are omitted) up to the 40 necessary to match the number of the sounds in the language to be read.

Why is there, we must ask ourselves, this contrast between the obvious success of his work for quicker writing and the apparent failure of his work for easier learning of reading?

I believe there are three reasons. First of all, that faster writing appeals to us because it benefits us, those who already read and write. Secondly, that easier learning benefits only those who have not yet learned to read. Let us face it, infants do not have votes and those more elderly, who have failed to learn, have no influence; so the difficulties of learning are ignored and submerged because there is no voice to call attention to them, and no desire on the part of those who already read and write to consider the plight of those who have not yet learnt or of those who have tried and failed. The third reason has been failure to recognize that changes in *form* do not matter. The conveyance of meaning is the *only* purpose. Moreover, if the changes in form are only temporary and not destructive of meaning, and are later abandoned, they ought to be used for learning. After all, many changes, and in major degree, have not only been tolerated but are now fiercely defended. We have changed the original Roman alphabet already twice and in consequence have no less than 10 variant forms of even the short word "bag"

BAG, Bag, Bɑg, bag, bɑg, *bag*, bɑg, bag, Bɑg, Bag

The social consequences of his life have been, or will yet be great. First of all, with much quicker writing, change has undoubtedly meant the emancipation of women. So long as a woman had to go begging her father or husband – "May I have some money to spend?" she was not a free woman. The moment she was earning her own money away from the roof of her menfolk – and she did so earn it through shorthand, and eventually typewriting – it was her money to spend and she became a person of independent mind, thought and action. Secondly, there has been, and is, his influence upon evening-class study. The evening institutes in Britain have been fed by the motivation to write more quickly and to earn money. Shorthand has brought literally millions of people to study intensively not only shorthand but also in the process the English language. Thirdly, in the Law, the Press and Business, shorthand has been of very great utility. A strike by all shorthand writers would be paralysing. Fourthly, the simplification of learning to read and write can be very helpful to our ordered Society. His proposals will come in time greatly to reduce class division – the division between those who can read and those who cannot: it will alleviate juvenile delinquency and crime. Ninety per cent of those in Borstals, Remand Homes and Prisons cannot read with understanding. They have failed and lost all self-esteem, man's essential need second only to bread. Finally, there is English as a world language. What Isaac Pitman did in the past will undoubtedly foster the spread of our great English language and increase the speed at which the world develops a common language.

His work was prodigious and that was, I think, because underlying his whole life and purpose was his tremendous religious faith. That final text in the Memorial at Bath reads: "The Lord is good . . . His truth endureth to all generations". It was part of one of his shorthand exercises in the first shorthand book that he published. It epitomizes his attitude and what he has achieved and will yet achieve.

THE LIFE OF
SIR ISAAC PITMAN

I

SIR ISAAC PITMAN, the inventor of the most widely used system of English Shorthand, and a lifelong advocate of Spelling Reform, was born on Monday, the 4th January, 1813. His birthplace was Trowbridge, in Wiltshire, but his parents were natives of Taunton, in the neighbouring county of Somerset, and his family name is one which has been borne with distinction by several West Country men. The father of the future shorthand author was Samuel Pitman; his mother's maiden name was Maria Davis. They migrated from Taunton soon after their marriage in 1808, and made their home at Trowbridge. This town has been engaged for many centuries in cloth manufacture, and as Samuel Pitman was by trade a hand-loom weaver, the reason of his settlement there is sufficiently obvious. For the next twenty years he acted as overseer of the cloth factory of Mr. James Edgell. He was an excellent business man, and had the satisfaction of managing a very prosperous undertaking. There can be no doubt that he possessed

more than average ability, and the recollections
of his children and friends reveal an individuality
as well worthy of biographical notice as an example
of a typical Englishman of the middle class, as
many on whom fortune showered more favours,
or circumstances brought into greater prominence.
Much that is distinctive in the character of Isaac
Pitman he owed to heredity, and some account,
therefore, of the influence which his father exercised may appropriately precede the story of his
son's life.   It should be added that the influence
of Isaac Pitman's mother was, in some respects,
equally important.   To her may be traced the
deep affection which united the family of eleven
children to their parents and to each other.   Of
this affection the family correspondence, which has
been preserved, furnishes abundant testimony.

Samuel Pitman had so little regular school
instruction that he thought it hardly worthy of
mention, but by self-education he attained to
considerable ability in some branches of knowledge.   He made a thorough study of astronomy,
and acquired the skill necessary to calcu-
late eclipses and other celestial phenomena.
The imaginary science of astrology was largely
cultivated in his time, and he was a diligent student
of Ebenezer Sibly's erudite quarto volume, " A
New and Complete Illustration of the Celestial
Science of Astrology."   As each of his children
was born he cast the infant's horoscope, which
was duly inscribed in the family Bible.   An

additional copy of the horoscopes of both parents and children was also made by him, and has been preserved in the family. In the case of his son Isaac, the horoscope did not indicate in any way

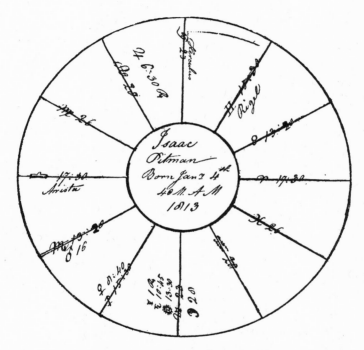

FACSIMILE OF SAMUEL PITMAN'S HOROSCOPE OF HIS
SON ISAAC

his future greatness as a shorthand inventor, and possibly this was one of the reasons which led Pitman père in later years to abandon his faith in the " celestial science." At a time when books were scarce and hard to obtain he was a diligent reader, and when he returned to his home after the discharge of the many active duties which formed his day's work, a book was invariably the companion of his leisure hours. He was consequently well informed, and his studies, coupled with his observation of life, made him tolerant in matters of religion. A man of sincere conviction in regard to the truths of Christianity, he practised his faith with conspicuous impartiality and broad-mindedness.

Each member of his family of seven sons and four daughters was baptised in infancy at the parish church of St. James, Trowbridge, the christening of his son Isaac taking place on the 11th April following his birth. Soon after this event, the Rev. George Crabbe, the poet, received his last clerical preferment, and was inducted Rector of Trowbridge on the 3rd June, 1814. Under the parson poet, Samuel Pitman became superintendent of the Church Sunday School, which Isaac and his brothers attended either as scholars or teachers. Their mother, who was a sincerely religious woman, and of a singularly equable temperament and kindly disposition, was a Baptist, and the family attended with her at Zion Chapel, which was not in its earlier days equipped with a Sunday School. Through the exertions of Samuel Pitman and others this defect was made good, and he became superintendent of this school, his eldest son Jacob and his next son Isaac acting as teachers there. On alternate

SAMUEL PITMAN
(*Father of the Inventor of Phonography*)

SCHOOL ATTENDED BY ISAAC PITMAN AT TROWBRIDGE

*(From a contemporary drawing in the possession of Mr. George
Lansdown of the "Wiltshire Times," Trowbridge)*

Sundays father and sons continued to discharge similar duties at the older school established in association with the parish church.

The interest of Samuel Pitman in educational advancement unquestionably had a great influence on the future career of his son Isaac. At this period, more than half-a-century before the Education Act of 1870, almost the only provision for popular education in England was in the form of the parochial charity school. But three years before Samuel Pitman settled at Trowbridge, Joseph Lancaster's efforts had resulted in the formation of the great society, which in a few years established throughout the land institutions designed for the children of the masses, and popularly known as British Schools. In Trowbridge the movement found an earnest pioneer in Samuel Pitman, through whose instrumentality subscriptions were obtained and a large school-house built, which, if not the first, was one of the earliest in the West of England. A few years later the infant school movement arose, and he promoted a scheme which brought the Pestalozzian system within the reach of the children of his fellow townsmen.

In another branch of social reform Samuel Pitman was a pioneer, namely, that of temperance —a good many years before the time when the men of Preston enriched the English language with the word " teetotal." Nearly half-a-century before free libraries were heard of in England,

Samuel Pitman—again well in advance of his age —had established a library for the work-people at his cloth factory, together with a reading-room. Interested as he was in these movements for the general welfare, he was in his home an excellent father, and not only set a good example there to his sons and daughters, but while firm and just in the discharge of the duties of the head of the family, he made use of all means which lay at hand for their moral and intellectual improvement.

Isaac Pitman was born in a house at the rear of the King of Prussia Inn, Trowbridge, which was many years ago pulled down, but his child-hood was spent at the next home of the Pitman family in the town, namely, Nos. 44 and 45 Timbrell Street. The testimony of his brothers shows that in his early youth he began to exhibit those mental and moral characteristics which were distinctive of his later life. His younger brother, Benn, says, " Isaac in his youth was of a diligent and studious habit. He was of a sensitive nature, inclined to be thoughtful, regarding life and its duties as matters of grave concern." His elder brother, Jacob, observes, " Isaac never had any of that rollicking nonsense about him peculiar to most of us boys, nor do I remember his ever stopping on his way from school to play, but home directly he went, either to his books or to his work." In the Pitman family the greatest regularity and punctuality were observed in regard to the daily round of duties ; the children were not permitted to loiter in the streets, and any infringement of regulations was followed by chastisement, administered by Pitman père with a strap. Recreative exercise was not, however, neglected, and took the form of country walks, and bathing and swimming ; in the last named pursuit his brother Benn bears record that Isaac showed courage and even daring.

The school days of Isaac Pitman began and ended at a comparatively early age. He received, he tells us, the rudiments of an English education in a day school of his native town : " From a list of the names of his pupils, kept by the master, Mr. Nightingale, it appears that Isaac Pitman left school on 8th October, 1825, in the thirteenth year of his age. The school contained from eighty to 100 boys, and the size of the schoolroom was about 25 ft. by 15 ft., and 8 ft. or 9 ft. high. A raised desk was placed against the wall on the window side of the building, high enough to allow of half-moon standing classes underneath. In the small space afforded by this high desk, and on the floor of the room about 100 boys were crowded together. The air was consequently so vitiated that young Pitman was frequently obliged to leave the schoolroom and go into the fresh air to recover from a fainting fit. His school days were thus early closed in consequence of these faintings. No one suspected that the schoolroom was in fault—so little were sanitary conditions of life then considered."

In a note to the above account Isaac Pitman records that the "fresh air" into which he was taken was "the churchyard, lying between the school and the church." This was, in fact, used as a playground by the scholars, and Benn Pitman has recollections of the games which were played by them among the monuments of the departed, "over which the boys chased each other in wildest glee." On Sundays the schoolroom was used as the Church Sunday School, to which reference has already been made.

The early termination of his school days was sincerely regretted by Isaac Pitman. He was at once initiated as a clerk in the counting-house of Mr. Edgell's cloth manufactory, and after a short experience there earnestly begged his father to allow him to return to school and resume his lessons, but the latter did not see his way to accede to his son's request. He advised Isaac to continue his studies at home, and indeed provided the means for doing so. Although the office hours were from six in the morning to six at night, the young clerk found time for systematic study. He and his brother Jacob rose at four each morning, and devoted nearly two hours to their books, till they left home to begin the duties of the day, and in the evening they gave one or two hours to study. It occasionally happened that there was no work to be done in the early morning at the factory office, and Isaac used such opportunities for study in the open air.

ST. JAMES'S CHURCH, TROWBRIDGE

(The site of the school attended by Isaac Pitman is the open space
in the foreground)

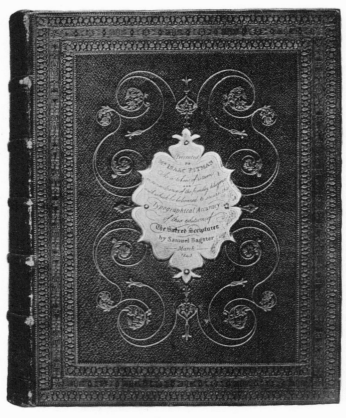

"COMPREHENSIVE BIBLE" PRESENTED TO ISAAC PITMAN
BY MR. SAMUEL BAGSTER

Among the authors who had a great influence in the formation of his habits and character was Isaac Watts, whose work on " The Improvement of the Mind " was a favourite volume of his early days. The well-known lines of this writer were especially applicable to Isaac Pitman :

> In books, or works, or healthful play,
>   Let my first years be past,
> That I may give for every day
>   Some good account at last.

There were two periods in the family history when Samuel Pitman arranged an evening school for his children, securing as instructor Miss New, a lady of good general culture and musical ability, who was daughter of the only bookseller in Trowbridge. Instruction was imparted in English subjects and in music. Music lessons were given for a considerable time to the young Pitmans on an antiquated triangular harpsichord. When some proficiency had been acquired in fingering, their father bought a Broadwood pianoforte of five-and-a-half octaves, to the keen delight of his son Isaac, who had from his early years a great fondness for music ; books and music, as he once observed, were his " two loves." At a later period a pair of globes was obtained, and Isaac profited by this addition to the means of instruction to such an extent that in subsequent years he was very successful in his school work in demonstrations by the " use of the globes."

Some of the particulars of Isaac Pitman's work of self-education recorded above are drawn from Mr. Thomas Allen Reed's " Biography." As this is the only account of this important period, we here make further extracts (revised by the subject of this narrative), which exhibit the young student unconsciously laying the foundations of his life work. " One of the books," Mr. Reed says, " which he made his companion in morning walks into the country, was ' Lennie's Grammar.' The conjugations of verbs, lists of irregular verbs, adverbs, prepositions, and conjunctions, and the thirty-six rules of syntax, he committed to memory, so that he could repeat them *seriatim*. The study of this book gave him a transparent English style. There was also a local library to which his father subscribed, one of the earliest lending libraries established in the country, and Isaac was one of its most diligent readers." " I went regularly to the library for fresh supplies of books," he observed in the course of a speech delivered at Manchester in 1868, " and thus read most of the English classics. I think I was quite as familiar with Addison, and Sir Roger, and Will Honeycomb, and all the club, as I was with my own brothers and sisters . . . . and when reading the ' Spectator ' at that early age I wished that I might be able to do something in letters." The perusal of the " Iliad " at this time gave him great delight. In addition to the lending library, occasional parcels of books were obtained from London,

Samuel Pitman having the advantage of buying them from the publishing house of Tegg, 73 Cheapside, at discount prices. Of this privilege Jacob Pitman says that his father " availed himself to a large extent, purchasing a number of books which he had never seen before, and this gave a great impetus to our studies."

" Isaac was in the habit," Mr. Reed tells us, " from the age of twelve, of copying choice pieces of poetry and portions of Scripture into a little book which he kept in his pocket, for the purpose of committing them to memory. Two of these little pocket albums have been preserved. Their contents are very various. One contains extracts from Pope, Milton, Cowper, James Montgomery, the Psalms, and Isaiah, interspersed with the Greek alphabet, the Signs of the Zodiac, arithmetical tables, and other items of useful information. This book is dated 31st May, 1825. The penmanship is extremely neat and distinct. A later pocket companion contains a neatly-written copy of Valpy's Greek Grammar, as far as the Syntax, which he committed to memory ; a chronological table, etc. In his morning walks [in 1832] he committed to memory the first fourteen chapters of Proverbs. He would not undertake a fresh chapter until he had repeated the preceding one without hesitation.

" Up to the age of sixteen he greatly increased his knowledge of books ; but he rarely had the opportunity of intercourse with educated persons.

One result of this was that, while familiar enough
with written words and their meaning, he was at
fault with regard to their pronunciation. A large
portion of the language of books he had never
heard in conversation, or at school, and the mis-
leading or ambiguous spellings of these words
often led him to pronounce them (mentally)
inaccurately. Happily, he was conscious of this
defect, and did his best to remedy it. Of many
hundred words, known by the eye only as dumb
symbols, he learned the accentuation by his
reading and passionate love of ' Paradise Lost.'
With characteristic energy and thoroughness, he
set himself a task, which to most persons would
be little less than repulsive, and which probably
few have undertaken. He carefully read through
Walker's Dictionary, with the double object of
extending his knowledge of words, and of correcting his errors in orthoepy. The words which he
thus discovered that he had mentally mispronounced were copied out with their proper diacritic
symbols of pronunciation. They numbered about
two thousand, and their correct pronunciation
had to be fixed in the memory by repetition. The
chief difficulty in this task lay in the fact that a
false pronunciation or accentuation had to be
unlearned. This reading of Walker was made
at about the age of seventeen. He read through
the book a second time, with the same object."
[In 1832-6.]

Soon after the first study of Walker, " With

that instinctive love of knowledge common to boys," Isaac Pitman says, " I began to study shorthand. I saw that it would be a great advantage to write six times as fast as I had been accustomed to, and I borrowed a book, read it through, copied the alphabet and ' arbitrary words,' and have written shorthand ever since." The story of his mastery and use of the stenographic art will be more conveniently narrated when we come to describe the invention of Phonography.

Isaac Pitman continued to hold the position of clerk in Mr. Edgell's factory until his father, in the year 1829 (when the subject of this biography was about sixteen years old), began business as a cloth manufacturer on his own account, and installed his son in the counting-house. The family moved to a house in Silver Street, Trowbridge, having a cloth factory adjoining it.   Isaac fulfilled the duties of clerk in his father's office until August, 1831, when he was a little more than eighteen and a half years old.   At that time his father, who, as we have already seen, was greatly interested in the movement for providing popular education, decided that Isaac should become a school teacher under the British School system. This selection of a profession for Isaac Pitman was the originating cause of his life's work, for it brought him in contact with those whose influence on his career was nothing short of remarkable.   In accordance with his father's decision, he was sent to the Borough

Road Training College of the British and Foreign School Society. Here he underwent a five months' training, and at the end of this time left the College, just after he had completed his nineteenth birthday, to take up his first appointment. The preparation was brief in point of time, but the young graduate was apt, and his training invested him for the rest of his life with all the best attributes of the schoolmaster, so that down to his latest years there was about him much that was distinctive of the manner and methods of the preceptor of youth. When Samuel Pitman applied personally to the Training College for the admission of another son, the Head Master, Mr. Henry Dunn, in granting his request, said, " You may send me as many more of your children as you can spare." Accordingly, in later years, five other members of the Pitman family were received at the Training College, namely, Jacob and Joseph of the boys, and Rosella, Jane, and Mary of the girls. All of these afterwards received appointments to schools in different parts of England.

As references to the various members of the Pitman family will occur in subsequent chapters of this Life, the present is a convenient opportunity for introducing them to the reader.

Samuel Pitman (b. 12 Sept., 1787, d. 2 Dec., 1863), married on 17 April, 1808, Maria Davis (b. 1784, d. 2 July, 1854). After the death of his first wife he married in 1857 Eliza Darton, relative

of a London publisher of that name. The children
of Samuel and Maria Pitman were as under :

Melissa (Mrs. Prior, later Mrs. Jones), b. 1809,
d. 1864.

Jacob, b. 1810, d. 1890.

Isaac, b. 1813, d. 1897.

Abraham, b. 1814, d. 1829.

Rosella, b. 1816, d. 1898.

Joseph, b. 1818, d. 1895.

Jane (Mrs. Hunt), b. 1820, d. 1896.

Benjamin (Benn), b. 1822, d. 1910.

Mary (Mrs. Webster), b. 1824, d. 1912.

Henry, b. 1826, d. 1909.

Frederick, b. 1828, d. 1886.

II

1832-1835

THE year which witnessed the passing of the
Reform Bill, saw Isaac Pitman enter on the
duties of his first appointment. Almost at the
end of his career, in a letter to Mr. Gladstone, he
reminded the veteran statesman of a coincidence
in their personal history : " We commenced our
public life," he wrote, " in the same year, 1832,
you as Member for Newark and I as Master of the
British School at Barton-on-Humber." Barton
is a small market town in North Lincolnshire,
six miles south-west of Hull, and the young schoolmaster arrived there on the 20th January. Many
a man who has been the architect of his own fortune
is proud to be able to boast that he began life
with the proverbial half-crown in his pocket. In
the case of Isaac Pitman the amount his purse
contained when he alighted from the coach to
take over his first charge was no more than three
half-crowns. With praiseworthy exactitude he
kept in a small pocket-book a complete record of
his income and expenditure from the date when
he began life at Barton. This account reveals the
above fact, and from it we are able to see with
what scrupulous promptitude he discharged every
liability he incurred, and out of his slender means

16

contributed to various useful objects. More than one entry bears eloquent testimony to the need of postal reform. Whenever a " letter from home " arrived, it cost its recipient the sum of 1s. 1d. !

The position to which Isaac Pitman was appointed was that of Master of what was known as Long's School, from the fact that the funds came from an educational bequest by an individual of that name. As the trustees at this time conducted the school in association with the Society which sent the Master to Barton, it became also known as the British School. The number of boys was about 120. The new Master began his duties at a salary of £70 a year, which was afterwards raised to £80. From the testimony of some of his old scholars, intelligent and trustworthy men, it is evident that he created a very favourable impression in Barton by his conduct and ability. One cherished till his latest years a prize volume awarded to him at the British School bearing an inscription in the Master's handwriting, and another had in his old age as vivid a recollection of the instruction imparted to him by the Master as he had when in early life he attended the old school (many years since converted into dwelling houses). Shorthand was not taught in the school, but by the aid of the blackboard Isaac Pitman trained the scholars in methods of correct pronunciation. The Lancastrian methods of education appear to have had the charm of novelty in this remote town, and the

circumstance lingered in the recollection of his
old schoolboys that the marching, which formed
part of the system, was done to the accompani-
ment of the Master's flute. Like many distinguished men who could be named, Isaac Pitman
found great delight in early life in playing this
instrument. In respect of discipline he is described
as having been in a mild way a martinet. He
seems, however, to have made little use of the
cane. Incorrigible boys were dealt with by
detention after school hours, and the tasks then
imposed had to be carried out under the eye of
the Master.

Outside his school Isaac Pitman appears to
have been active in his efforts for the mental
and moral improvement of the inhabitants of
Barton.   He gave popular lectures on astronomy,
and his addresses on this subject seem to have
been highly appreciated.   He took a lively interest
in Temperance Reform, directing his attack on
the use of ardent spirits.   A Temperance Society
was formed at Barton, under the regulations of
the British and Foreign Temperance Society,
and he filled the post of secretary. Work was
commenced by the circulation to every house-
holder of a tract written by Isaac Pitman, dated
5th November, 1834, in which the evils of intem-
perance were described in vigorous language.
The tract was headed " Gin, Rum, Brandy, and
Whisky," and the opening sentences were calculated
to arrest attention.   Its author wrote :   " Ardent

spirits, pure or mixed, are pronounced by the highest authorities in our land to be evil spirits. This is not generally believed : faith is weak because knowledge is imperfect. Not till lately has the old-fashioned falsity been exploded, that ' a comfortable glass does one good.' Sir Astley Cooper says, ' Spirits and poisons are synonymous terms.' " An appeal was especially made to Christians to aid in the work. In those early days of temperance advocacy, the tract caused some stir at Barton, and the views set forth in it met with opposition. A Nonconformist minister, residing in the neighbourhood, published some strictures on it. But it happened that these were circulated before the original had been sent out to the public, and consequently Isaac Pitman utilized the blank leaf of his tract for the purpose of replying to his too eager opponent. From that time his interest in the Temperance Reformation never abated.

He attended the services at the Methodist place of worship, and on 19th April, three months after his arrival, he was admitted on trial into the Wesleyan Methodist Society, Barton Circuit. After nearly three years' membership, his name was placed on the plan of circuit preachers for 1835-6. This plan Isaac Pitman wrote out with copper-plate neatness on an extremely minute scale, and it is interesting to notice among the names that of one who was in frequent communication with him in later years, namely, the Rev. Joseph

Hudson, who took orders in the Church of England, and was for many years Vicar of Dodworth, near Barnsley.

In the course of his ministrations at the villages around Barton, Isaac Pitman, in October, 1835, conducted the services in the Methodist chapel at Ulceby, and he there saw for the first time a copy of Bagster's " Comprehensive Bible," in the house of his host, Mr. John Hay, a substantial farmer. Hitherto the young schoolmaster had used for his private reading the well-known octavo Reference Bible, issued by the Bible Society, which had been presented to him by the Committee of the Borough Road College. A careful study of this volume had led to the discovery of certain errors in the references, and as he was desirous of ascertaining whether the " Comprehensive " repeated any of these mistakes, he borrowed the volume and took it home with a view to instituting a comparison. He found that of thirty-eight errors, which he had detected in the Bible Society's edition, fifteen appeared in the " Comprehensive." A letter was addressed to the Bible Society giving a list of the thirty-eight errors. Though the communication was not acknowledged, the Society in subsequent years corrected the errors which had been pointed out in their Reference Bible.

On the same date he wrote to Mr. Samuel Bagster, the founder of the well-known publishing house of Bagster & Son, whose publications in association with the Holy Scriptures, it has been well said, "earned for him the esteem of all Biblical scholars." As this letter brought Isaac Pitman in touch with one whose influence on his life work was very considerable, it will be of interest to relate the circumstances which led to their early acquaintance. The communication addressed to Mr. Bagster was dated 15th October, and called attention to the errors which the writer had discovered in references in the "Comprehensive Bible." "I have made it my custom," Isaac Pitman said, "for two or three years in my morning and evening reading of Scripture, to refer to every parallel place ; in some measure appreciating the value of the plan. If you would like to place a copy of your Bible under my care, to be considered your property, I would make a constant and careful use of it, and give you the benefit of the corrections and mistakes which I might discover in reading it through."

The next coach from London brought a prompt reply from Mr. Bagster, accompanied by a copy of his "Comprehensive Bible," and subsequently a second copy, divided into seven portions, each to be returned when read, was forwarded at Isaac Pitman's suggestion. Some idea of the magnitude of the self-imposed task may be gathered from the fact that the marginal references in the work amount to a total of five hundred thousand. The young schoolmaster made a careful estimate of the amount of reading and revision he could accomplish daily, and came to the conclusion that he could complete the undertaking in three years from the latter part of October, 1835 ; as a matter of fact he reached the end well within that period, for it was in August, 1838, that the work was finished. Moreover, these were years in the life of the reviser when hindrances were to manifest themselves that he could not at this time anticipate, which, with any less steadfast worker, would have effectually brought all progress to a standstill. Benn Pitman states that at least five thousand hours of the closest mental and physical application were devoted to this revision, and that it was religiously pursued every day till completed. Mr. Bagster, he also tells us, offered to pay any sum which Isaac Pitman might name for his services, but the ardent searcher of the Scriptures would take nothing. To a friend who suggested that he ought to accept payment he replied, " I offered to do the work freely ; and, of course, I would not now accept anything for it ; it has been a great satisfaction and a benefit to me ; but now, when I want to give my whole attention to my Phonetic Shorthand, I am only too grateful that it is completed."

These laborious investigations resulted in the discovery of at least one error per page, sometimes more, in the references, and when the Bible was afterwards printed with all these emendations duly made, the grateful publisher presented to his voluntary helper a superbly bound copy of the large edition of the " Comprehensive Bible," on the cover of which was a silver plate bearing this inscription : " Presented to Mr. Isaac Pitman as a token of esteem, and in remembrance of the friendly diligence with which he laboured to secure the Typographical Accuracy of this edition of the Sacred Scriptures, by Samuel Bagster, March, 1843." The Bible revision had resulted in a lasting friendship between publisher and reviser, and had, as will be seen later, a very important bearing on the invention and propagation of Phonography.

At Chapel Brigg (Glamford Briggs) on 5th January, 1835, Isaac Pitman was married to Mrs. Mary Holgate, a lady of good birth and education, the widow of Mr. George Holgate, solicitor, of Barton. Her late husband had left her an income for life, so that Isaac Pitman and his wife were able to establish a well-appointed home, such as would have been impossible on the slender stipend of his scholastic post.

III

1836-1837

In the ancient Gloucestershire town of Wotton-under-Edge, lying at the foot of the Cotswold Hills, and situated in a district famous alike for its scenery and its associations, a number of the inhabitants—in emulation, no doubt, of what was being done elsewhere—decided to provide facilities for popular education. A Nonconformist school committee was formed, and at the invitation of this body Isaac Pitman, in January, 1836, went from Barton to take up the duties of Master at the new British School established at Wotton. The salary was the same, and the school was of similar size. Personal reasons appear to have strongly influenced him in making the change. His elder brother, Jacob, had married and settled in a pleasant house with grounds, situated at North Nibley, not far distant from Wotton, and here Jacob's wife, who had formerly been a governess, conducted a ladies' school. Isaac was glad of the opportunity of residing near his brother, and within easy distance of the rest of his family. His younger brothers, Benn and Henry, lived with him at Wotton and attended his school.

It was about this period that Samuel Pitman

24

KINGSTON HOUSE (OR THE HALL), BRADFORD-ON-AVON

ISAAC PITMAN'S SECOND SCHOOL AT WOTTON-UNDER-EDGE

removed his weaving business from Trowbridge to the neighbouring town of Bradford-on-Avon (where water power could be utilized), and for some years occupied Kingston House. This famous structure, which Aubrey described as "the best house for the quality of a gentleman in all Wiltshire," was built towards the end of the sixteenth century. The architect is unknown, but the design has been ascribed to John of Padua. After it ceased to be the home of the Pitman family, it was used as a farm-house, but passing into the hands of Mr. Stephen Moulton in 1848, was admirably restored, and is now justly admired as a fine example of the architectural taste of the period in which it was built.

The length of Isaac Pitman's residence at Wotton was three years and a half, and in many respects this was the most important epoch of his life, for its whole course and aims were determined by what then happened. In the present chapter we propose to deal with the earlier portion of these eventful years only, namely, the period of less than two years which preceded the invention of Phonography.

Very little either in the nature of narrative or anecdote is now obtainable concerning Isaac Pitman's conduct of his second British School. In the turmoil which arose over the religious difficulty referred to below, his educational work seems to have been all but forgotten. But that it was very successful the following facts will

show. The School Committee engaged a " long
room " called " The Folly," in Sim Lane ; for
about a year the school was conducted in this
room, when it was found necessary, in consequence
of the increase in the number of scholars, to remove
to larger premises. These were found in the
first floor of a disused factory in what was known
as " The Steep," at the bottom of Long Street,
a building which afterwards became a Church
Institute.

The change in Isaac Pitman's religious convictions which led to the " difficulty," came about
under the following circumstances. In his journey
from the North to Gloucestershire, he made the
acquaintance on the coach between Birmingham
and Wotton, of Mr. John Kingwell Bragg, of
Clifton, an uncle of a well-known Birmingham
citizen. Mr. Bragg says, in a published letter,
that his stage-coach companion led the way to a
conversation on religious subjects and authors,
and " I ventured at length to ask him," he goes on,
" if he had ever read any of the writings of
Swedenborg." The young schoolmaster replied
that he had read with delight a work by the Rev.
John Clowes (Rector of St. John's, Manchester),
in which some of the doctrines of the Swedish
seer were explained, but confessed that prejudice
had prevented him from studying the revelations
at first hand in the works of the author. A
fortnight later Isaac Pitman paid a visit to Mr.
Bragg, when the works of Swedenborg were

further discussed.   A correspondence ensued, beginning with a letter dated 9th February, 1836,
from Isaac Pitman.   The letters were published in
the *Intellectual Repository*, between the following
September and March, 1838, and in them the
inquirer's full acceptance of the doctrines discussed
was set forth.

A controversy of some bitterness arose over
Isaac Pitman's change of faith, which it would
serve no useful purpose to describe at length.
As he did not retire from his connection with and
work for the Wesleyan body, he was ejected from
it ;   and strong condemnation of his views was
expressed from the pulpit of the Congregational
chapel, when he was among the worshippers.
During the remainder of his residence at Wotton,
therefore, he attended divine service at the parish
church.   On first doing so, he considered it
necessary to protest aloud at the invocation of the
Trinity in the Litany, but the Vicar, the Rev.
Benjamin R. Perkins, B.C.L., a clergyman of
Christian wisdom and tolerance, allowed the
interruption to pass unnoticed, and became, in
fact, on very amicable terms with his parishioner.
The Vicar's friendship was highly appreciated by
the Pitman family from that time until they left
Gloucestershire.   Consequent on Isaac Pitman's
acceptance of Swedenborg's revelation, the School
Committee dismissed him from his Mastership.

In some " Reminiscences " dealing with his
religious views, published by himself at the close

of his life, Isaac Pitman says that the two seemingly casual events, the visit to Ulceby (which led to the friendship with Samuel Bagster), and the coach ride from Barton (which resulted in the change in his scholastic position), "under the guiding hand of the Divine Providence shaped the course of my life." They were, as we shall see, amongst the causes of the invention of Phonography, or Phonetic Shorthand, of which he has stated that his early study of Walker was the "first step."

During these years of storm and stress, it is characteristic of the man that he went on uninterruptedly with the revision of the "Comprehensive Bible," in accordance with the plan he had formulated at Barton. His views on total abstinence deepened. About the year 1837 he knocked the bung out of his beer barrel and poured its contents down the sewer, and for the rest of his life discontinued the use of intoxicating liquor in any form. It was at Wotton that he adopted a vegetarian diet. An unsuccessful attempt to kill a fowl for the cook led to humanitarian reflections, and a resolve to dispense with animal food. There was also the influence of example—two ladies who resided at Ebworth Park, near Wotton, with whom he was acquainted, were vegetarians. A literary influence must not be overlooked, namely, the reading of Shelley's "Queen Mab," and to such a diligent Bible reader Genesis i, 29 was a command. Following the adoption of a vegetarian diet came relief from dyspepsia, from which he suffered severely at this period of intense application to the work to which he had set his hand.

At this time George Jacob Holyoake (1817–1896), then a young man following the occupation of a whitesmith, won a prize for mathematics, which was presented to him at the Birmingham Mechanics' Institute in 1836. The prize was the gift of a certain " Mr. Pitman," but although Mr. Holyoake believed this individual to be the Inventor of Phonography, there seems to be no doubt that he was mistaken, and that Isaac Pitman never came into personal touch with the apostle of Co-operation.

IV

1837-1839

DURING the early part of 1837 Isaac Pitman opened a private school at Wotton-under-Edge, and secured suitable premises for the purpose at the top of Long Street, the British School from which he had been dismissed being at the opposite end of the same street. There was an opening for a school of a higher grade than that which he had just left, and in a very short time he derived a larger income from his new enterprise than the salary he had previously received from the Committee. Shorthand was among the subjects in which he decided to impart instruction in his new school. He had made much use of the art since he acquired it. From the year 1833 he had written out all his correspondence in shorthand in a letter book, afterwards transcribing these letters in longhand for despatch to the addressees. Letters to the Press and other literary productions were also first composed in shorthand, and he was in the habit of taking notes of sermons and speeches in which he was specially interested, as he could write at a fair though not a high speed. But he had not hitherto attempted to teach the art in the British Schools he had conducted. Now, in a position of greater freedom, and with a superior class of scholars to that attracted to the elementary schools, instruction in shorthand was introduced in his own school.

The shorthand method which Isaac Pitman mastered in the course of his youthful studies was William Harding's edition of the system of Samuel Taylor. An account of the circumstances under which he learned the art will appropriately preface the story of his earliest attempt in the domain of shorthand authorship, in which he was destined to become famous. In the year 1829 a copy of the system mentioned above was lent him by his cousin, Charles Laverton, a young man of great promise, who had acquired shorthand as an aid to his study for the ministry. The cousin was a son of William Laverton, who married a sister of Isaac Pitman's mother, and it is of interest to mention, in passing, that other sons of William Laverton, and cousins of the subject of this biography, were Mr. Abraham Laverton, some time Member of Parliament for Westbury, Wiltshire, and Mr. Frederick Laverton, the founder of the well-known Bristol house furnishing business. Isaac Pitman and Charles Laverton were of a similar studious bent ; they helped each other in their studies, and a close attachment existed between them. This friendship was broken in a tragic way by the accidental death of Charles Laverton. He had left England for America, intending to study at Harvard University, but when about to land he slipped from the plank connecting the vessel with the wharf, and was drowned.

The feature of Harding's publication which stimulated Isaac Pitman to make himself proficient in the art was an essay by William Gawtress, of which he thought so highly in later years that he quoted it in his own " Manual of Phonography " in many successive editions of that work. " Phonography," he long afterwards wrote, " with all the intellectual and social benefits that follow in its train, has resulted from the seemingly trifling circumstance that the author, at the age of seventeen, learned Taylor's system of shorthand from Harding's edition, and that he was incited to the study chiefly by the perusal of the eloquent enumeration of some of the advantages arising from the practice of the art, from the pen of Mr. Gawtress, the publisher of an improved edition of Byrom's system."

Taylor's shorthand was taught by Isaac Pitman to a class of the more advanced boys in his school; but he soon discovered that it was necessary, if shorthand was to become a subject of instruction, as he desired it to be throughout the schools of the country, that a suitable treatise should be available at a much lower price and in a more concise form than the cheapest edition of Taylor then known to him. He accordingly prepared a small instruction book on this system, which he supposed could be published at the low figure of three pence, and submitted the manuscript to his friend, Mr.

ISAAC PITMAN'S HOUSE AT WOTTON-UNDER-EDGE
(*The " Birthplace of Phonography "*)

Plate 1.

Stenographic Sound Hand.

Vowel Sounds	Single Consonant Sounds h, l, r & y, are upstrokes, s, up or down.			
e' the, thee,	B	be, been, by.	S	self, so, us.
a· (and	D	do, done,	T	it, out, to,
a· a, an,	F	for, if, off.	V	ever, of, over,
au' awe, law,	G	go, God, good,	W	we, will, with,
o, 'O, owe.	H	hand, have, he	Y	yet, you,
oo, who.	J	Jesus, judge,	Z	as, is,
i' eye, I, thy,	K	can, Christ, come,	wh	where which,
u· ewe,	L	all, always, Lord,	sh	change, child
oi, boy, voice	M	may, me, my,	esh	shall, ship
ou' how, thou	N	in, know, no,	th	thought
	P	up, upon,	TH.	that them
	R	are, or, our,	zh.	usual, "ing

Prefixes & Affixes \dis, dom, — a ‴ — mont inter under ent recom, circum sub, super, trans, tive tude, sion [pen tchun] sion a tion [shun] sion [zhun] ly

Representatives into, unto, world, &c. word, ward,

Double Consonant Sounds

bl		below	gw		language	tr		truth,
br		breadth	gz		example	twr		twice,
dr		direct,	kl		call.	vl		evil.
dw		dwell,	kr		care.	vr		every,
fl		full,	ks		except;	shr		short,
fr		from	krw		question,	thr		through
gl		glory	pl		people.	THr		their, these
gr		great	pr		person,	zhr		treasure

Drawn by Isaac Pitman, Stenographer.

FACSIMILE OF PLATE 1 IN "STENOGRAPHIC SOUND-HAND"

Key to Plate 2 on opposite page.

Inscription over the Diagram.—This alphabet contains sixteen vowel sounds, twenty-five single consonants, and twenty-four double ones; total sixty-five letters, including every vowel sound in the language, and every combination of consonants that will commence a syllable, all drawn from this diagram.

Examples.—1*a*, The plainest practical plan of putting pen to paper for the production of peerless poems or profound and powerful prose for the Press or for private pursuits ever published. 3*h*, Tea, tin; pay, pet; father, fat; daw, dot; show, shut; coo, could; fine, duke, boy; vow. 5*a*, Fear thou the Lord in thy youth; hate and avoid evil; love and pursue good; and so walk in the paths of life. 7*f*, Anguish bb, bd, bf; 8*a*, db, dd, df; 8*d* sp, st, sf, sk, sr, sm; 9*a*, sb, sd, sf, sg; 9*e*, rbl, pkr; 9*g*, ff. mm, prpr; 10*a*, least, all, oil; right, our, raw, case, us, see; among, owing; 11*c*, sprain, strong, screw; 11*f*, splinter, swing; 12*b*, principle, instruct: 12*g*, possible, toaster, whisper; 13*a*, maxim, sticks; 13*c*, queen, request; 13*e*, exist, languish; 13*g*, lm,; 14*a*, beyond, statistics, open, alter, altitude; 14*f*, mood, tune; 15*a*, transact, wisdom; childhood, without, forward, professions contents,

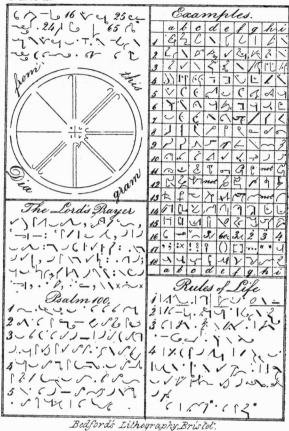

FACSIMILE OF PLATE 2 IN "STENOGRAPHIC SOUND HAND"

Key to Plate 2 (continued).

incomplete, missionaries ; 16a, thoughts, comes, thou mayest ; 300, 60,000, 300,000, second, third, fourthly ; 17a, comma, semicolon, colon, period, admiration, in errogation, irony, parentheses, brackets, hyphen, quotation marks ; 17i, notwithstanding, nevertheless, indispensable, incomprehensible, satisfactorily ; 18e, as it is said, there are, kingdom of heaven, His Majesty's ministers, practice of the Court.

Rules of Life.—1. To read often and to meditate well on the Word of God.

2. To be always content and resigned under the dispensations of Providence.

3. Always to observe a propriety of behaviour, and to preserve the conscience clear and void of offence.

4. To obey that which is ordained, to be faithful in the discharge of the duties of our employment, and to do everything in our power to make ourselves as universally useful as possible.

Always to remember "The Lord will provide."

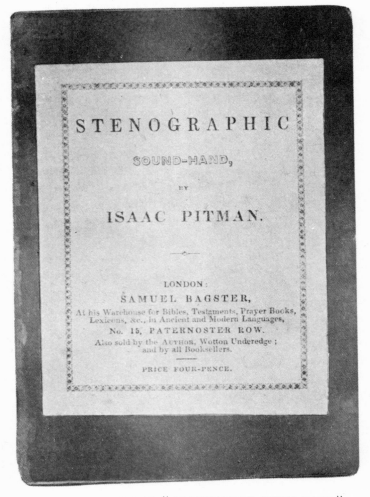

STENOGRAPHIC

SOUND-HAND,

BY

ISAAC PITMAN.

LONDON:
SAMUEL BAGSTER,
At his Warehouse for Bibles, Testaments, Prayer Books,
Lexicons, &c., in Ancient and Modern Languages,
No. 15, PATERNOSTER ROW.
Also sold by the AUTHOR, Wotton Underedge;
and by all Booksellers.

PRICE FOUR-PENCE.

TITLE AND COVER OF "STENOGRAPHIC SOUND-HAND"
PUBLISHED IN 1837

Bagster, accompanied by a letter dated 24th April, 1837. Mr. Bagster readily agreed to undertake the publication of the work, but before taking any practical steps submitted the manuscript to a professional reporter for his opinion. This was communicated to Isaac Pitman, and was to the following effect :

The system Mr. Pitman has sent to you is already in the market ; now if he will compile a new system, I think you will be more likely to succeed in your object to popularize shorthand ; there will be novelty about it.

The name of this sagacious and impartial adviser, who, no doubt, himself used one of the old stenographic methods, has not been handed down to us. He deserves the gratitude of the English-speaking world for making the suggestion which led Isaac Pitman to become a shorthand inventor. But if we cannot pay him the honour which is his due, we can at least give praise to Samuel Bagster, not only for having elicited this epochal proposal, but for his friendly offices during the next few years in advising the inexperienced young schoolmaster on many practical points which contributed to the success of the new system. "I had no intention of becoming a shorthand author," the Inventor of Phonography remarked at Manchester, "the ambition of appearing before the public in that capacity never entered my mind, until it was suggested to me as a means of accomplishing my end."

The opinion above quoted appears to have been

communicated to Isaac Pitman in the month of
May. He at once took steps to carry the idea into
effect, and started on the enterprise with the
sanguine enthusiasm which was such a marked
feature of his mental temperament throughout his
long life. " When the phonetic idea had taken
lodgment in Isaac's brain," observes his brother
Benn, " we talked of nothing else on our way to
and from school, and in our occasional morning
walks, and intense was the joy of my brother at
the completion of his long task (on the ' Comprehensive Bible ') and the opportunity it afforded
him to give his time and thoughts, as well as heart,
to new ideas in the field of experiment and
usefulness then opening up to him."

The summer months of 1837 were consequently
exceedingly busy ones in the life of Isaac Pitman.
In addition to his school duties and the completion
of the Bible revision, he embarked on the work
of constructing a system of shorthand based on the
sounds of the English language, with the analysis
of which his study of Walker's " Principles of
Pronunciation " had rendered him, as we have
seen, thoroughly familiar. All the spare time not
occupied in other duties appears to have been
devoted to the construction of shorthand
alphabets, and to experiments with them ; even
the Midsummer holiday of three weeks was
occupied in the task. It is interesting to note that
Isaac Pitman was most deeply engrossed in experiments with his system on that momentous day

when Queen Victoria succeeded to the throne, so that the art is coeval with the opening of the Victorian Era, of which it proved to be one of the most useful inventions.

In setting about the construction of a new system of shorthand, the inventor turned his attention first to the representation of vowel sounds. This is a feature in which preceding systems were either imperfect, because they essayed to represent only the five vowels of the common alphabet ; or ineffective, because their vowel signs were impracticable. For some time Isaac Pitman pondered over the advisability of introducing into his proposed system the vowel scale now so widely known, and proved by the experience of millions of shorthand writers to be the best practical method of representing the vowels ever devised for English shorthand. It was with " fear and trembling " he has himself told us that he framed the scale which ran originally, *ee, eh, ah ; aw, oh, oo ;* and *i, e, a ; o, u, oo,*

| ˙| *ee* | ·| *eh* | .| *ah* | ¯| *aw* | -| *oh* | _| *oo* |
| || *ĭ* | ⊣| *ĕ* | ⌋| *ă* | ⌐| *ŏ* | ⊣| *ŭ* | ⌟| *ŏŏ* |

and also provided signs for the representation of four diphthongs.

He had little confidence in the usefulness of this method of representing the vowels, but he had, in fact, found the most serviceable arrangement. When this vowel scale was decided on, it was clear that the new method of shorthand

must be " writing by sound," and that the same
principle must be followed in the construction of
the remaining portions of the system. " I saw
the truth," he exclaims, " practised it, and it
became delightful. In a few months I got clear
of the shallow waters and breakers of our present
orthography, and committed myself to the
boundless deep of phonographic writing."

The story of the invention of his alphabet for
representing the consonant sounds of the language
has been several times told by Isaac Pitman. It
was related in detail in a paper entitled " The
Genesis of Phonography," which he read on 28th
September, 1887, at the first International Shorthand Congress held in London, when, after
remarking that the system was " on the anvil " for
six months, he said :

" The shorthand alphabet given in the first
edition of Phonography contains the elements of
the present matured system, but in several of its
details it was imperfect, because it proceeded from
a finite mind. These imperfections were discovered by experience and removed. As a skilful
anatomist can, from three or four bones, construct
the entire skeleton of an animal, so from three or
four shorthand signs or letters that have been
acknowledged from the commencement of shorthand writing as the best for certain letters, we can
construct a natural shorthand alphabet. The
three leading bones in the shorthand skeleton are
| t, ⌣ n, ╱ r, struck upwards. The form or
direction of stroke in t determines all the other
letters of the same class. They must be either

/ *p*, | *t*, \ *chay*, — *k*, or \ *p*, | *t*, / *chay*, — *k*.
The first set was adopted in the first edition of
Phonography (but *chay* was curved instead of
straight) and the second and more practical set in
the second and subsequent editions. The positions of the four right lines to represent the
explodent consonants determine the positions of
the curves to represent the continuant consonants
that are made with the same organs. Thus, ⸦ *f*
(labial, written in the same direction as the labial
\ *p*), (*ith*,) *s* (dental letters, written in the
same direction as the dental *t*), ⸦ *ish*, (a palatal
written in the direction of the palatal / *chay*).
These light letters for light sounds determine the
forms of the corresponding heavy sounds, which
are represented by corresponding heavy letters,
namely :—

\ *b*, | *d*, / *j*, — *gay*, ⸦ *v*, (*thee*,) *zee*, ⸦ *zhee*.
"*N* ⸦ is settled in this form by shorthand usage,
and this determines the form of *m*, because the
two letters frequently follow each other as
⌣ *mn*, ⌢ *nm*. The nasal ⌣ *ng* is related to *n*,
and is written thus. The two liquids *l* and *r* are
letters of frequent occurrence, and require the
convenience of strokes that have both an upward
and downward movement, that they may conveniently unite with other consonants. This
double direction is provided by giving *r* the spare
downward curve ⟍ *r*, in addition to its historically
settled form ⟋ *r*. *L* ⸦ is represented by a curve
in the *r* direction, written either up or down.
There remain but three other letters to consider,
namely, the two hybrids or vowel-consonant
letters *w*, *y*, and the aspirate *h*. *W* ⟍ and *y* ⟋
receive forms from what may be called the waste
material of the *pl* and *pr* series of double

consonants ; and the aspirate takes the two forms
〗 ⌒ which are two unused signs taken from the
spr series of treble consonants. Thus the shorthand alphabet is complete, and there is a good
reason why every stroke should represent the
letter to which it is assigned. The making of the
phonographic alphabet is really another version
of Columbus's egg. Anybody could make an egg
stand on end by first giving it a tap on the table ;
and a ' schoolboy ' could have made the phonographic alphabet if he had noticed the three letters
│ *t*, ⌣ *n*, ╱ *r*, running through the history of
shorthand, and had put all the other letters in
their places by the side of these three, paying
regard to the placing of the straight lines and
curves in the four possible directions corresponding
to the four seats of articulation in the mouth for
the production of consonants, namely, the lips,
teeth, palate, and throat ; and allowing the
gutturals and nasals both to take the horizontal
direction."

The consonant portion of the alphabet of 1837
differs, as indicated above, from the " more
practical " allocation adopted after the system
had been in actual use. Further, the inventor
was content with the arrangement *b*, *d*, *f*, *g*, and
so forth, following the order of the Roman letters,
but he promised an " alphabet according to
nature " if the first presentation of his system met
with acceptance. This anticipation was happily
fulfilled, and in subsequent editions the consonants
were arranged in their natural order, *p*, *b* ; *t*, *d* ;
ch, *j*, and so on. But the three distinctive merits

of Isaac Pitman's treatment of the consonants
were exhibited in his first work, namely, (1) an
extension in the number of characters which
(following the analysis of Walker) gave a sign for
each consonant sound ; (2) an economy of stenographic material, by using light and heavy strokes
respectively for the paired sounds ; and, (3) the
production of an alphabet of simple strokes for
single consonants, thus rendering possible a super-
structure of abbreviating devices for indicating
two or more consonants by a single inflection,
which is a distinguishing merit of the system.

In regard to the last named point, we have in
the first edition the introduction of the hook signs
which so greatly aid the writer, by enabling him
to represent two characters by a hook attached to
a stem. The representation of the frequent
recurrence of *l* or *r* with other consonants was, for
example, provided for in this way. The large
initial hook standing for *tw* or *dw* was, however,
soon discarded, though it has survived in America.
In imitation of some older systems, " Stenographic
Sound-Hand " was provided with certain arbitrary
characters bearing no resemblance to alphabetical
signs, but these happily disappeared from all
subsequent editions. In a crude fashion—following the lead of older systems—the consonant
signs were allocated to the representation of
common words, but a far better and a more
scientific method of representing words of
frequent occurrence was adopted later on in the

"Grammalogues." There is a suggestion relative to a method of contracting frequently occurring words with long outlines, but the plan was not of practical utility, and was not a feature of subsequent editions. The method of " phrasing," by which the signs for several words are written without lifting the pen—one of the most successful features of the Pitman system—is suggested in a direction on " joining little words together." The advantages of halving or doubling the length of characters was not yet recognized by Isaac Pitman, who refers to the principle as " objectionable."[1] In this and in many other directions, the practical experience of subsequent years suggested useful improvements and additions to the Pitmanic system which were undreamt of by its inventor in 1837. In later years he was disposed to characterize his first essay in shorthand authorship as crude and imperfect, and so by comparison with later editions it undoubtedly is, but sufficient has been said to show that " Stenographic Sound-Hand " contained the fruitful germs from which the perfected system sprang.

The new shorthand system was introduced to the world in the form of a booklet of crown 16mo size (3½ in. by 5 in.), consisting of twelve pages of letter-press and two lithographed plates, enclosed in a drab cover of thin cardboard, on the

---

[1] Before he left Wotton, however, Isaac Pitman had tested the halving principle and decided to adopt it. He wrote the Bible in his system from the reading of his brother Henry, and in this experiment employed the half-length device.

front of which was a label bearing the only title the treatise possessed.

The production of this small work appears to have been a dual effort on the part of author and publisher. The plates were printed at the establishment of Bedford, a Bristol lithographer. They were executed under the personal supervision of the author—a precaution absolutely necessary to ensure the accuracy of the characters—and this part of the work is from a technical point of view of considerable excellence. The letter-press part was printed in London, by the firm of Stevens and Pardon, of Bell Yard, and was no doubt arranged for by the publisher. The edition was one of three thousand, and the author undertook himself to get his book placed in covers and stitched. The first portion of the edition was despatched to Mr. Bagster from Wotton on 14th November, and on the following day, the 15th November, 1837, " Stenographic Sound-Hand " was published in London. In a letter written to Mr. Bagster on the date first named, Isaac Pitman communicated the following particulars to his publisher :

" I have sent," he wrote," 200 'Stenographies' for present sale, and the rest, to make up 1,500, will follow by wagon in about a week. I think I shall want 1,500 for myself. Please let me know in a month or two how they sell. I must beg pardon for the manner of sewing in this 200. The next will be dark coloured thread, and done properly. Also the labels will be more nearly in the centre. The stitching was done by the elder boys in my

school, who have learned the system.   They are
quite delighted to spend two or three days in this
sort of half play.   Since this first essay we have
had a lesson on the subject from a stationer."

Before its publication, the new system of shorthand had been extensively used by its inventor.
In Isaac Pitman's letter book (previously kept in
Taylor's system) he made the first entry in his own
phonographic method on the 7th September, 1837,
all subsequent entries being recorded in it.   His
elder brother Jacob (who left London for South
Australia in the month in which "Stenographic
Sound-Hand" was published), took 100 copies
from Bagster's with him to Adelaide, and made
himself proficient in the system.   Joseph Pitman
was presented with a copy on 16th November,
"with the author's affectionate respects," and
soon after became a skilful writer of the method.
Benn and Henry at Wotton had watched every
step of their elder brother's inventive efforts, and
had learned "Sound-Hand" while it was still in
the manuscript.   "Before the system was sufficiently developed to warrant its publication,"
writes Benn Pitman, "my brother Isaac and I
prepared a set of cards, containing the alphabet,
exercises, and reading practice, from which I
taught a class of more than twenty boys in the
school.   I was then only between fourteen and
fifteen years of age, but my brother manifested full
confidence in my acquaintance with the system,
for he sent me to Bristol, then a full day's journey

ISAAC PITMAN'S LETTER TO SAMUEL BAGSTER

(Facsimile of original entry in his letter book.   For Key see page 41)

ISAAC PITMAN'S LETTER TO SAMUEL BAGSTER
(Rewritten by him in present-day Phonography. Facsimile)

from Wotton-under-Edge, to superintend the correction of the plates that accompanied the first edition of Isaac Pitman's ' Phonetic Shorthand.' " Not long after its appearance, Samuel Pitman, father of the inventor, who was then in his fiftieth year, learned the system and, after a few days' practice, wrote a letter in its characters. Isaac's brothers and sisters all acquired the art.

The Pitmanic system was introduced to the world quietly and without advertisement. As far as can be discovered its author engaged in no special efforts to make it known. He was, indeed, far more concerned in effecting improvements in his work for the contemplated second edition. In association with the statement of Benn Pitman quoted above, it is curious to note that Isaac Pitman in its pages speaks of his first work as " this *card* " which, he adds, " contains the *principles* and is thrown out as a *feeler*." For a little over eighteen months after the publication of " Stenographic Sound-Hand " he continued to reside at Wotton, and through his own efforts the first edition of his system was almost exhausted. As has been more than once pointed out, the success of the method was without doubt greatly promoted by the fact that it was issued by the eminent Bible publisher, whose name was a guaranty that it was of a meritorious kind, and not of a " catchpenny " nature. The actual sales of the first edition at Paternoster Row were, however, small.

V

1839-1840

ON the 30th June, 1839, Isaac Pitman took up his residence at No. 5 Nelson Place, Bath, and in this Western city he made his home for the rest of his life.   Several reasons appear to have influenced him in his settlement at Bath on leaving Wotton-under-Edge.   He was not insensible to the beauties which Nature and Art have lavishly bestowed on the " Queen of the West," for not long after he wrote : " Of the many beautiful cities in this fair country, Bath is unquestionably the *most* beautiful," and he proceeded to describe its characteristic features in eloquent terms of appreciation.   He probably also regarded Bath as a suitable place for the establishment of a private school.   Yet another, and without doubt an important consideration, was the fact that there had been founded in Bath ten years before a society of receivers of the doctrines of Swedenborg, which under the name of the New Church has had a continuous existence down to the present day.   At this period the Church worshipped in a room in Chandos Buildings, and Isaac Pitman and his wife were admitted into membership soon after they settled in the city.   In this congregation,

NELSON PLACE, BATH

(*From a drawing, about 1840*)

THE FIRST PHONETIC INSTITUTE, NO. 5 NELSON PLACE, BATH

(The street lamp shown in the picture is immediately in front of No. 5)

as the years passed, the Inventor of Phonography made lifelong friends, some of whom
became his valued assistants in enterprises which
have yet to be described in these pages. Mr.
James Keene, who was the New Church minister
(unpaid) at that time and for many succeeding
years, was also the editor of the oldest newspaper
in the city, *Keene's Bath Journal*, established in
1742, of which the brothers John and James Keene
were the joint proprietors.

In one of his early periodicals Isaac Pitman
gave an illustrated account of his first Bath
residence at Nelson Place. He described it as
situated in the western part of Bath, and as,
together with Norfolk Crescent and the river
Avon (which flowed by), enclosing a triangular
lawn bordered with trees. The view from his
windows looking south over this lawn, and taking
in verdant fields gradually rising to Combe Down,
is described in appreciative language and pronounced " very fine." But since the time when
this description was penned, the " verdant fields "
have been largely obscured from view by the
growth of suburban Bath. At Nelson Place he
opened a " school for young gentlemen," and one
of the privileges of the boarders, which he mentions in the circular he issued, is that of " walking
in the lawn in front of the house." The usual
subjects were taught in his school, with, in
addition, the author's system of " writing by
sound."

During the summer of 1839 Isaac Pitman visited his friend and publisher, Mr. Samuel Bagster, at the latter's beautiful residence at Old Windsor. One evening during his stay with him they talked about the issue of a second edition of the shorthand treatise, the first having been by this time nearly exhausted. "We both wished," writes Isaac Pitman, "to give it a shorter title than the lumbering one by which the first edition was known—'Stenographic Sound-Hand.' I remarked that a compound of two Greek words, $\phi\omega\nu\eta$, *sound* or *voice*, and $\gamma\rho\alpha\phi\eta$, *writing*, combined as 'Phonography' accurately described the new method of writing, but the word was not in existence in English. So I thought at the time. 'That must be the title,' said Mr. Bagster, 'it is a new name for a new thing.'" Having obtained this emphatic approval of his proposed new title, Isaac Pitman on the 7th of September, 1839, issued a crown folio prospectus, which was printed by the Messrs. Keene, announcing that the second edition with the title "Phonography, or Writing by Sound, being also a New and Improved System of Short Hand," was in preparation There was not the novelty about the word "Phonography" which Isaac Pitman and Mr. Bagster supposed when they discussed the matter at Old Windsor. In 1701 a certain John Jones, M.D., published a work entitled "Practical Phonography," which was designed to assist persons to read and spell the ordinary longhand. But in 1839 Isaac Pitman had very little, if any, acquaintance with the works of any other author except Walker in the field of phonetic science, though as regarded the stenographic art he had a fairly representative collection of the works of older and contemporary authors.

Some interesting glimpses of the development of his own system by Isaac Pitman are afforded in the prospectus before alluded to, in which we are permitted, as it were, to see Phonography " in the making." In 1839, on the 3rd of January, and again three months later, we find correspondents writing to Isaac Pitman in his own system, which they had learned from " Stenographic Sound-Hand," and bearing enthusiastic testimony to its excellence. To these communications there is a foot-note by the author, who says that since the dates of his correspondents' letters his system has been " touched up and modified," and practised extensively for the sake of trial almost every day (the entire Bible had, as already stated, been transcribed by Isaac Pitman in the characters of Sound-Hand). Then follows this significant passage : " In the beginning of May about thirty double consonants sprung up as of their own accord, from principles previously acknowledged as in the system ; nothing was deranged by this, but they fell into their places, like the keystone of an arch, and completed the whole." We are further told that " the author of Phonography is no mere theorist, but was a shorthand writer of

extensive practice before he published." He
possessed, he says, over thirty of the previously
published systems of shorthand : " But they all
fail in the grand principle of giving a mark for
every sound, and never using it for any other."

He makes announcement in the same prospectus
of what, outside his own school, was probably the
first public class for the mastery of the system.
He notifies that he teaches a " Phonographic, or
Shorthand Class," at the Mechanics' Institute,
No. 3 Bath Street, Bath, every Wednesday
evening, and announces that after school hours
he attends ladies and gentlemen at their own
residences for instruction in his art, while for those
at a distance postal tuition is offered. It is also
announced that : " The publication of Phonography is delayed for four months, that it may be
still more fully proved, and receive every amend-
ment it is capable of receiving before being
engraven in enduring steel."

In Isaac Pitman's second prospectus the publication of " Phonography " is announced as a
" Companion to the Penny Post." It is difficult
in the present day to realize the enthusiasm with
which the great boon of penny postage was greeted
when Rowland Hill's ideas were fully carried out,
and it became possible to send a letter under half
an ounce in weight for one penny. In response
to a Government offer of a prize of £200 for a
suggestion for the best method of collecting
the pence for prepaid letters, Isaac Pitman in

September, 1839, submitted to the Lords of the Treasury a proposal for penny postage stamps, printed from engraved plates in sheets containing 240, which could be used for affixing to letters, and as remittances for small amounts. Benn Pitman says that " he further recommended—and this was the unlucky stroke of economy that proved his undoing—that the stamps be used for sealing the letter or envelope. The inconvenience of cancelling the stamp, when affixed at the back of the letter, gave the much coveted prize to another competitor, who repeated Isaac's idea, but with the suggestion that the stamps be affixed on the face of the letter, at the upper right-hand corner, as is the convenient practice of to-day." When it is remembered that the average cost of a letter sent by post under the old arrangement was $9\frac{1}{2}$d. for a single sheet of paper, no enclosure of any kind being permitted, it will be seen how far-reaching was the reform brought about by the new regulations, which permitted anything in the nature of written or printed matter to be sent through the inland post at the rate of a penny per half-ounce, and how beneficial the concession was to Phonography and to other forms of popular instruction in which written communications play an important part.

The work of designing the " Penny Plate " involved considerable ingenuity and labour. In his early life Isaac Pitman had a great fondness for minute writing, but the " Penny Plate " far surpassed his pen and ink efforts in this direction, as will be seen. His original design for this conspectus of his system was written with extreme neatness within a ruled space 9 in. by 11 in. in his letter book and journal, and this design was produced very early in the year 1839. The heading is as follows : " Phonography, or Writing by Sound, being a New and Improved System of Shorthand." The space is divided into four quarters. In the top left-hand quarter is the table of " Vowels," " Long " and " Short," and " Double Vowels," in three parallel columns, and underneath the table of " Consonants " in the *p, b ; t, d ; ch, j,* order, thus arranged for the first time in connection with English shorthand. In the bottom left-hand quarter are the " Double Consonants " of the *pl, pr,* order, etc., each character being designed as the logogram for representing several more or less common words. In the top right-hand quarter is a " Joining Table of Consonants " ; a table illustrative of the vowel places, and the phonographic design which appears at the top of the " Penny Plate." The bottom right-hand quarter consists of two columns, one containing Psalm I, the Lord's Prayer, and the Lord's Invitation, in small shorthand characters, and the other " Rules for Writing " in very small longhand.

Although it is closely written, there is considerably less matter in this manuscript presentation of the second edition of his system than Isaac

Pitman a few months later managed to pack into a space of 6½ in. by 8 in. on the " Penny Plate." This steel plate was engraved by S. J. Lander, of High Street, Bristol, and in order to secure accuracy Isaac Pitman walked to and fro to Bristol—a city distant eleven miles from Bath, and as yet unconnected with it by railway—in order to watch the engraver at work, a precaution absolutely necessary in order to ensure accuracy. Many of the characters in this closely packed plate are so microscopical as to require a magnifying glass to read them. The improvements in the system are, however, fairly obvious to the initiated. The table of consonants is arranged in the order indicated above, which was for the future adopted in the author's works, and initial hooks to the consonant stems are systematically introduced to represent the additions of *l* or *r* respectively. The halving of consonant strokes to indicate the addition of *t* or *d* is first introduced. " The beautiful discovery of the sets of double vowels, *ye, ya, yah ; we, wa, wah*," also makes its first appearance in the system. It is stated on the " Penny Plate " that it was " invented and drawn by Isaac Pitman," and it also bears the name of his London publisher.

This production formed the Second Edition of the system and was published on the day Penny Postage was introduced, namely, the 10th January, 1840. A copy of the plate came into the hands of Mr. Reed, then a thirteen years old schoolboy

at Bristol. " I found it," he says, " too hard
a nut to crack. The system was presented in so
condensed a form, and with so few explanations,
that I laid it aside as transcending my powers of
comprehension." The majority of people, we
believe, concur in Mr. Reed's opinion, and the
prospect of Phonography achieving its future
triumphs would have been meagre indeed had the
system only been presented to the public in what
its author termed a " minutely engraved plate."
But the cheerful faith of Isaac Pitman's publisher
in the new system must be recorded here. At
this time Mr. Samuel Bagster expressed his
appreciation of Phonography in the following
verse—

> Artists and scribes no more delight,
>   Their arts imperfect found,
> Daguerre now draws by rays of Light,
>   And Pitman writes by Sound.

VI

1840-1842

THE introduction of penny postage enabled Isaac
Pitman to conduct through the post an active
propaganda on behalf of the art he had invented.
He first sought to interest the schoolmasters of
Somerset and Gloucestershire by sending to each
a copy of the " Penny Plate," with the request
that they would either study it themselves or hand
it to any pupil who was likely to take an interest
in the art.   There was undoubted novelty in the
issue of a system of shorthand which was entirely
comprised on a steel plate of moderate dimensions,
and letters to the inventor which have been preserved show that in the early months of 1840 his
heart was cheered by appreciative communications
from many quarters.   Then the statement on the
plate that " any person may receive lessons
from the author by post gratuitously," resulted
in numerous inquiries. [1]   And when postage stamps
were introduced in connection with the penny
post early in May, 1840, Isaac Pitman issued

---

[1] The earliest impressions bore the words, " Any person may
receive lessons from the Author by post at 1s. each to be paid
in advance, and enclosed in a paid letter," but in two or three
months' time the plate was altered by substituting the above
words.

the following announcement : " The Author will also feel great pleasure in correcting gratuitously, any shorthand exercise or lesson that may be forwarded to him. After the student has learned the shorthand letters, committed to memory the words which they represent, and read through the exercises, he may write a portion of Scripture, and forward it to the Author, with a postage stamp enclosed. The lesson will be returned corrected, with observations and references to the rules for writing."

At the end of 1840 Isaac Pitman with timely sagacity published the Third Edition of his system, in the form of a demy 8vo text-book with printed rules and explanations, illustrated by phonographic characters engraved on wood. Similar matter was also issued as a quarto sheet printed on both sides. For the first time in English stenographic treatises, the rules for writing the system were illustrated by shorthand characters printed in the letter-press, instead of by plates entirely apart from it, a singularly inconvenient plan. A series of " Exercises " in phonographic reading was also published in two forms— either bound up with the text-book or issued separately.

In the three weeks vacations of his school at Christmas and Midsummer respectively, Isaac Pitman travelled and lectured in connection with his system. The first enterprise of this nature was arranged for the Christmas holiday of 1840, concerning which there is this entry in his letter book : " Left home to lecture on Phonography, 23rd December." His return is noted on the following 15th January, 1841. This expedition was planned on a considerable scale. Posters and leaflets were arranged for, and a number of secretaries of institutions were written to in regard to places of meeting which might be used free of charge. An itinerary containing the names of thirty-five towns was drawn up, but for reasons not now discoverable, a more limited tour seems to have been actually carried out. Isaac Pitman has himself told us that what happened was that he started out from Bath early on the morning of 23rd December, and walked over the snow-covered roads to Stroud, thirty miles distant, carrying in his knapsack a supply of phonographic literature weighing 15lb. He gave a lecture at Stroud, and on the following day walked to Oxford, where he visited most of the colleges, left copies of his " Penny Plate " and other literature, proceeded through High Wycombe and other towns to London, and from thence returned to Bath.

Manchester was also visited during this tour, and the art introduced to the inhabitants in a series of lectures. Isaac Pitman's first visit to this city, in which in subsequent years his shorthand system has been so thoroughly appreciated and so generally taught, has been rather strangely overlooked. But the Inventor of Phonography has himself preserved a complete record of it in the form of a letter which he addressed to two Manchester newspapers. The editors declined to insert it, and its author's comment on this conduct reveals the thoroughgoing reforming spirit in which he had entered on the campaign. " Another instance," he writes, " is here added to the list of persecutions which truth has had to endure from the prejudice and selfishness of men." As this is Isaac Pitman's first letter to the Press concerning his system it is important, apart from its biographical interest. We reproduce it below :

" To the Editor.

" Sir,—At the commencement of the present year four lectures were delivered by me in the town of Manchester on Phonography, a method of writing all languages by means of *signs* that express *sounds,* two to the members of the Mechanics' Institute, Cooper Street, and two to the members of the Christian Institute in the Town Hall, Grosvenor Square. They were well received by the audiences, and the exposition which I gave of this new science called forth repeated plaudits. At the close of the last lecture given in the Town Hall, Grosvenor Square, on the evening of Tuesday, 12th January, Mr. P. B. Templeton, a shorthand writer and author, and formerly reporter for the *Manchester Times,* made some remarks attempting to show the inutility and even the impracticability of Phonography ! ! But he could not persuade the audience to think with him. During his address on the demerits of Phonography (!) he laid down five points with respect to the science :—

1. That no more could be done by the phonographic alphabet in the expression of sounds than by the common alphabet.
2. That the system was applicable to no foreign language.
3. That admitting it to be applicable to foreign languages, it was of no value in the absence of a knowledge of such languages.
4. That as a system of shorthand it was utterly impracticable.
5. That, if at all practicable, it was less expeditious by two-thirds than half-a-dozen systems already published.

" Immediately after Mr. Templeton had brought forward these false charges, before I had made any reply, he gave me a challenge to prove the worth of Phonography publicly, proposing that its merits should be discussed in any large room in Manchester, advertised in all the Manchester papers, and that if he failed to establish each and all of the five propositions, he was to bear the whole expense of the room and the advertising, and in addition would either be bound to purchase one thousand copies of my book, or to pay £20 to the Manchester Royal Infirmary.

" I answered that my time was much better employed than in running about the country on so foolish an errand, that I was so constantly engaged in my school here in Bath, that I *could* not accept the challenge, and that if I were otherwise situated I *would* not, as I should be performing a much greater service to society by teaching Phonography than in trying to prove to Mr. Templeton that it is a real science fit for the expression of any language and is a system of shorthand shorter than any other system extant.

" I took down notes of the five charges (in the 'impracticable' system of Phonography !) as they came from his lips, and when he had done gave an answer to them to the entire satisfaction of the audience. My reply was this :—

" 1. That it is true the common alphabet can express in a certain bungling way all the sounds that Phonography can. But it is by the expedient of using two letters to express one simple sound with respect to both vowels and consonants, and that in no less than ten instances—the names of which two letters it must also be remembered have little or no connection with the sound they are made to represent. Thus, the two letters *a u* are put together to signify the simple vowel sound *awe*. It is also necessary to put over the vowels the marks of quantity, a horizontal stroke to signify the long sound and a curve to express the short sound. In addition to this, in the common alphabet the vowels and consonants, whether single or double, are all placed together in complete confusion, whereas in Phonography every sound is placed in its true position, the whole forming the nature alphabet. Every simple sound is expressed by a simple mark, and every double and treble sound derived from it is expressed by a mark derived from the simple mark by some slight change of form.

" 2. That Phonography was applicable to the writing of all languages proof was given in the published ' Exercises in Phonography,' wherein the 100th Psalm was written in French, German, Italian, Chinese, and Hebrew, every sound being expressed by the appropriate phonographic sign so perfectly that the professors of those languages assured me there was no mistake whatever in the pronunciation. Proof of this fact has also been given in Mr. Templeton's hearing by the writing of German and Welsh dictated by the audience.

" 3. It was not professed that Phonography imparted a knowledge of languages unknown before ! It merely gave a means of expressing them as to their very sounds on paper by the same signs that are used to write English.

" 4. That Phonography was ' utterly impracticable ' was already shown to the meeting to be ' utterly ' *false* by my having written with chalk upon the blackboard two or three dozen separate words and sentences which that very audience, whose understanding Mr. Templeton was abusing, had dictated. The practicability of Phonography was also shown by the publication of a collection of ' Exercises in Phonography,' at the cost of a few pence, consisting of ten octavo pages of extracts from Scripture, engraved in a bold style of phonographic shorthand, and in which every word was written correctly according to the alphabet and the rules laid down in the system, which was also in print at the cost of a penny for one edition and eight pence for another. Anyone on opening the ' Exercises ' would see that the shorthand consisted of easy strokes which any person could make who could handle a pen.

" 5. That I had a collection of about fifty systems of shorthand, including every one of note that had been published, and there was not one of them that could be compared with Phonography ' in point of expedition.' Mr. Templeton had not *named* any system that was shorter, so I put *my* assertion against *his*, having proved to the audience in many instances that *Phonography* was considerably briefer than *his* system.

" After giving this answer to Mr. Templeton's charges, and assuring him that I should accept his challenge no further, he still opposed my system of writing, and that in so violent and outrageous a manner that he was hissed down by the audience. Among other indecent expressions by which the auditors felt disgusted, he said that Phonography was an ' imposture ' and that I was ' foisting ' it upon the public. The people knew too much to be willing to bear this ; I had been in the town above a week, and had given four lectures, sold many hundred copies of the work, and distributed gratuitously several thousand publications, and the system was sold in one form for a penny. In teaching if anything it was evident to all that I was not humbugging them and putting money in my pocket. Mr. Templeton endured their scorn as long as he could, his voice being frequently drowned in hisses and the unqualified expression of their contempt for his remarks, insomuch that it was necessary for Mr. Grundy, Secretary to the Christian Institute, and myself, to interfere in order that he might obtain a hearing. He could not possibly mistake the feeling of the meeting.

" Indeed he *felt* the withering influence that was around him, and spoke once to this effect :

" ' If you will not hear what I have to say I cannot help it, I am merely stating facts and they are for your benefit.' However, he could not persuade them that ' He, as an individual, could not have the slightest possible reason for bearing me any ill-will.' He said he bore me none, ' but having been for some time connected with the Press, in the capacity of a shorthand writer, he thought he was sufficiently qualified to pronounce a decided opinion on the merits of the system which had been propounded.'

"When he was leaving the room, the audience insisted upon his recanting his expressions that Phonography was an 'imposture' and that it was 'foisted' upon the public. After a great deal of talk to no purpose, wishing to avoid the recantation as the audience was determined to have it, he at last admitted that he had spoken 'without consideration' or 'without due consideration.' He also acknowledged that he had not read through the whole of my little book, and that he did not understand it. Still he had had the impudence to lay down the above five positions.

"Knowing what kind of 'farewell' he would receive from the company, he made up his mind that on leaving he would *order* the people to do what he well knew they were determined to do, namely, to laugh at him. As he was leaving he said, 'Now, gentlemen, laugh!' which they did in good earnest, and then bought my books more readily on account of the stir.

"Now, Mr. Editor, you will ask, 'What is all this to me or the Manchester public now the affair is over?' Nothing at all, and so I thought at the time, and never intended taking any notice of it, feeling sure Mr. Templeton would not, and that he would have more prudence than to publish his own shame. Judge, then, sir, how surprised I was the other day on receiving an article cut from the *Manchester Times* of January 16th, and measuring above a foot in length, entitled 'Phonographic Lecturer's Extraordinary Challenge.' In this document (furnished by Mr. Templeton, I suppose) I am described as having been completely foiled. The charges and the challenge are given in a style of triumph, Phonography is pronounced by this knight of the quill to be ' the veriest mass of absurdity that ever was written by mortal on paper.'   And it is said that after hearing the awful charges brought against me, I ' looked considerably astonished, declined the challenge, and after some conversation of no interest, the matter ended.'

" This ' conversation of no interest ' consisted of a recantation which Mr. Templeton was compelled to make, the loudly expressed reprobation of the public for his course of conduct, and his humiliating retreat.   These things were, of course, of ' no interest ' to him, but he should in his statements respect the rights and feelings of others. To *me* and to the audience they were of equal interest with the false charges and the boasted challenge.   I thought the one was the balance of the other, and intended to say nothing about the matter.

" Instead of looking ' considerably astonished ' at Mr. Templeton's bravado, I was mightily amused at the Quixotic expedition in which he had embarked, and could not help smiling at it.   Indeed, it was remarked to me after the affair was over that while he was speaking I *looked* an answer to his heated vapouring, and that if I had not spoken the audience would have been perfectly satisfied that all the hubbub was nothing more than a little professional rivalry and jealousy.

" I call on you, Mr. Editor, to do justice, not so much to me and Phonography, as to truth and honesty.   A scandalous misrepresentation has been put forth by the Press, and as an Englishman I claim the privilege of being heard in my own defence.

" ' But why did you not send this refutation to

Mr. Templeton's report as soon as the *Times* of
January 16th appeared ? ' I never saw it, nor
had an idea of its existence till above three months
after the time. I remain, Sir, Your obedient
servant,

"ISAAC PITMAN.
"5 Nelson Place, Bath.
"5 May, 1841."

If we may judge from the correspondence received a short time afterwards, the merits of
Phonography were fully recognized at Manchester.
Among incidents of the lectures was a demonstration of the ease with which a sentence in Greek,
dictated by a member of the audience, could be
recorded on the blackboard. This was done as a
proof of the fact that the " Alphabet of Nature "
was adapted to the representation of other
languages besides English. To a Manchester
correspondent, " T. W." (Walker) (who dictated
the Greek sentence), Isaac Pitman wrote : " It is
the author's intention to make known Phonography by lecturing and other means of instruction, in every town in the Kingdom, should the
Divine mercy give him length of days and
opportunity."

During the Midsummer holiday of 1841, Isaac
Pitman undertook a second and longer lecturing
tour, spreading over twenty-three days, in the
course of which he visited and gave addresses
at Devizes, London, Ipswich, Norwich, Hull,
Barton-on-Humber, Leeds, York, Newcastle

(twice), Edinburgh (three times), and Glasgow.
He returned to London by steamer, and from
thence proceeded to Bath by the Great Western
Railway, which had been opened for traffic not
long before. Of this series of lectures Mr. Reed
has recorded some interesting impressions, which
have a unique interest from the fact that no other
account of them exists.

"At Edinburgh," Mr. Reed says, "he could
only sell a few copies of the system. At Newcastle
he received greater encouragement. He had large
and attentive audiences, and made many converts,
one of them being the late Alderman T. P. Barkas,
who himself shortly afterwards became an active
propagandist of the new faith ; for as such it had
now come to be regarded ; and a bond of brother-
hood was established among its adherents. This
was largely due to Isaac Pitman's own indomitable
energy, his enthusiastic, yet quiet temperament,
and his profound belief in the ' cause ' which he
had initiated. At that time his highest hope was
the popularizing of shorthand. . . . His
shorthand scheme was propounded not as a mere
professional instrument in the hands of the reporter, or an occasional aid to the student, but as
a method of saving a large proportion of the time
ordinarily spent in writing. He boldly asserted
that his system was applicable to all, or almost all,
the purposes to which longhand is applied, and he
especially advocated its use for all kinds of
correspondence. Enforcing the maxim that ' to

save time is to prolong life,' he invited all his countrymen to become phonographers, and waxed eloquent on the benefits that would inevitably flow therefrom."

One gratifying result of the visit to Edinburgh was that the Brothers William and Robert Chambers gave the new invention favourable mention in their popular serial work, " Information for the People." In No. 62, in which various methods of communicating ideas were discussed, Phonography was mentioned with approval, as " it does away altogether with the tedious method of spelling, because it has distinct signs for all the sounds of the human voice." The art had now begun to attract the notice of the Press, and attention may here be called to an able review of the system from the pen of Mr. Ebenezer Austin (1818-1884)—afterwards a well-known Bristol shorthand writer and journalist—which appeared in the *Bath and Cheltenham Gazette,* on 27th July, 1841. The superior utility of a system with " signs for all the distinct sounds of the human voice, arranged in their natural order," as compared with one based on the " common roundabout way of spelling," was fully recognized, and the greater ease and certainty with which Phonography could be used was clearly pointed out. The reviewer ended with a prediction which has been abundantly fulfilled : " We are," he wrote, " sanguine enough to anticipate the day when Phonography will to a great extent supersede every mode of abbreviated writing, and be the system of shorthand in general use."

In the Christmas holidays of December, 1841, and January, 1842, Isaac Pitman arranged another lecturing tour, in the course of which he revisited Manchester in December. At the office of Messrs. Bradshaw & Blacklock he made his first acquaintance with the art of lithography. George Bradshaw, the head of the firm, and a member of the Society of Friends, was an engraver and lithographer, and had just before started on a small scale the railway time table with which his name has since been identified. Keen interest in improved means of producing his shorthand system led Isaac Pitman to Mr. Bradshaw's office. The method of producing lithographic matter by means of transfer paper was explained to him, and he was given a sheet. After an hour's trial with the lithographic pen, he wrote at his lodgings eight pages of transfer, forming No. 1 of the *Phonographic Journal*, dated January 1842, and the matter was printed by Messrs. Bradshaw and Blacklock.

The first number of the first shorthand periodical ever published in this country opened with a manifesto by its editor and lithographer setting forth the objects for which the new journal was established. One article dealt with the reasons for giving the title only in the common style of printing, and another article was given dealing with the older systems of English shorthand. The

No.1   *JANUARY, 1842.*   Price 2^d or
3^d by Post. paid

THE

PHONOGRAPHIC JOURNAL.

EDITOR. *Isaac Pitman, 5, Nelson Place, BATH.*
PUBLISHER *Bagster, 15, Paternoster Row, LONDON*
Sold also by all Booksellers

FACSIMILE OF THE FIRST PAGE OF " THE PHONOGRAPHIC
JOURNAL "

Key.—The sure word of prophecy uttered by Our Lord and Saviour Jesus Christ, " Behold I make all things new." is every day receiving its fulfilment. Within the last eighty years almost everything has been made anew, or is in progress towards it. But till within the last four years nothing new has practically appeared in the art of writing. It is most remarkable that that art which is the mainspring of all civilization, has remained stationary from the very period of its introduction. This is, however, in accordance with the general law of order prevailing throughout the universe, that the best things are of the slowest growth. We at the present day communicate our ideas with no more rapidity than did the Romans, the Greeks, and the Hebrews, except that we have more suitable materials for writing. By leaving a space at the end of each word and the insertion of stops, we have an advantage over them in *reading*, but in *writing* we have none. It must be acknowledged that something is gained in the Greek and Roman alphabets, but chiefly in the *small* letters, compared with the Hebrew, but this advantage is overbalanced with respect to ours and of the other nations that have adopted the Roman alphabet through the introduction of a most " cumbrous orthography," so that what we gain

ADRL'S

TU ΔU MLMBURZ OV ΔU "FUNOGRAFIK KORLSPONDIU SOSΛ'LTI,"
AND ΔU SUBSKRΛBURZ TU ΔU FUNLTIK FUNT.

DIR FRLNDZ,—IT IZ WIΔ PLL'ZURABUL FILIUZ OV NO Θ'RDINURI KΛND
ΔΛT Λ ADRL'S U IN FUNO'TIPI, AND ΔUS OFUR U ΔU RIZU'LT OV ΔU FURST
LKSPL'RIMLNT MLD WIΔ ΔU FUNT HWIL UR LIBURΛ'LITI HΛZ LNLBULD
MI TU PROVΛ'D. TU U WIL FULUR LJIZ LUK, ΛZ BIIU, UNDUR DIVΛ'N
PRO'VIDLNS, ΔI INTRODUSURZ OV Λ KORL'KT MOD OV RΛTIU AND
PRINTIU : ΔI INSTRUKTURZ OV ΔU SI'VILΛZD WURLD IN ΔU TRU
PRI'NSIPILZ OV ΔΛT ART HWIL⁻IZ ΔU MLNSPRIU OV SIVILIZL'ZUN:
ΔI IMΛ'NSIPLTURZ OV ΔI INFΛNT MΛND FROM ΔU GOLIU LLNZ OV ΔU
PRLZLNT SISTLM OV ΘRΘO'GRAFI : AND ΔI L'LIVLTURZ OV ΔU GRLT MΛS
OV MANKΛ'ND FROM ΔU LOLST DLPΘS OV I'GNORΛNS AND SUPURSTI'ZUN
TU ΔU PLLZURZ OV SΛLNS, AND ΔU DILΛ'TS OV VURLU.

ALU' MI TU KONGRΛ'LULLT U, ΛZ Λ DU MOST SINSIRLI, ON ΔI
LSTΛ'BLIZMLNT, AND RΛPID GRΘΘ OV ΔU "FUNOGRΛFIK KORLSPONDIU
SOSΛ'LTI:" IT IZ, UNKWL'SLUNABLI, WUN OV ΔU MOST USFUL ASOSIL'-
ZUNZ ΔΛT KΛ'RΛKTURΛZ ΔU PRLZLNT DL. NOTWIΘSTANDIU ΔU SOSΛ'LTI
HΛZ BIN IN LGZISTLNS BUT TLN MUNΘS, IT ΘLRLDI BLRZ SUL HΛ
PROMIS, AND MΛ'NIFLSTS SO MUL L'NURJI, TΛLLNT, AND Λ'PTITUD FUR
ΔU WURK HWIL IT HΛZ UNDURTLKIN,—ΔU RL'FΘRMLSUN OV UR RITIN
AND PRINTLD LΛUGWIJ,—ΔΛT Λ HL'ZITLT NOT TU LKSPRL'S MΛ FURM
BILI'F, ΔΛT IT WIL PRUV LFL'KLULL FΘR ΔU SΛLVLSUN OV ΔU LI'TURURI
WURLD FROM ΔU BONDIJ UNDUR HWIL IT GRΘNZ.

"NUΘIU HWOTLVUR IZ MOR TU BI DIZΛ'RD, ΘR MOR DILΛTFUL ΔΛN
ΔU LΛT OV TRUΘ : FΘR IT IZ ΔU SURS OV WIZDUM. HWLN ΔU MΛND
IZ HΛRΛST WIΔ OBSKU'RITI, DISTRΛKTLD BΛ DUTS, RLNDURD TΘRPID
ΘR SΛDLND. BΛ IG'NORΛNS ΘR FΘ'LSITIZ, AND TRUΘ IMURJIZ ΛZ FROM
A DARK ABI'S, IT LΛNZ FΘRΘ INSTΛNTL'NIUSLI, LΛK ΔU SUN DISPURSIU
MISTS AND VLPURZ, ΘR LΛK ΔU DΘN DISPLLIU ΔU ZLDZ OF DARKNLS."
PURHΛ'PS ΔLR IZ NUΘIU MOR FRΘT WIΔ LRUR, ΔΛN ΔU PRLZLNT MOD OV
ALFABL'TIK RΛTIU : AND ΔI IVILZ ΔΛT FLO ΔLRFRΘ'M AR INU'MU-
RΛBIL. DR· PRISTLI OBZU'RVZ, "ΔI IMPURFLKSUNZ OF ΘL Λ'LFABLTS,
(ΔU HIBRU BΛ NO MINZ LKSLPTLD,) SIM TU ARGU ΔLM, NOT TU HΛV
BIN ΔU PRODUKT OV DIVΛ'N SKIL, BUT ΔU RIZU LT OV SUL A KONKURLNS
OV Λ'KSIDLNT AND GRΛ'JULL IMPRUVMLNT, ΛZ ΘL HUMAN ARTS, AND
HWOT WI KΘL INVLNSUNZ, O ΔLR BURΘ TU : FΘR SU'RTINLI, ΔI ΛL'FA-
BLTS IN US, BLR NO MARKS OV ΔU RLGULΛ'RITI OV ΔU WURKS OV NLLUR:
ΔU MOR WI KONSIDUR ΔU LATUR, ΔU MOR RIZIN WI SI TU ADMΛ'R ΔLR

FACSIMILE OF FIRST PAGE PRINTED IN PHONETIC SPELLING
(1844)

last page was devoted to intelligence respecting the progress of the art (at this time incorrectly termed a "science") which shows that, in spite of the opposition already referred to, and the hostility of the Manchester local press, the students and practitioners of the art already numbered one thousand. No. 1 of the *Journal* ran to a second edition, and from this issue we quote below a transcription of portions of the first article, as follows :—

" Till within the last four years nothing new has practically appeared in the art of writing. It is most remarkable that that art which is the main-spring of all civilization, has remained stationary from the very period of its introduction. This is, however, in accordance with the general law of order prevailing throughout the universe, that the best things are of the slowest growth. We at the present day communicate our ideas with no more rapidity than did the Romans, the Greeks, and the Hebrews, except that we have more suitable materials for writing. By leaving a space at the end of each word and the insertion of stops, we have an advantage over them in *reading*, but in *writing* we have none. . . .

" The following must suffice to show how concise is the *pronunciation* of our beautiful English tongue and how prolix is its orthography. *Through* contains two letters, a double consonant and a single vowel, yet it requires seven letters to express it, *t-h-r-o-u-g-h !* *Weight* consists of two sounds but needs six letters in the common spelling, *w-e-i-g-h-t !* Here again neither of the letters except the final *t* is heard in the word.

" *Stricken* is composed of three letters, a treble consonant, a single vowel and a double consonant, but it requires eight signs to represent it to the eye in the common way of writing, *s-t-r-i-c-k-e-n* ! Once more, *though* is formed of the two sounds *thee* and *ō*, but not less than six letters will express the word in longhand—*t-h-o-u-g-h*.

" We may here be met with the remark that shorthand has been known in England 250 years, and that this is a *great* improvement in the art of writing. ' Why then has it not come into general practice ? ' No other answer can be given than this : ' Because it is impracticable according to any of the systems that ever appeared previously to 'Phonography.' We shall often have the opportunity in our pages of showing the reason why shorthand based upon *a, b, c,* cannot become universal, and that it may become universal when founded upon the phonetic principle.

" It is now only four years and a half since the principles of Phonography began to be developed to the mind of the editor of this Journal. In three months, namely in Nov. 1837, it was given to the world in a small work entitled ' Stenographic Sound-Hand,' made as perfect as other and what appeared more important engagements would allow of. In Jan. 1840, it was republished with considerable improvements, suggested during two years' use of the science. . . .

" A new era has now dawned upon the science— the establishment of this Journal—and we have no doubt that the thousand phonographers that are now in existence will be doubled during the present year. This will be attributed chiefly to this publication.

" The Journal will appear monthly, and we are

confident that we shall receive the support of every phonographer. The general expression of delight which greeted the announcement of the work is a pledge to us that it will be a source of pleasure and usefulness to all readers of the science, and one of the best means whereby to extend its blessings to others. At the same time that it will convey interesting phonographic intelligence, it will give extensive practice in *reading* the science, which is at present much needed."

Of the first number of the *Phonographic Journal* one thousand copies were printed. Some hundreds were circulated in Manchester, and a portion of the impression was sent to Mr. Bagster, for publication in London.

Isaac Pitman went from Manchester to Glasgow, where he devoted the remainder of his winter vacation to lecturing on and teaching Phonography. He reached Glasgow on the 7th and left on the 20th January, and during that time delivered six lectures at the following places, namely, the Glasgow University, the Andersonian University, the Grammar School, the Mechanics' Institution, the Anderson Popular Institution, and at Laurieston. From the audiences a total of eighty entered on the study of Phonography, and their instructor records that at the close of the third lesson the greater part could write the system with tolerable readiness. The lecture at the University was delivered in the Common Hall, and was attended by about three hundred students ; of these, thirty-three had a course of lessons at the

University, and a dozen attended other classes. Before he left Glasgow, the following unsolicited testimonial was handed to him, signed by two distinguished professors of the University. It was published by its recipient in his *Journal* for February, 1842, and was in the following terms :—

GLASGOW COLLEGE,
13*th Jan.*, 1842.

We have examined with care and interest Mr. Pitman's analysis of the sounds of language which is made the basis of his system of Phonography, and we consider it not only ingenious but also as founded throughout on correct philosophical principles. His system of Phonography we have not had time to examine, but as it rests on so good a basis, we can have no doubt of its possessing great merit.

JAMES THOMSON.
WILLIAM RAMSAY.

Professor Thomson's two sons were instructed in Phonography at their home. One of these scholars, William, became the world famous scientist, the late Lord Kelvin ; the other was the late Professor James Thomson. Many years after Isaac Pitman met his old pupil, Lord Kelvin, on a visit of the latter to Bath, when he expressed himself as still interested in Phonography, though he had not kept up his practice of the art.

There were no further lecturing and teaching tours undertaken by the Inventor of Phonography in the school vacations. The success of the system resulted in a large demand for instruction books, and these were produced in several styles and in greatly improved form by Isaac Pitman during 1842. In this year the popular " Pocket Edition " was brought out, and also the first text-book to which the title of " Manual of Phonography " was given. He had in addition to undertake single-handed the literary work and the then novel task

DESIGN ON THE COVER OF THE " POCKET EDITION " OF PHONOGRAPHY (1842)

of transfer writing of the pages of his monthly *Journal*, issued in lithographed shorthand, and the provision of a large amount of propagandist literature in the ordinary print. All these pro-ductions were printed and bound in Bath, under the personal supervision of their author.

Mr. Joseph Pitman in the summer of 1841 entered the field as a travelling lecturer on and teacher of his brother's system.   In a tour in the West of England, the city of Worcester was visited, where the oldest existing English provincial newspaper *Berrow's Worcester Journal* (founded in 1709) in its issue of 3rd February, 1842, pronounced the new system to be " undoubtedly unique, clever, and complete," though it was not convinced of the feasibility of phonetic writing.   In 1842 Mr. Benn Pitman came out as a phonographic lecturer. Other instructors were at this time beginning to issue circulars, and the regular teaching of the system may be said to have definitely begun.

VII

THE WRITING AND SPELLING REFORM—THE FIRST INSTITUTE

1843

At the beginning of 1843 Isaac Pitman discontinued the private school he had conducted since his settlement in Bath, in order that he might devote his whole time to the production of the various books, periodicals, and leaflets connected with his system of Phonography, and early in the year he added to the text-books already noticed " The Reporter's Book " his first special adaptation of the system to verbatim reporting. There was now a steady and increasing demand for treatises on the art, and a large portion of his time was henceforward devoted to the production of successive editions of his shorthand works. His residence was now designated the " Phonographic Institution " on his publications and on all that he sent out. He had at this time a large correspondence, which was swollen by great numbers of exercises from learners sent for correction, and involving a vast amount of voluntary labour. But his work was attacked and disposed of from day to day with unabated energy, and he was invariably successful in imparting a portion of his own intense enthusiasm for his invention to those who had mastered it, who now numbered some thousands

of active workers in all parts.   Early in this year
(1843) a youthful disciple, destined to become a
famous exponent and writer of Phonography, paid
a visit to Nelson Place.   Mr. Reed, the visitor in
question, was a boy of sixteen and living at Bristol
when he first saw Isaac Pitman.   " He was then,"
Mr. Reed tells us, " a young man, tall, slim, active,
springy in all his movements," and his cheerful,
ready explanation of the work to which he was
devoting all his time, from five or six in the morning till nine or ten at night, made a lasting
impression on young Reed.

Had it been possible, it was no longer necessary
for the Inventor of Phonography to travel and
lecture personally on his system, although at
intervals he attended gatherings of a special
character, as will be described in due course.   A
number of additional lecturers had entered the
field early this year, while those already engaged
in such work were extremely active throughout
1843.   In most of the towns they visited the
subject had the charm of novelty, and almost
invariably attracted large audiences, among whom
the fervent enthusiasm of the lecturers was
successful in enlisting a band of adherents who
afterwards practised and taught the art.   The
early workers in this field (in addition to Joseph
and Benn Pitman) were George Withers, a nephew
of Mrs. Pitman ; T. A. Reed and F. E. Woodward,
afterwards partners in the well-known London
shorthand writing firm ;   T. P. (afterwards

Alderman) Barkas, of Newcastle-on-Tyne; William
Hepworth Dixon, afterwards famous as an author
and editor (1853-69) of the *Athenæum ;* T. Walker,
of the Commercial Bank of England, Manchester ;
W. G. Ward, who afterwards became Mayor of
Nottingham ; and later on James Clarke, after-
wards editor and proprietor of the *Christian
World ;* H. S. Brooke, J. H. Mogford, G. R.
Haywood, C. Sully, J. Hornsby, and F. Carson.
There were many others in all parts of Great
Britain who within a few years from this date
publicly lectured on and taught the system, and
among them were the two younger brothers of the
Inventor, Henry and Frederick Pitman.

A suggestion was made by Mr. Reed in February,
1843, which resulted in the establishment of the
first society in connection with the phonographic
art. He proposed to the Inventor that he should
" introduce, by letter, some friends whose time is
not fully occupied, to other friends in different
places, thereby establishing a correspondence
between phonographers in different parts of the
kingdom." " The same thing," Isaac Pitman
observed, " was proposed to us last year by another
correspondent, who very properly recommended
the *Journal* as the repository of the addresses of
such as wished thus to exchange ideas." He
expressed his full concurrence in Mr. Reed's
proposal, and observed that it would be well to
form a society entitled " The Phonographic Corresponding Society," with the names and addresses

of members published in the *Journal*, " the
society," he added, " may be made very useful by
taking part of our own labours, which have really
become too heavy for any one person to perform
well. It is that of correcting the lessons of
learners through the post gratuitously." In
response to an invitation twenty-seven individuals
sent their names and addresses. These were
published in the *Journal* for March, and thus
formed the first list of members of the new society.
By the end of 1843 there was a total of 300
members, and from this time onward the society
vastly increased in numbers and in usefulness.

But even in the pursuit of the most useful
branch of knowledge, human nature seems to be
so constituted that occasional relaxation is absolutely necessary. A pause must be made now and
then in order to discover what progress has been
achieved, and to gain encouragement for renewed
exertions. It was for a purpose of this kind that
the phonographic festivals appear to have been
instituted. The first took place at Manchester on
15th March, 1843, and attracted 100 friends of
Phonography, who partook of tea and indulged in
speech-making. Mr. George Falkner, editor of
Bradshaw's Journal, was unable to preside, but
sent a letter in which he said, " I feel it a depriva-
tion to be absent from this epoch in the history of
Phonography—this erection of the first milestone
in the path which is to conduct to its universal
recognition."

The second festival was held at Nottingham on 6th June, and here about 450 sat down to tea, and the number afterwards increased to 600. The *Nottingham Mercury* gave a report of the proceedings in the Exchange Hall, and as the account furnishes a very good idea of what the festival proceedings were like, we quote a short descriptive passage. The writer observes :—" The management of the festival was under the direction of a committee, who are a body of spirited phonographers, and who, for their strenuous exertions to make the festival both pleasing and instructive, deserve the greatest praise. Four tables, extending the whole length of the room, were tastefully laid out with numerous massive glass vases, containing the choicest flowers, and urns decorated with garlands of no small beauty. At the upper end of the room was placed a cross table, intended for Mr. Isaac Pitman and his brothers, together with phonographers from distant places. In fact, the whole presented an exceedingly pleasing appearance ; the usual splendid fascinations of the hall adding *their* charms to the scene. Never was a miscellaneous party more highly honoured with

Sparkling eyes and happy faces

than the present." The editor of the *Journal* adds that the tea was very well served, and that when the tables were cleared, a platform was erected for the speakers. There was music by a select choir, and a " high-toned piano " enlivened the proceedings. The orators on the occasion included Mr. Barkas, Mr. Joseph Pitman, Mr. Benn Pitman, Mr. Reed, and Isaac Pitman. The speeches were of a most enthusiastic description, and appear to have carried conviction to the minds of the audience. As the " platform " did not desire to monopolize the whole time of the meeting, the audience was invited to participate in the oratory, with the result that " a gentleman in the body of the room then stood upon his seat and addressed the assembly in a very humorous strain. He stated that he had come fifteen miles to attend the festival ; that he had lately commenced the study of Phonography, and was more pleased with it than with anything else he had ever met with. He urged its study upon the attention of the young, and forewarned them of the bitter regrets they would feel hereafter, if they should now neglect it." When the speeches were over, " many of the youthful part of the company remained to enjoy themselves with music and a festive dance."

The third festival was held at Birmingham on the 18th July, and to the enjoyable accompaniments of tea and music, but without the dance as a finale. Again speeches were made fully as enthusiastic as those which had been delivered at the previous festivals. The tea-party numbered 170, but how many attended the subsequent meeting is not recorded. Dr. Melson presided, and the other orators included Mr. T. W. Hill, the father of the eminent Post Office reformer, Mr.

Joseph Pitman, Mr. Benn Pitman, and Isaac Pitman. The speech of the last named contained some interesting references to the origin of Phonography.

" It originated," Isaac Pitman observed, " with myself so far as this, that I knew nothing of an attempt to write by sound having been made by any one else till three years after I had published the first edition of Phonography, under the title of ' Stenographic Sound-Hand.' I then met with the work of Mr. George Edmonds, of this town, aiming at the same object. I have since seen several others ; and I may refer particularly to a system of phonetic writing, constructed by a gentleman now present, T. W. Hill, esq., honoured and respected for his age and virtues, and particularly so, as being the father of our great benefactor, Rowland Hill.

" You will perhaps be led to inquire, How is it that the authors that have published such systems have all failed in their attempt to gain writers, while Phonography, in the course of three years, has attracted the attention of many thousand persons, a Journal being printed in it, to which there are already a thousand subscribers, and the number daily increasing ? I can account for it only in this way. The framers of other systems did not possess a thorough acquaintance with all the materials for swift writing ; they did not know the comparative value of every stroke and dot ; neither had they observed the analogy between the four positions in which a line may be placed, and the four seats of articulation, the lips, teeth, palate, and throat ; they did not give single marks for the double vowels *ye, ya, yah, yau, yo, yoo ;*

we, wa, wah, wau, wo, woo ; nor did they hit upon
the beautiful expedient of halving the consonants
to signify the addition of *t* or *d.* There are some
other minor points that might be noticed in
connection with this subject, such as the hooking
on of *l* and *r* to all the letters, etc."

There were many other gatherings of a similar
kind, but an enumeration of them is unnecessary.
All who took part in these proceedings were very
much in earnest, and their enthusiasm no doubt
occasionally betrayed them into some extrava-
gances of language.   But what great movement
ever made satisfactory progress without the
momentum which enthusiasm engenders ?

The enthusiasm for Phonography was partici-
pated in by its London publisher.   On reading in
Timothe Bright's dedication of his " Characterie "
to Queen Elizabeth that Cicero contrived a shorthand and Seneca improved it, Samuel Bagster at
this time sent the following verses to the Inventor
of Phonography :—

TO MR. PITMAN, OF BATH,

*On his Invention of the Phonographic Art, and successful
Efforts in spreading a knowledge of it.*

Were Cicero's sweet voice now heard,
This art would gather every word,
            Nor leave one thought unwrit ;
Were Seneca's deep knowledge taught,
(A wisdom that a nation sought),
            To gather it, 'tis fit.

Had Cicero's admirers known,
Or, Seneca the science shown
         Of Phonographic art ;—
The world would now have held a prize,
And *all* this wisdom met *our* eyes,
         And not, as *now*, A PART.

Mr. John Bright was among those who were at this period impressed with the value of Phonography, and he defrayed half the expenses of a lecture delivered at the Rochdale Theatre on 15th September, 1843, by Mr. Joseph Pitman. After witnessing the practical demonstrations of the use of Phonography given by the lecturer and Mr. Reed, Mr. Bright, who presided, addressed the audience in the following terms :—

I am greatly astonished at what I have seen. I think no person can have been at this lecture or attended the one that was given this day week, without being convinced that all that has been promised by this science may easily be performed ; and that it is so exceedingly simple as to be easily learned by everyone of ordinary capacity ; and if it be learned by a very large number of the people, the public benefits to be derived from it are entirely incalculable. It may be said, also, that, to make it very valuable, it is necessary that great multitudes should learn it. Shorthands are of very little use if they are only known to a select few ; for men are not writing always to the same men ; and if ever it is to come into general use, it must be, I think, by very large multitudes learning it ; and I see no reason why, in this town, we should not have a class of four or five hundred, or more. If five hundred knew it well, and used it, many thousands would be forced to learn and practise it from necessity. In this age, when we are talking so much about education—when we ought to be doing so much more than we are—this science appears to me likely to tend to increase the love of reading and writing, and of education generally ; and it seems to have sprung up at a

time when, like many other improvements, it was most needed;
and when, in all probability, it will be seized upon with the
greatest avidity.   I may say for myself that I am extremely
obliged, personally, to the Inventor, and to the gentleman
who has come among us and given us these lectures ; and
hope to be much more so, when I become acquainted with the
science. We are extremely indebted to them for the very
handsome manner in which they have come forward, in
offering to teach, gratuitously, all such as find it difficult to
pay ; and, unfortunately, there are too many such in these
days. I trust there will be no want of those who can pay,
to remunerate them for this handsome offer which they have
made towards those who cannot pay.   I shall be glad if this
town, which, on many occasions, has stood foremost among
the towns in Lancashire on some other questions, should not
be behind in one so important as this.

In later years Mr. Bright's eldest daughter
(afterwards Mrs. Clark) learned Phonography and
became her father's amanuensis, often writing
from his dictation.

The testimony of two well-known journalists
to the merits of Phonography demands record
here.   Mr John Harland, a famous reporter, and
afterwards one of the proprietors of the *Manchester
Guardian*—who wrote a system of his own—was so
much impressed with its practical merits, that he
stated that Phonography " contains within itself
the power of becoming superior to all " systems
of shorthand extant.   Mr. John King, proprietor
and editor of the *Suffolk Chronicle*, in addition
to hearty advocacy of the system, started a
phonographic magazine.

In this year (1843) the first practical steps were
taken to realize an idea which had originally

occurred to Isaac Pitman in the preceding spring.
Why, he asked himself, should not the phonographic alphabet, so successful for writing, be
employed in printing the English language ? In
August, 1842, he mentioned in his *Journal* a
proposal for a printing alphabet to consist of all
the separate phonographic signs for the simple and
compound forms of consonants and vowels in his
system. As this would need a total of 115 distinct
characters, leaving " upper case," or capital
letters, out of sight altogether, it was obviously
impracticable for use in the printing office, while
the disjoined geometric characters when assembled
in words would have presented a far from harmonious appearance. But out of this idea arose
a practicable plan for adding additional signs for
unrepresented simple consonants and vowels to
the Roman alphabet. In 1843 Isaac Pitman
issued his periodical in two sections, one the
Phonographic Journal, lithographed in Phonography by its Inventor, and the other, the
Phonotypic Journal, for the advocacy of Spelling Reform. The proposition was enunciated
that " As Phonography becomes the general
medium of written communication, phonotypic
printing must follow. We shall, therefore," he
said, " advocate Phonography as a means for the
attainment of the great need—Phonotypic Printing." From this time he regarded his system of
shorthand chiefly as an introduction to Spelling
Reform ; and to the advocacy of a phonetic

notation he devoted the strenuous efforts of a
lifetime and his own means without stint, while he
had also the moral and pecuniary support of a large
number of adherents in all parts of the country.
Of these the most distinguished was Mr. (afterwards Dr.) Alexander John Ellis (1814-1890), then
residing at Dorking, who having had his attention
called to Phonography by a notice in the *Athenæum*
of the Birmingham festival, wrote in the following
terms to Isaac Pitman in a letter dated 6th August,
1843 :—

Although I have for some years, and especially during the
last fifteen months, bestowed considerable attention on the
phonetical analysis of languages, it has so happened that
I never heard of Phonography till two days ago. I have been
diligently reading the " Manual " and the last number of the
Journal, and am delighted to find that our labours do not
clash. You have bestowed your principal attention on the
phono*graphic ;* I on the phono*typic* division of the subject.
It was my chief object to produce an alphabet which should
be easy to *print ;* and I think that I have succeeded at last in
forming an alphabet of the eighty-two primitive sounds of
the principal European and Oriental languages such as could
be set up by any country compositor at any country press.

On 12th September, Mr. Ellis again wrote to Isaac
Pitman making certain practical suggestions for
increasing the fund which had been opened to
provide for the cost of the first phonotypic
alphabet. After considerable discussion, the new
forms for the first phonotypic letters were agreed
upon, and an order was given to Messrs. V. and J.
Figgins, typefounders, who produced a fount of the
new letters before the close of 1843.

VIII

PHONOTYPY INTRODUCED—PHONOGRAPHY AND THE SPELLING REFORM ATTACKED AND DEFENDED

1844-1845

IN spite of his many activities at this period, Isaac Pitman found time to edit and lithograph a second monthly shorthand magazine, entitled the *Phonographic Correspondent*, which began its course in January, 1844, and at the close of the year took the place of the phonographic section of the *Journal*. Next to his industry, his versatility at this period of his life is little short of astonishing. Hardly any of the earlier or contemporary reformers of English spelling—however excellent may have been the schemes they formulated in their treatises —had, or aspired to have, a practical acquaintance with the art of printing, which is so greatly affected by projects of this description. The Inventor of Phonography, however, acquired in the office of his printers, the proprietors of the *Bath Journal*, practical skill in typesetting, and was thus enabled to " set " with his own hands the first page of phonotypic printing produced in this country. This practical knowledge of the art of letterpress printing was destined to prove of the utmost service in succeeding years, both in Spelling Reform experiments and in the production of his shorthand instruction books. His typographical attainments in connection with Phonotypy were the necessary complement to his lithographic transfer writing ability in association with Phonography. But for his skill in these two classes of work, the history of Phonography and Phonotypy might have been widely different.

Isaac Pitman's first Annual Address to the Phonographic Corresponding Society and to subscribers to the phonetic fount, appeared in the early days of January, 1844, and filled two pages of phonotypic printing, the first put in type from the new phonotypic fount (in small capital letters only), provided in part by subscriptions from supporters of the movement, and in part paid for by its originator. " Many attempts," he reminded his supporters, " have been made to reform the errors of our written language, but hitherto without success. . . . There was no desire created in the public mind for a consistent system of orthography ; now, by your benevolent exertions in spreading abroad the truths of phonetic writing, a desire has been created for phonotypy, a desire that will increase by that on which it feeds." The work of reforming English orthography was, in a word, set about under the inspiration of a noble desire to aid the march of the human intellect.

The Reading and Writing Reform, now fully inaugurated, was brought before the public at a time when several great movements which profoundly interested the nation were occupying attention. There was a world's Anti-Slavery Convention in London in the autumn of 1843, and among those who attended from America was the eminent Abolitionist Stephen Pearl Andrews (1812-1886), a member of the American Bar, a linguist and philologist of no small attainments, and the inventor of a universal language to which he gave the name of " Alwato." He addressed a meeting in London, and thus describes what followed, when he descended from the platform :—

Somebody, I never knew who, pressed into my hands a package of books and pamphlets, and whispered to me an earnest request that I would examine them and use my influence to get the subject of which they treated introduced to the American public. On my return to my lodgings I partially examined the package, and for the first time saw the name of Isaac Pitman, and the words Phonography and Phonotypy. I was too busy to give the matter more attention then, and carelessly threw the package into my trunk with other documents. It was not until I was on my way home, on the steamer, that I fairly opened the package and examined it. Years before in New Orleans I had discovered the irregularities of English orthography, and resolved some time to devote myself to reforming it. There I found the same idea, before wholly my own, already under way, and it interested me profoundly. It was the Spelling Reform Branch, and only in a very secondary way, at first, Phonography, which fixed my attention. I made the study of the two, however, my main business on the voyage. Landing in Boston, I found myself a good deal of a lion there. . . . I became a lecturing agent for the Massachusetts liberty party, but at the same time I resolved to become a propagandist of the Pitmanian project in this country. I established my headquarters at 21 School Street, Boston, second floor, front room, with its bow window, from which locality the new phonetic gospel was first promulgated to Americans. I availed myself of my notoriety with the Press to crowd on the public the most enthusiastic accounts of Mr. Pitman's great discovery, and advertised for pupils.

Mr. Andrews soon had a large band of American students and disciples. At the start he put himself in communication with Isaac Pitman, who, he observes, " Backed me very nobly, giving his books freely or selling them at cost. He must have invested many thousand dollars beyond actual returns in planting this American branch of the movement." In 1844 Mr. Andrews produced at Boston the first American instruction book published on the Pitmanic system.

In the following year (1845), Phonography became associated with the Free Trade movement. There was an Anti-Corn Law Bazaar at Covent Garden Theatre, London, on 12th May, when the claims of Phonography were brought prominently before the notice of those who attended by a supply of special literature at one of the stalls. At the end of this year an Anti-Corn Law Demonstration was held at Bath. Isaac Pitman attended a public meeting in the Guildhall and reported the speech of Richard Cobden for the *Bath Journal.* There were in the printing office of this newspaper several compositors who had been instructed in Phonography by its Inventor, and he determined to try an experiment which was at that time quite unique, and is described in the *Bath*

IZAC PITMAN,

INVENTER OV FONOGRAFI.

*Dédicated, tu de Fonografic Corespóndiŋ
Sosjetiz ov Grat Briten and America
bj dar Obedient Servant,
Jamz B. Cen.
(J.B.Keene.)*

Ogust 1846.

Ǝ FONETIC NIUZ.

CONDUCTED BƆ ƎE PROPRIƎTUR, ALECSANDER J. ELIS, B.A.

NR 1.]   SATÉRDA, 6 JANUERI, 1849.   [PRIS 4½d. STAMPT.
Per Cwarter in advans, 4s. 6d.

FACTS FOR SPELLERS OF THE OLD SCHOOL.

READER! Do you ask why we propose to change the English orthography? We reply:

1. IT IS A FACT, that no one can tell the sound of an English word from its spelling.

Proof.—To *read* the book he has *read*; to *present* a *present*, the *slough* of a snake found in a *slough*; *lead* me to the *lead* mine; *refuse* the *refuse*, &c.; the words in italics are pronounced differently, that is, are different spoken words, according to their meaning alone; and there are 201 words of this kind in our language, which are pronounced in 406 different ways:—2. The same combination of letters has very different significations in different words: compare *hear, heard, heart; here, where; hie, shie; sine, sinne* (so), *sloth; eyed; keyed, conveyed, journeyed*; and so on, in an infinite number of cases.—3. There is a very large number of words concerning the pronunciation of which even orthoepists are not agreed: as, *knowledge*, (nol-ledge, no-ledge); *leisure*, (lee-zhur, lezh-ur); *inimical, inimical*, and so on.—4. No one can be sure of the pronunciation of any word he has not previously been taught: let the reader try the unusual words, *batman, leasoffe, rowlock, boargeoise* (type); and the names of places and persons, *Beaulieu, L'-Isidost, Hecklebeys*, and so on. Turn the page and read—
ψαλτηρολογοι 'βαβλοι 'ασφαλειη 'υψηφι 'ασασαιηφι

2. IT IS A FACT, that no one can tell the spelling of an English word from its sound.

Proof.—1. There are 406 spoken words, spelled in 537 ways, but the variations of the spelling never depend on the sound, and cannot be learned from it.—2. There are upwards of 1350 words, about the spelling of which authors are not agreed.—3. The style of spelling cannot even be predicted from a knowledge of etymology: compare *fancy phantom, concede succeed, island bay, husband house, rhyme, ghost, city, flyr flier, burgess bourgeoise burgher*, &c., &c.—4. No sound in the language is uniformly represented by the same sign.—

ǞHE ENGLISH PHONETIC ALPHABET.

The letter written	prnd	is always sounded as		The letter written	prnd	is always sounded as
	E e	er in eel			P p	p in pole
	A a	a . . ale			B b	b . . bowl
	A q	a . . alms			T t	t . . toe
	O o	o . . all			D d	d . . doe
	U u	oo . . food			ch . . cheer
	I i	i . . ill			c . . came
	E e	e . . ell			g . . game
	A q	a . . olive			F f	f . . fear
	O o	o . . .			V v	v . . veer
	U u	u . . up			th . . thigh
	U u	oo . . foot			th . . thy
	I i	i . . isle			s . . real
	O o	oi . . oil			z . . real
	U u	ou . . owl			sh . . vicious
	U u	u . . mule			z . . vision
					R r	r . . rare
					L l	l . . lull
	Y y	y . . yea			M m	m . . mum
	W w	w . . way			N n	n . . nun
	H h	h . . hay			ng . . sing

The sign (') is prefixed to *i, l, m, n*, to show that they form syllables by themselves; thus, *idl'l, apos'l, 'yt'l* = little, spasm, open. The parentheses (†) indicate that the inclosed words are not spelled phonetically.

Journal of 8th December, 1845, in the following terms :—

In connection with the report of the excellent addresses, delivered at the great demonstration on Thursday of the opinions of a very large majority of the citizens of Bath, which will be found in our columns this week, we would call the attention of our readers to a fact indicative of Reform in other matters as well as in the Corn Laws. By the kindness of Mr. Isaac Pitman of this city, whose systems of writing and printing by sound have made such astonishing progress in all parts of the kingdom, we are enabled to give a nearly verbatim report of the excellent speech of R. Cobden, Esq., which our compositors have set up from Mr. Pitman's phonographic notes, there being no necessity for their transcription. With all other systems of shorthand writing, not only was there never known such a thing as a reporter passing over to the compositor his notes of a speech an hour and a quarter in delivery, but he is often unable to decipher them himself. All that was necessary in this case, Mr. Pitman has assured us, was to give the speech one reading the next morning, and fill in a few vowels. We are convinced that we shall in a few years, by this invaluable system, save all that immense amount of toil which our present reporters have to undergo in deciphering and transcribing their notes for the press. [1]

For various reasons the anticipations of the writer of the above notice have not been realized. The first and most important cause why they have not is that it is hardly ever possible for the speech of any speaker, even when reported fully, to be presented to the public without receiving a certain

---

[1] At this time a portrait in oils of Isaac Pitman at the age of 32 was painted by Mr. J. B. (afterwards Colonel) Keene (1823-1910), son of the then Editor of the *Bath Journal*, and one of the earliest writers of Phonography. A steel engraving was produced of this portrait, an impression from which faces this page.

amount of " editing " from the reporter. But with the present general knowledge of Phonography, much newspaper and book " copy " might be written in shorthand, and a great saving of time and labour effected.

Phonography at this period attracted the attention of two poets, James Montgomery and Bernard Barton ; the former manifested his friendship for the new art, the latter his hostility to it. Both expressed their thoughts in poetry, and brief extracts from their respective utterances will indicate their views. James Montgomery, when the system was introduced to his notice by Messrs. Joseph Pitman and Reed, gave them a practical dictation test, and satisfied himself as to the efficiency of the new system. At one of their meetings held in the Cutlers' Hall, Sheffield, on 28th February, 1844, he recited from the chair a poem which opened thus :—

> Mind is invisible, yet when we write,
> That world of mystery comes forth to sight ;
> In vocal speech, the idle air breathes sense,
> And empty sound becomes intelligence.
> PHONETIC ART hath both these modes outdone,
> By blending sounds and symbols into one.
> Take one step more, and science may define
> How spirits discourse without a word or sign ;
> And teach mankind their feelings to impart,
> Unseen, unheard, by pulses of the heart ;
> While souls by sympathy the world embrace,
> And hold communion, free of time and place ;
> Or, unembodied, with survivors keep
> Sweet intercourse, both when we wake or sleep,

> Glorious, and good, and wonderful such powers !
> And who shall say they never can be ours ?
> They're ours already in the parent root,
> The stem, the branch, the flower,—and then, why not
> the fruit ?

Bernard Barton penned a tirade against Phonography at the time Isaac Pitman visited Ipswich to attend a phonographic soirée in 1845. In "An Epistle to a Phonetic Friend ; or, A Few Words on Phonography," prefaced by the quotation,

> A thing of sound (not fury)
> Signifying nothing,

appeared the following amusing lines :—

> The New System saves much time.   Indeed !
> Must we then write, read, spell, by rail-road speed ?
> 'Tis bad enough, whene'er we go abroad,
> That fire and smoke must urge us on our road,
> And, for the music of the birds and spheres,
> To have that horrid whistle din our ears ;
> Must we not *ride*, alone, as if we flew,
> But the same haste adopt in all we do ?
> " *More haste worse speed*,"—The proverb still holds true !

> I wish that Pitman, Reed, and all their crew,
> Or better taste, or better manners knew ;
> To one accustomed to the olden lore
> Their boasted *System* is a dreadful bore,
> Though trumpeted, with empty acclamation,
> A READING, *Writing*, *Printing* REFORMATION !
> Misses and masters in six lessons taught
> What a life's labour to our fathers brought ;
> Can write in shorthand, or like parrots speak,
> Chaldee or Coptic, Sanscrit, Hebrew, Greek ;
> But the sum total of this parrot lore,
> Appeals to sight and sound, and little more.

This attack on Phonography provoked several rejoinders. Isaac Pitman replied in prose, and there were four poetic answers, one of which was composed by Mr Reed. Mr John Dallenger headed his reply with an apt parody of Barton :—

> Phonography her simple page
> Impartially unfolding,
> Prohibits neither saint nor sage
> Its beauties from beholding.

In the course of his reply he thus retorted on the Quaker poet :—

> I wish Phonographers may soon subdue
> All snarling critics, and the satirist crew ;
> When vulgar prejudice shall vote no more
> A perfect system as a dreadful bore ;
> But Poets hail, with joyous acclamation,
> This truly splendid WRITING REFORMATION ;
> And future ages shall, in truth, be brought
> To estimate the system PITMAN taught ;
> Write in its praise, and of its beauties speak,
> In sterling English—not in Poet's Greek ;
> For Poets cite the tongues, to show their lore,
> And know as much as parrots—little more.

Several other literary men and many journalists took an active interest in the new method of writing, and in some instances learned Phonography. Dr. Robert Chambers, whose first acquaintance with the art is noticed in Chapter VI not only learned it but wrote an article on it in *Chambers's Journal* of 5th October, 1844, which proved of great service to the movement. Some journalists were favourable and some distinctly hostile, and there were about this time challenges and contests which provoked a great deal of interest and possibly amusement. The extravagance of language of certain champions of Phonography, who seemed to regard it as nothing short of a new dispensation, led the Rev. Edward Bickersteth (father of Dr. Bickersteth, sometime Bishop of Exeter), in his book entitled " The Promised Glory of the Church," to class Phonography with other things which he denounced as " stalking horses behind which the most Satanic lies and the most absurd blasphemies are sent forth against the Word of God ! " The rev. gentleman received an assurance that nothing was further from the thoughts of its Inventor, at any rate, than to dishonour the Divine Word, and Mr. Bickersteth readily withdrew Phonography from the black list in the second edition of his book.

The Post Office Reformer, Mr. (afterwards Sir) Rowland Hill, whose father had two years before shown his interest in the movement (see Chap. VII) presided at a phonographic soirée held in the Town Hall, Brighton, on 28th February, 1845, in connection with the visit of Messrs. Joseph Pitman and Reed. In lamenting the fact of our cumbrous system of orthography, Rowland Hill said :—

" I therefore attach very great importance to attempts such as these made by the Messrs. Pitman to improve and reform our writing and printing."

In association with phonographic correspondence, manuscript magazines written in shorthand
were started in 1840, when the first of the kind,
called the " Family Messenger," circulated among
the nine brothers and sisters of the Pitman family
then resident in England. This production was
of very small size, in order that it might go through
the post in a half ounce letter for a penny postage.
In 1844 the number of these magazines in circulation among phonographers was fairly large, and
they then received the distinctive name of
Evercirculators.

By the end of 1845 the Phonographic
Corresponding Society was receiving large acces-
sions of members, and Isaac Pitman deemed it
advisable that those who desired membership
in future should, as a preliminary to enrolment,
submit a specimen of their Phonography.

IX

A DEPARTURE IN PRINTING AND PUBLISHING—
MR. A. J. ELLIS AND THE " 1847 ALPHABET "

1845-1848

AT the Ipswich soirée held on 14th May, 1845,
when Mr. Robert Ransome and Mr. W. D. Sims
were among the speakers who bore eloquent testimony to the value of Phonography, Isaac Pitman
gave a long address on the origin and development
of his system. Some of the more important statements and facts contained in that speech have
been reproduced in the earlier chapters of the
present narrative, but his remarks on that occasion
contained some interesting facts bearing on the
extent of the movement in 1845, which will be
appropriately noticed here. Isaac Pitman informed his Ipswich audience that from the Institution at Bath he was sending out seven hundredweight of books per month, and was receiving ten
thousand phonographic letters a year. Ten lecturers were constantly employed in teaching the
system, and over a thousand members of the
Phonographic Corresponding Society were engaged
in its private dissemination. Phonography was now
in the Seventh Edition ; many improvements had
been made in its presentation as new editions were
called for, and it was abundantly evident, if we
may use a colloquial expression, that it had come to

stay. Its originator saw in all these evidences of appreciation of his work proof that it had become a "national movement," and he was justified in that assumption. With the practical sagacity which was a striking feature of his character, he perceived that in order to provide most successfully for what would, in all probability, be an ever-growing demand for the books and periodicals connected with the phonographic art, and for the purpose of carrying on his experiments in phonotypy, it was essential that he should have a printing establishment under his own direction.

Accordingly, in December, 1845, the Inventor of Phonography set up his first printing press at his residence, and henceforward his many publications in ordinary letterpress with woodcut short-hand illustrations, and in phonotypy, bore the imprint 5 Nelson Place. Writing in 1852 Isaac Pitman observed that those who had seen some of the millions of books and papers printed at that address "will learn with astonishment that (from 1845) the whole business of the Writing and Printing Reform, so far as the production of English books was concerned, was, until March, 1848, carried on in two rooms—a long one on the ground floor, measuring 34 ft. by 12 ft. for the compositors and bookbinders, and a small room underground (adjoining the kitchen, and commonly termed the housekeeper's room) just large enough to take a printing press. . . . During the winter of 1849-50, eighteen persons were engaged in these two rooms, sixteen in the compositors' and binders' room, and two in the press room. When it is considered that all the stock of books and paper, as well as the men and tools had to be crowded into this place, it may be said that the Reform was projected, and successfully carried on for seven years—reckoning from January, 1844, when phonetic printing first appeared in the *Journal*— in a bee-hive."

The narrative quoted above is the earliest account we have from the pen of Isaac Pitman concerning his Institute and staff. From a later statement of his we learn that a third room in his home was afterwards devoted to the business of the Reform.

Changes in regard to the London publishing arrangements occurred almost simultaneously with the alterations in production at Bath. Messrs. Bagster & Sons found that the handling of the phonographic publications interfered with their Bible publishing at No. 15 Paternoster Row. They accordingly in 1845 opened a shop at No. 1 Queen's Head Passage, adjoining their establish- ment in the Row, and here the phonographic books and periodicals were published. The name of Bagster was for the future omitted from the phonographic books, and the new place of publica- tion was designated the "Phonographic and Phonotypic Depot." In 1846 Mr. Benn Pitman took charge of the "Depot," assisted by his two younger brothers. In the following year

Mr. Frederick Pitman, then but nineteen years old, superintended the business. About the time that he came of age (October, 1849), Mr. Frederick Pitman took No. 20 Paternoster Row, set up in business on his own account as a publisher, and from this time to his death was the publisher of his brother Isaac's phonographic books and periodicals. " Some risk," Mr. Reed says, " was expected to attend the experiment apart from the Messrs. Bagster, with whose house Phonography had been identified for nine years, but the result amply justified the change. Here, as at Queen's Head Passage, Mr. Fred. Pitman was assisted by his father, Mr. Samuel Pitman, who, in his old age, had the satisfaction of witnessing the success of his sons, and giving them the benefit of his co-operation. Those who visited the depot in those days will not forget the shrewd and sagacious sayings and doings of Pitman père, who was for some years a well-known character in the Row."

In 1845 a Phonetic Council, which had been organized some little time previously, was engaged in deliberations on various points in relation to the phonotypic alphabet. Isaac Pitman was the President of this body, and of the twelve members Mr. Ellis was incomparably the most distinguished as a scholar, a phonetician, and an author. His contributions to the *Journal* during this period were among the ablest and most convincing arguments on behalf of phonetic spelling that have ever appeared. In addition to works such as " The Alphabet of Nature," and " A Plea for Phonotypy and Phonography, or Speech-writing," Mr. Ellis was the author of adaptations of Phonography to no less than fourteen languages, living and dead. " His scholarship," as Mr. Reed observes, " was a great acquisition to the cause." With the aid of subscriptions, a complete long primer phonotypic fount of type had been produced (followed later on by larger and smaller sizes), and one of the first uses to which Isaac Pitman put the new type was to begin the printing of a " Phonotypic Bible," but when the publication had proceeded serially as far as Exodus XX, the printing was stopped, owing to changes which had been introduced in the vowel notation of phonotypy, and all that had been produced became so much waste paper. ˙Innumerable phonotypic experiments, both before and after this time, were submitted to the Phonetic Council, but in June, 1846, the " Absolute Completion of the Phonotypic Alphabet " was announced in these terms :—

" Messrs. Pitman and Ellis distinctly pledge themselves not to make any further alterations in the forms or uses of the letters of the practical Phonotypic Alphabet of the English language given in this number of the *Journal,* or in the theory upon which it is founded. Whatever books they publish in Phonotypy will be printed in accordance with this alphabet and no other."

This decision was arrived at after experiments extending over three years. A few slight improvements in the Pitman-Ellis alphabet were introduced within the next eighteen months by Isaac Pitman and the Phonetic Council. During this period Mr. Ellis was residing in Germany, but by the end of 1847 he had returned to England, and came to reside at No. 4 Lansdown Crescent, Bath, with the design of taking a leading part in a movement for bringing the new spelling before the nation in a fashion not hitherto attempted.

The initial step in this change was announced in a notice which appeared in the *Phonotypic Journal* at the end of 1847. Isaac Pitman informed the readers of his retirement from the control of the *Journal* he had created, and the contemplated appearance in 1848 of a new series, with the title of the *Phonetic Journal*, under the editorship of Mr. Ellis. The announcement closed with the intimation that " It gives Mr. Pitman much pleasure to think that all these experiments have been commenced and brought to a satisfactory termination while the *Journal* was under his management." The phonotypy thus referred to became known in subsequent years as " the 1847 alphabet."

In pursuance of this project Mr. Ellis in November, 1847, purchased the printing plant used in the production of the *Journal*, and took over the composing staff at Nelson Place. In March, 1848, he removed the printing establishment to larger premises at Albion Place, in the Upper Bristol Road, Bath. Mr. Reed states that "One of the conditions of the purchase was that Isaac Pitman was to have the joint use of the office and plant, paying 5 per cent on the cost of production for wear and tear." He was also to edit the "Intelligence" department of the new series of the *Journal*.

In the first number of the *Phonetic Journal* for 1848, Mr. Ellis described at length the origin of the phonetic alphabet, and his narrative includes a passage of considerable historical and biographical interest, as follows :—

The alphabet was reduced to a satisfactory working state in January, 1847. So many persons have taken part in bringing the alphabet to its present state of perfection that it is impossible to name any one as the sole inventor. To Mr. Isaac Pitman, of Bath, unquestionably belongs the merit of the idea, and of the practical form in which a Phonetic system of spelling was so cleverly clothed even in the earliest editions of his system of Phonography, the success of which alone could have paved the way for the introduction of Phonetic Printing. The first form of the Phonetic Printing Alphabet, and the determination to use a variation of the Roman alphabet, are also entirely his ; but most of the letters were invented, and the theory of their use laid down in conjunction with the Editor of this Journal, who had occupied himself with phonetic investigations and attempts at forming a universal alphabet for several years before he had heard of Mr. Pitman's labours on the same ground, and who has taken an active part in all the experiments and investigations made since August, 1843, when accident first made him acquainted with Phonography. He eventually became the chief proposer of further experiments, and starter of theories on which to found them, while Mr. Pitman with unparalleled industry, and perseverance,

and practical tact, worked them out, and was mainly instrumental in bringing their merits to the test of experience.
The improvements in the theory on which the alphabet was
first formed, and its extension to embrace Foreign Sounds,
both in Phonetic Printing, and Phonetic Short Hand, are also
entirely the work of Mr. Ellis.   During the last two years of
experiments, much assistance in reducing the printing alphabet
to a practical working form has been derived from the labours
of the Members who compose the Societies, called the General
Phonetic and Executive Council, and the Phonographic
Corresponding Society, so that the English Phonetic Alphabet,
both in its short hand and its printing forms, must, when
completed—and we hope that we now lay it before our readers
in a complete form—like most great practical inventions, be
rather regarded as the growth of time, than the sole work of
one or two individuals.   And although it may, with great
justice, be called the joint invention of Isaac Pitman and
Alexander John Ellis, yet, as great inventions take their name
from those who first started and gave a practical form to the
idea, even though the completion of their inventions may
have been wholly or partially the work of others, *future
generations must look up to Isaac Pitman the inventor of Phonetic
Short Hand, as the Father of English Phonetic Spelling.*

The italics are Mr. Ellis's.   He conducted the
Journal for just a year, and then discontinued it
under circumstances which will be described in
our next chapter.

Apart from phonotypy, Isaac Pitman was
engaged in several not inconsiderable enterprises
during this period.   His " History of Shorthand,"
the most popular and comprehensive survey
of stenographic invention in ancient and modern
times, first appeared serially in the *Journal*
in 1847.   Since that date it has been published
several times in book form, with considerable

additions.   At the end of 1846 he completed, as a
supplement to the " Ipswich Phono-Press " (a
shorthand magazine produced by lithography),
the first " Phonographic Dictionary of the English
Language, containing the most usual words, to the
number of twelve thousand." This work was
also greatly expanded and improved in later years.

There were two notable utterances on phonetic
shorthand writing and printing at this time.   The
first was an able and appreciative review of Isaac
Pitman's labours which appeared in the *Athenæum*
on 19th December, 1846.   The second was a
speech by Mr. George Dawson, the minister of the
Church of the Saviour at Birmingham, and widely
known as a popular lecturer, who presided at a
phonographic gathering at Birmingham on 24th
August, 1847.   He mentioned incidentally that
his chief secretary (he was referring to Mrs.
Dawson) wrote a different system of shorthand to
that which he himself employed.   " We have
therefore agreed," he added, " to throw away the
two old systems and take to the new one ! "   With
prophetic instinct he remarked that " Phonography being first undeniably good in itself, and
then its advantages being based on the highest
principle man knows—duty—it will succeed."

X

"THE PHONETIC NEWS" AND WHAT FOLLOWED
1849-1850

THE appearance of the first number of the *Phonetic News* on the 6th January, 1849, was the most notable event in the history of the Spelling Reform movement of the last century. For the first five months of the year, and for the greater part of that time every Saturday morning, there was issued under the title mentioned above a twelve-page newspaper very similar in size and style to the weekly newspapers of that period, but produced from phonetic printing type. Mr. Ellis conducted the paper with conspicuous ability. He did not make it the organ of either political party, but the Parliamentary and other great reforms which were at that time before the country were either advocated or favourably noticed. All kinds of news, home and foreign, was given in reformed spelling. Every number had in a prominent place a statement in the ordinary orthography treating of the necessity and advantages of a reformed spelling, with an explanation of the 1847 phonetic alphabet, in which the *News* was printed.

The *Phonetic News* brought the Spelling Reform very much under the notice of the country. Mr. Reed has borne testimony that it " drew public attention to the anomalies of English spelling, and the necessity of a change, in quarters to which previous publications had rarely, if ever, obtained access." The *Westminster Review*, which was then a power in the land as an organ of liberal thought, devoted thirty pages of its April issue to " The English Spelling Reform," its remarks being suggested by Mr. Ellis's writings, and more particularly by the appearance of the *Phonetic News*. The article was of a very appreciative and encouraging character, but the new organ of Spelling Reform had at an earlier date been somewhat caustically criticized in *Punch*, which friends of the reform were disposed to think a little remarkable for the following reason. In conversation with Hepworth Dixon, one of the best known contributors to *Punch*, namely Douglas Jerrold, had approvingly remarked, " It is one of *my* reforms." Some other member of the *Punch* staff (the paper was then edited by Mark Lemon) was probably responsible for the article which characterized reformed spelling as " decidedly the most insane thing out of Bedlam." Mr. Ellis took criticism of this kind with perfect good humour, and controverted whatever arguments were offered against reformed spelling in the columns of his own *News*, and in the much derided reformed characters.

Although the *Phonetic News* appealed to a wide constituency, it is doubtful whether it was calculated to help the movement for reformed spelling so effectively as the smaller periodicals printed both in phonotypy and phonetic shorthand, which

Isaac Pitman had been issuing for some years in various cheap forms, and in considerable variety. The *Phonetic News* was published at the weekly price of 4½d. stamped, each number bearing at the bottom right-hand corner of its front page the penny red stamp which was a familiar feature on our newspapers down to the introduction of half-penny postage. The price was a prohibitive one for a propagandist journal, but it would appear from various statements in its pages that there must have been a large gratuitous distribution.

A month after the *Phonetic News* had begun to appear, Isaac Pitman discovered that the discontinuance of the *Phonetic Journal* by Mr. Ellis at the end of 1848, left the Society practically without an organ. Though it was true that a certain amount of space was devoted to news of a phonographic and phonetic character in the *Phonetic News*, yet as Mr. Ellis published his newspaper not as the organ of the workers in the movement but rather as a journal appealing to the general public, it was inevitable that such matter could only be inserted to a limited extent. Isaac Pitman therefore again set up a printing press at Nelson Place. In March, 1849, he resumed the publication of the *Phonotypic Journal*, which henceforth appeared fortnightly instead of monthly, as was previously the case. In his resuscitated *Journal* published at the beginning of May, he announced the failure of Mr. Ellis's

effort to popularize phonotypy in the following
terms :—

" The altogether unexpected and regretful
intelligence has just been communicated to us by
Mr. Ellis that the *Phonetic News* does not pay its
expenses, and that it will therefore give place to a
smaller publication." " Deeply," he went on,
" as we shall regret the discontinuance of the
phonetic broad sheet, yet we cannot but acknowledge it is better that the *News* should be discontinued, than that the proprietor should sustain a
heavy loss by it. *Only as a business can the
Reform now succeed ;* and in order to this, the
continued exertions of the members of the rapidly
increasing Phonetic Society are indispensable."

In this year the Phonographic Corresponding
Society, which had taken such a considerable share
in the phonotypic branch of the movement, was
re-named the Phonetic Society. Under this new
name, as the years passed, it gained in importance
and influence. In the announcement from which
we have quoted, Isaac Pitman proceeded to refer
to the services which his co-worker had rendered
to the Reform. He was not a man who indulged
in idle compliment, and therefore when he speaks
of the " rare generosity " of Mr. Ellis in giving to
the Spelling Reform not alone his scholarly
advocacy, invaluable as that was, but also no
inconsiderable portion of his means, we may feel
assured that he is speaking with his accustomed
sincerity. The amount which Mr. Ellis lost over

his "too sanguine" enterprise—to quote Mr.
Reed's phrase—was between six and seven
thousand pounds.

It is a pleasure to be able to record, however,
that there is no note of despondency or disappoint-
ment in Mr. Ellis's valedictory address to the
readers of the *Phonetic News*, although his health
had unfortunately suffered by his considerable
literary labours in connection with its production.
He acknowledges the generous way in which those
interested in reformed spelling had subscribed
towards the fund for type matrices, and had in
various ways laboured for the common cause.
" It would be very wrong and very ungrateful in
us," he says, "to overlook those who have so
nobly, disinterestedly, and indefatigably worked
for us in the cause of *Spelling Reform*." In the
first rank of these he places Isaac Pitman, and he
mentions with special appreciation the services of
the first lecturer on phonetic spelling purely, Isaac
Pitman's kinsman Mr. George Withers, and in a
similar capacity his brother Mr. Benn Pitman.
Finally he announces the publication of a successor
to the *Phonetic News* of a less ambitious character,
to be entitled the *Spelling Reformer*. This
periodical appeared on the 15th June ; in all eight
numbers were published, the last being dated
Friday, 18th January, 1850. In this issue Mr.
Ellis regrets that in obedience to the strict injunction of his physician he is obliged to intermit
the publication. He hopes that a few months'

perfect repose will enable him to resume his attention to the cause of the Spelling Reform ; he will give due notice of the resumption of the *Spelling Reformer* in Isaac Pitman's *Journal.* But that notice never appeared. At the end of 1850, owing to his continued ill-health, the *Reformer* was " finally abandoned."

Mr. Ellis removed to Clifton directly after the *Phonetic News* was discontinued, and his phonetic type (the " 1847 alphabet ") was sent to a London printing establishment. The following announcement was at this time made by Isaac Pitman :—

" The style of phonetic spelling employed till towards the close of 1848, was adopted with the mutual consent of the two parties who had the principal share of the labour of maturing the alphabet. Many of the schemes and peculiar spellings were, however, professedly tried as mere experiments. From that time Mr. Ellis has assumed the entire control of this matter, and in consideration of the large sums of money he has invested in the Reform, we intend in all the phonetic printing we send out, till the close of next year (1850) to follow the system laid down in his Phonetic Spelling Rules."

In accordance with the intimation quoted above, a very different phonetic printing alphabet was in due course introduced in the books published by Isaac Pitman, of which he was practically the sole inventor. But with recovered health Mr.

Ellis issued new publications in the alphabet of his choice, until his phonetic type was destroyed in a fire at the office of his London printers. He viewed with strong disfavour the later developments of phonotypy at Bath, and when Isaac Pitman approached him in 1853 with an appeal for phonotypic unity by his acceptance of his late colleague's developments, he answered briefly, " I have no inclination to propose any alteration in the 1847 alphabet." To later overtures he made practically the same answer.

Early in the last year (1850) of Isaac Pitman's labours at Nelson Place, he printed and published the largest volume which had yet appeared in reformed spelling. This was " The Holy Bible, containing the Old and New Testaments, according to the Authorized Version. Printed Phonetically, in Paragraphs and Parallelisms." The production was in the form of a handsome demy 8vo volume of nearly 750 pages, with two columns of matter on each page in minion type. A vast amount of work was entailed in the revision of the transliteration and in the correction of the pages for the press, but, as the Preface indicates, this was with its producer a labour of love. The actual cost of printing and binding was no more than £200. The edition consisted of one thousand copies.

THE SECOND PHONETIC INSTITUTE, UPPER BRISTOL ROAD, BATH

(From a drawing, about 1851)

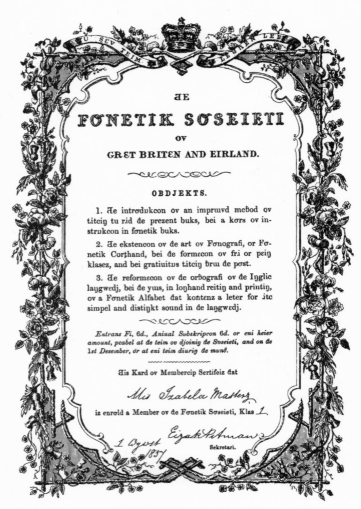

ĐE

FƟNETIK SƟSEIETI

OV

GRꜱT BRITꜱN AND EIRLAND.

OBDJEKTS.

1. Đe introdʋkcon ov an impruʋd meƀod ov titciŋ tu ꞧid đe prezent buks, bei a kɔꞧs ov instrʋkcon in fɔnetik buks.

2. Đe ekstencon ov đe art ov Fɔnografi, or Fɔnetik Corþhand, bei đe formꜱcon ov fꞧi or peiŋ klasez, and bei gratiuitʋs titciŋ þhru đe pɔst.

3. Đe reformꜱcon ov đe orƀografi ov đe Iŋglic laŋgwꜱdj, bei đe yʋs, in loŋhand ꞧeitiŋ and priꞧtiŋ, ov a Fɔnetik Alfabet đat koꞥtenz a leter for ꞧtc simpel and distiꞥkt sound in đe laŋgwꜱdj.

Entrans Fꞇ, 6d., Aniual Subskripcon 6d. or eni ꞓeier amount, pꜱabel at đe teim ov djoiniŋ đe SƟseieti, and on đe 1st Desember, ɔr at eni teim diuriŋ đe munþ.

Ꞓis Kard ov Membercip Sertifeiz đat

Mis Izabela Masterz

iz enrɔld a Member ov đe Fɔnetik SƟseieti, Klas 1

Eizak Pitman

Sekretari.

1 Ɵgʋst 1857

XI

WHEN Mr. Ellis gave up his printing office and left Bath, the premises known as No. 1 Albion Place remained unoccupied for something like eighteen months, and this fact led to the dissemination of a statement that " the phonetic printing institution at Bath had ceased to exist," owing to the loss sustained by Messrs. Ellis and Pitman over the *Phonetic News* " speculation." Isaac Pitman at once issued a statement giving the actual facts, and showing that his own printing and binding establishment at Nelson Place had been engaged uninterruptedly in the production of the literature of the movement. " Our own printing office," he wrote, " is in full work, and employs eighteen persons, eleven in the printing department and seven in the binding department. In addition to this force, three lithographic presses are kept constantly employed upon the shorthand periodicals and other works at the large lithographic establishment of Mr. Hollway in this city." Some months after this, in January, 1851, he rented the vacant premises at Albion Place, which henceforward became the second Phonetic Institute.

The first of May, 1851, is memorable as the day which witnessed the opening of the Great Exhibition in Hyde Park. There have been many exhibitions since that day, but none have so greatly aroused public interest as this pioneer enterprise. In his *Journal* published on the date given above, Isaac Pitman answered the question, " Will the arts of Phonography and Phonotypy be found in the Exhibition ? " with an emphatic affirmative. Knowing that space was valuable, he had preferred a modest request for one square foot of counter space for a glass case, and for twelve square feet of hanging space for a chart. What was asked for was readily granted ; indeed, on a second application, twenty square feet of hanging space was obtained. The exhibit took the form of " a neat piece of cabinet work," consisting of a mahogany stand, with " four tastefully turned and twisted pillars supporting a sloping frame," in which, under a plate glass cover were an open Phonetic Bible and an open Shorthand New Testament. Other phonetic books and a copy of the " Manual of Phonography," were attached to the stand, and underneath was a supply of free literature. The exhibit cost £10, and an appeal was made to all interested in the Spelling and Writing Reform to contribute to a fund to provide a supply of free literature at the stand while the Exhibition was open, at a cost of £50. The exhibit was awarded a bronze medal.

During the summer of 1851 people thronged to London from all parts of the country, and the time was therefore an especially appropriate one for holding in the metropolis a meeting of those interested in the Reform. Accordingly on the 6th August what was known as the London Phonetic Soirée was held in the Minor Hall of Exeter Hall. The chair was taken by Mr. James Simpson, of Accrington (President of the Vegetarian Society), and the other speakers included Messrs. Isaac Pitman, A. J. Ellis, Benn Pitman, and T. A. Reed. In writing about the meeting Isaac Pitman observed: " In that room met, for the first time, many friends who, by means of correspondence in phonetic shorthand, had known each other intimately for many years, in some cases for eight or ten years ! It was indeed a meeting for the overflowing of affection, rather than for exhibiting the bright sparklings of intellect." But for all that the speeches were marked by a vigorous advocacy of the objects of the Reform. It is significant that the London daily papers devoted a liberal amount of space to reports of the meeting, while the *Morning Chronicle* gave a leader on it, the tone of which may be gathered from the not very polite designation of the speeches as " *ex parte* spouting." Mr. Reed wrote a letter in reply, which demolished a good many of the arguments of the leader writer. It was to Mr. Reed's arrangements that the success of the soirée was largely due. He has left it on record that some difficulty was experienced in obtaining one of the rooms of Exeter Hall for the purpose of the meeting. " The movement was looked upon with suspicion by some of the authorities," and he says that he " well remembers the trouble he had in persuading them that the proposed reform was not of the revolutionary character attributed to it, but simply a means of rendering reading and writing a pleasure rather than a toil."

There had been established at Preston in the previous year, as the outcome of a visit of Messrs. Benn and Henry Pitman, a Phonetic Sunday and Week Evening School for teaching the unlettered to read by means of phonotypic instruction books, and its anniversary was commemorated on 22nd September, 1851, by a tea party. It was announced that " many who were totally unable to read and write on entering the school are now well versed in these indispensable arts." Isaac Pitman attended and gave an eloquent and practical address, and, as at the Exeter Hall meeting, a resolution was passed acknowledging the labours of Mr. Ellis and himself in promoting the Spelling Reform.

Early in 1852, Mr. John Cassell, the founder of the well-known publishing house, made an announcement in his " Popular Educator," which was then making its first appearance in weekly numbers, that the subject of Phonography would be taken up in it in due course. Isaac Pitman's attention was called to this by Mr. John H. Younghusband, of the Liverpool Institute (an able advocate of Phonography by voice and pen) who favoured the idea, and some correspondence followed with Mr. Cassell. The last-named proposed that the Inventor of Phonography should prepare a course of lessons for the new serial, " to perfect the learner in the phonographic art without a master," and that such course " for such sum as may be agreed upon " should be the copyright of the proprietor of the " Popular Educator." This proposal Isaac Pitman declined to accept, but not exactly on the ground of the average successful author. If, he pointed out, he did not need the profits arising from the copyright of Phonography to enable him to bear the expenses attending the introduction of phonetic printing, he would willingly comply with the request, but without the profits arising from the sale of his shorthand books he had no means of meeting the heavy expenses of continuing phonetic printing. Mr. Cassell therefore went elsewhere for a series of shorthand lessons, and secured these from Mr. Alexander Melville Bell, who had just published the system associated with his name under the title of " Steno-Phonography." It cannot be said that this feature of the "Popular Educator" was a success. The firm of Messrs. Cassell, Petter & Galpin ultimately decided to discontinue it, and applied to Isaac Pitman for permission to give lessons in Phonography in the " Educator," agreeing to the terms which had been offered to Mr. John Cassell seventeen years before. The permission was readily given, and since that time lessons in Pitman's Shorthand have been a leading feature in the " Educator " and have given many thousands of young people their first introduction to the phonographic art.

During the years 1852 and 1853 the reconstruction of the phonetic printing alphabet was the subject of innumerable experiments and of vigorous correspondence on the part of advocates of rival proposals. The British Phonetic Council, a body of fifty phoneticians (of which Mr. Ellis was President ; Isaac Pitman, Editor ; and Mr. C. Gahagan, jun., Secretary), was very actively engaged at this period in giving decisions on various points. The expenditure with the type-founder over these experiments was very considerable—a few large donations, many subscriptions, and a large proportion of the revenue derived from the profits on the shorthand books, appear to have all gone in the promotion of the branch of the Reform which did not " pay expenses."

Most of the lecturers and travelling teachers whose names have figured in the earlier pages of this biography had now retired from the field. Their labours had been highly successful from the time when Mr. Joseph Pitman took up the work relinquished by the Inventor of Phonography in 1842, down to the retirement of Mr. Benn Pitman from the lecturing field late in 1852, in order to emigrate to the United States. " At that time," Mr. Benn Pitman says, " I was the only remaining lecturer and teacher who had for nearly ten years made the dissemination of Phonography and Phonetics successful enough to yield a frugal living." Before this time most of the other lecturers whose names have been mentioned had found a more permanent source of livelihood than the precarious income which travelling lecturing afforded. The causes that at the outset attracted crowded gatherings had to a great extent ceased to operate. Speaking of the early lecturing work Mr. Reed has observed, " We had the great advantage of having something of the nature of a novelty to bring before our hearers. We had not only a new system of shorthand to expound, we had a new system of spelling to advocate." But with local teachers of shorthand and champions of the Spelling Reform springing up in all directions, it became less and less possible to break new ground, and accordingly the early lecturers sought other callings in life. Mr. Joseph Pitman entered a position of trust in the firm of Messrs. Jonas Brook & Bros., at Meltham, which he held for thirty years. Mr. Reed, after filling two or three provincial appointments as a newspaper reporter, came to London and founded the well-known firm of professional shorthand writers now entitled Messrs. T. A. Reed & Co. Mr. Henry Pitman combined newspaper reporting with professional shorthand writing and a considerable amount of teaching work, eventually settling in Manchester. Here Mr. William Hunt, who had married Isaac's sister Jane, for some years also engaged in teaching. Mr. Frederick Pitman, as we have seen, became the London publisher of his brother's books, and in addition developed a large music publishing business. Mr. Withers became for a period private secretary to Sir James Matheson (who at one time represented Ashburton in Parliament), but later on he settled in Liverpool as a shorthand teacher. Other lecturers and teachers readily found openings on the newspaper press as reporters, when the repeal of the Stamp and Advertisement Duties made a cheap press possible, and there was a considerable demand for reports of public proceedings such as could only be furnished by reporters who were expert shorthand writers. At this time also phonographic reporters were beginning to make their way into what had hitherto been a close preserve of the writers of the older systems—namely the Galleries and Committee Rooms of the Houses of Parliament. We find Isaac Pitman writing that he is " acquainted with the names of three gentlemen engaged on the *Morning Post*, with one on the *Morning Chronicle*, and one on the *Morning Advertiser*, who use Phonography in the House of Commons ; and with one employed on *The Times*, who reports Committees of the House, etc."

The travelling lecturers had done their work well and thoroughly ; there was hardly an important

town in the country in which their voices had
not been heard.   They were succeeded by resident
teachers and voluntary workers, in most cases
their own pupils, under whom Phonography made
great and continuous progress, and it became a
considerable undertaking to provide literature in
the shape of instruction books, exercise books,
reading books, and periodicals.   But Isaac Pitman
went about this work with steady and unwearied
regularity.   On 3rd January, 1852, the *Phonetic
Journal* was enlarged in size and was issued as a
weekly periodical.   At this period an enlarged
edition of the " Phonographic Dictionary," entitled " A Phonetic and Pronouncing Vocabulary
of the English Language " was prepared with the
shorthand characters lithographed on pages facing
the letterpress.   In this work Mr. Reed assisted,
and " many phonographic outlines and sets of
outlines were tried in ordinary writing for the
purpose of selecting the best."   Isaac Pitman was
fond of giving statistics, and in association with
his lithographic work he mentions that at this
time during four years he lithographed 4,800 pages
of Phonography.   His work as a shorthand transfer writer has never been excelled.   But when
he had been engaged in this way for ten years he
published in 1852 this singularly modest estimate
of his own abilities.   " He never hoped," he said,
" to be able to produce anything in this way that
could be considered excellent, because his ' transfers ' were, from the stern necessity of his business.

produced in a short time, and often amid interruptions. Moreover, he had not been trained to the work—had never written anything merely for practice, but lithographed the first number of the *Phonetic Journal*, in 1842, after an hour's trial with the lithographic pen, and never afterwards wrote anything but for the purpose of its being printed."

From year to year the Phonetic Society showed considerable growths in membership, its objects being at this time defined as "For the general introduction of Phonetic Spelling, both in Writing and Printing, in order to render the arts of Reading and Writing accessible to the whole Population." The only official of the Society since its establishment had been its Secretary, Isaac Pitman, who continued, in fact, its working head throughout. But in 1854 he invited Mr. George Dawson to become its President, and that gentleman took office. The membership was at this time about 4,500, and a re-classification of members being projected it occurred to Isaac Pitman to offer the Presidency of the Society to Mr. Ellis "notwithstanding the differences of opinion existing between them in reference to the 1847 alphabet." The following correspondence took place, which speaks for itself :—

Isaac Pitman to Mr. Ellis.

I believe I speak the sentiments of every phonographer when I say that your acceptance of the office of President of the Phonetic Society would be hailed with delight by every one of the thousands of spelling reformers in this country and in America. . . . For the interest of the phonetic cause in America especially would I urge the propriety of your accepting the office of president of a Society which I have from its commencement, eleven years ago, served in the capacity of secretary. There, where party feeling on most subjects runs high, they suppose that you and I are at variance as men because we have different opinions on phonetics. It is in your power to remove this impression, which is as hurtful to the interests of morality as to the phonetic reform.

Mr. Ellis to Isaac Pitman.

I have read over your article on the proposed new organization of the Phonetic Society, and also your letter to me asking me to be President. It is quite impossible for me to accept the office ; indeed, I am not even aware that it is vacant, having recently seen the name of Mr. George Dawson printed as that of the President of the Phonetic Society. You must excuse me from entering upon my other reasons for declining to allow my name to be placed at the head of your Society, to which in my own opinion no other name but your own could be prefixed, as it is emphatically a Society of your own creation and upholding. I will only say that I do not decline from any party feeling on the subject of alphabets, any dislike to the soonest possible advent of some phonetic spelling, any disapproval of Phonography in its present state, or any personal feeling against yourself.

No change was made in the Presidency of the

Phonetic Society, and Mr. Dawson continued to fill that position.

In 1855 Isaac Pitman removed his private residence from Nelson Place to No. 2 Lansdown Terrace, Bath, situated at a much higher level than the home he had vacated, and on the steep road ascending from the city to the famous heights of Lansdown. He was also at the same time obliged at considerable inconvenience to remove the Phonetic Institute from Albion Place. The building he occupied had been acquired for the Western Dispensary, and he had at short notice to

THE THIRD PHONETIC INSTITUTE, PARSONAGE LANE, BATH
The entrance " through dark passages and up narrow flights of stairs."

find suitable premises elsewhere for the accommodation of his considerable printing plant and
growing staff.   In Parsonage Lane, in the centre
of Bath, there are some substantially built and
capacious buildings used for a variety of industrial
purposes, and in one of these Isaac Pitman secured,
at the low rental of £15 a year, a room on the top
floor 53 ft. by 28½ ft., which was lofty and well

A CORNER IN THE THIRD PHONETIC INSTITUTE

lighted, though there were very serious dis-
advantages and discomforts which made it a far
from ideal place for conducting the varied pursuits
of author, reformer, transfer writer, printer, and
publisher.   The lane in which the building is
situated was at that time far from being a credit
to the City of Bath, while the approach to Isaac
Pitman's office from the entrance " through dark
passages and up narrow flights of stairs " was the
reverse of prepossessing.   But the spacious room

occupied as the third Phonetic Institute was in delightful contrast to its surroundings. From its neatness and order it was a model office, and here for the next eighteen years Isaac Pitman did some of the best work of his life in the popularization of his system of shorthand, and in the development of phonotypic printing.

During 1855 there occurred what Isaac Pitman designated as the " Websterian discussion on the right of the Secretary of the Phonetic Society to disseminate his religious opinions." It had been a regular custom of the Inventor of Phonography to furnish all who desired phonographic or phonetic publications with a modicum of New Church literature in addition, and the *Journal* was also made the vehicle for a similar propaganda. When attention was directed to the matter by Mr. William Webster, of Dundee, a number of prominent phonographers and phoneticians belonging to different communions gave expression to emphatic opinions to the effect that they did not desire the Reading and Writing Reform associated with the propagation of any particular religious tenets. Among those who expressed this view were two Cambridge undergraduates who later on assumed leading parts in the phonographic and phonetic movement. One of these was Mr. C. H. E. Wyche, who became a clergyman in the Church of England, but met with an untimely death in South Africa, being drowned while crossing a river. The other was Mr. F. J. Candy (wrangler in

1854) who took up a professorship of Mathematics at Bombay, and was throughout his long life an ardent phonographer and spelling reformer. Isaac Pitman had strong views as to the duty incumbent on him to " scatter the seeds of truth," but finally hit on a compromise to which no reasonable objection could be taken. While not yielding his freedom of action as an individual, he agreed that in his official capacity as Secretary of the Phonetic Society he would no longer seek to propagate his particular religious views.

XII

THE TENTH AND ELEVENTH EDITIONS OF PHONOGRAPHY

1857-1862

BETWEEN the publication of the Second Edition of Phonography, in 1840, and the last issue of the Ninth Edition in 1855, the art had become the most widely and generally used system of English shorthand ever invented. Apart from the literature produced by Isaac Pitman and sent out from the Phonetic Institute, there was a considerable output of periodical and other productions lithographed in the characters of the system and issued by various phonographers. The Pitmanic text-books, published in different forms, had attained large sales. The " Manual of Phonography " was in its one hundred and fortieth thousand, and the popular introductory text-book —the precursor of the " Phonographic Teacher " —was in its two hundred and thirtieth thousand. While the system had been untouched in its main features, the period had been one of experiment, which had resulted in simplifications and useful additions. For example, the half length principle had been reduced to order, and the double length principle introduced and applied to curved consonants. The representation of the aspirate had been improved, and consonant forms, which were badly needed for *w* and *y*, had been adopted. At the same time several crudities had disappeared. Thus far the evolution of the system had given satisfaction. Improvements had been effected after full consultation with the phonographic body, and it was generally felt that they added materially to the usefulness of the method without any serious interference with the writing habits of those who had acquired Phonography from the earlier editions.

During the autumn of 1855 Isaac Pitman began a series of experiments with the vowel scale of Phonography, which had a most remarkable effect on the future development of the system in this country and in America. In this project he had the co-operation of Mr. Charles Bagot Cayley (1823-1883), the poet, and brother of Mr. Arthur Cayley, the eminent mathematician. Mr. C. B. Cayley came to Bath and resided with Isaac Pitman for about a year while engaged at the Phonetic Institute in the experiments above mentioned, and afterwards in the considerable labour of introducing the changes in the text-books and other literature of the system. A less courageous and determined man than Isaac Pitman would have hesitated to introduce improvements which could not fail to alienate a large number of his most influential supporters ; to be attended with much personal inconvenience to himself ; to prove, moreover, a source of considerable loss in his publishing business, not only while the changes were being introduced, but for a long time after the appearance of the much criticized Tenth Edition towards the end of 1857. But he never allowed such considerations to hinder the development of Phonography.

The improvement proposed in the system was the following altered order of the vowel scale :—

OLD VOWEL SCALE.   NEW VOWEL SCALE.

1 ee	1 ĭ		1 ah	1 ă
2 eh	2 ĕ	to	2 eh	2 ĕ
3 ah	3 ă		3 ee	3 ĭ

This change involved a corresponding alteration in the *way* and *yay* series, while the positions of some half-dozen grammalogues were affected. And the alteration, of course, revolutionized the vowel notation and the observance of position. The Ninth Edition writer had to partly change his habits of writing in order to adopt the Tenth Edition. A considerable number of phonographers in this country and the bulk of American phonographers of that generation never used the new scale. But the improvements were twice submitted to the vote of the Phonetic Society with favourable results. In 1857 a total of 214 voted for the new scale against 45 who were opposed to it ; and in 1858, after a vigorous hostile campaign, the votes were : For 191 ; against 58 ; neutral 38. These majorities, consisting largely of teachers who were specially interested in the future propagation of the system, confirmed the Inventor of Phonography in the conviction that the improvement in the vowel scale was in the best interests of the system and its practitioners. It was one of those changes in which philosophic desirability is happily associated with practical expediency, and the improvement without question makes the Tenth Edition one of the great landmarks in the progress of Phonography.

"So radical a change as this," Isaac Pitman wrote in introducing the new vowel scale to phonographers, "would not be proposed on slight grounds, nor for any reason that I did not consider imperative. The alteration *must* be made now or at some future time." He held that the old vowel scale violated a fundamental principle of phonetic writing which he had discovered in Dr. Latham's work, but there was a far more practical reason furnished in some observations Isaac Pitman made early in 1858, when the controversy was at its height. "Phonography, as regards the vowel scale," he wrote, "started on a different principle from that more or less employed in the formation of other systems. In other systems *a* and its cognate vowels were regarded as naturally the first in the scale, because of the position of *a* in the romanic alphabet. This reason did not appear satisfactory, and it was proposed on philosophic grounds that *ee*, *ĭ*, should be the first vowels. These grounds have now been found untenable, and it has been decided that the arrangement sanctioned by common usage is also the most philosophical. How can it then be expected that if we now adopt the *ah, eh, ee* scale, we shall ever be called on to discard it? The opposite scale, as long as it is employed, may produce division among phonographers, may increase the difficulties of the learner in acquiring a notion of, or a liking for Phonography, but can never afford a permanent basis for a system to be as widely employed among mankind as Phonography aims at being." The Tenth Edition of Phonography, in addition to having the new vowel scale, introduced the large hook for -*shon*, the small hook which had previously done duty for this termination being assigned to *f* and *v*.

In spite of the support by a majority of the Phonetic Society of the new vowel scale, the opposition to it was both strenuous and vigorously expressed. Mr. Reed was the protagonist of the opposition in England. Mr. Ellis took no active part in the controversy, but (unlike Mr. Reed) adhered to the Ninth Edition throughout his life. Isaac Pitman replied at length to Mr. Reed's objections, and pointed out with considerable force that the new and natural vowel scale formed a complement to the natural arrangement of the consonants, which had been adopted in the Second Edition of Phonography. Many examples of vocalized words were used as illustrations during the discussion, and the form for *ability* ∨ἰ was again and again cited as an example of the advantage

ISAAC PITMAN
1859 (*age* 46)

BLONDIN OUTDONE (?)

CARTOON PUBLISHED IN THE "PHONOGRAPHIC LUMINARY" ·IN 1862

of giving the vowel ă its natural first position, and ĭ its natural third position, rather than the positions they assumed under the old vowel scale, in which *ability* was vocalized thus, Ⅴͳ At the end of 1858, Mr. Reed, while still believing the alteration unnecessary, announced his decision to adopt the new vowel scale, rather than perpetuate the want of harmony which had prevailed for a considerable period. But he added significantly, " This will be the last occasion on which we shall adopt any material alteration in the system which we do not regard as a substantial improvement, and worth the labour involved in the change."

A well-known London phonographer, Mr. Charles Gahagan, editor of the *Phonographic Examiner* and other periodicals, who had opposed from the outset the introduction of what he was pleased to describe as " the inverted or non-natural vowel scale," continued the teaching and advocacy of the Ninth Edition long after Mr. Reed had come to the decision mentioned above, and as time passed showed himself a most persistent and determined foe to the new vowel scale. He not only taught the Ninth Edition extensively, but in 1858 he collected the votes of 767 phonographers— presumably outside the ranks of the Phonetic Society—and declared 648 favoured the retention of the *ee*, *eh*, *ah* arrangement of the vowels. He also promoted the British Phonetic Union, with the Rev. Canon Gray, of Ripon Cathedral, as

President, " to unite phonographers upon the old
and tried vowel scale."

In America the discussion on the new vowel
scale created a great amount of interest and
excitement in phonetic circles. Mr. Benn Pitman
addressed his brother in vigorous terms on the
subject though, as regarded the improvement itself,
he expressed the opinion that it would yield " a
slight advantage in point of speed," and he also
somewhat grudgingly admitted that " the proposed alteration of the vowel scale is a nearer
approach to a philosophic alphabet," but for
perhaps five or seven years he would continue to
publish his brother's Ninth Edition " without a
particle of alteration." As a matter of fact the
waiting policy was never departed from by the
younger brother of the Inventor of Phonography.

The " Battle of the Styles " continued in
England for some years. Teachers who insisted
on having Ninth Edition books, were supplied
with them, but the stock was not inexhaustible,
and in time only the current Tenth Edition was
procurable. Those who objected to the transition
from the Ninth to the Tenth Edition did not
foresee that ere long other and almost as fundamental improvements would be introduced for
their acceptance. There were still some changes
to be made ere Phonography was brought to the
standard of perfection designed by its Inventor.
In the summer of 1861 further proposals were
submitted to the judgment of phonographers, on

which Isaac Pitman and Mr. Cayley had been for
some time experimenting. After an interval for
discussion, the Eleventh Edition of Phonography
was published in 1862, in which the improvements
introduced included alternative consonantal signs
for *w*, *y*, and *h ;* the prefix *in-* to the consonantal
form of *h ;* and large initial hooks to curves for
indicating the addition of *l*—an effective and
harmonious employment of hitherto unused
phonographic material.

The reasons given for the introduction of large
hooks into the system did not, however, commend
themselves to Mr. Reed's judgment, and he
accordingly carried into effect the resolution
already quoted. He declared himself a Tenth
Edition writer, and as there were many teachers
and writers who shared his objection to the big
hooks, a further schism in the ranks of phonographic workers was created, which was not closed
for many years. " We see no sufficient reason,"
Mr. Reed wrote, " for changing to the Eleventh
Edition, with the prospect before us of having ere
long to change to the Twelfth and Thirteenth,
and so on *ad infinitum*." Mr. Reed's criticism
led the Inventor of Phonography to discontinue
the designation of new issues of his text-books as
" Editions " after the Twelfth. Isaac Pitman did
not favour attempts to perpetuate and propagate
Tenth Edition Phonography, and intimated that
he considered it " somewhat selfish " on the part
of teachers and writers not to recommend the

Eleventh Edition. The phrase was hardly an agreeable one, and Mr. Reed naturally rejoined that those who differed from the Inventor of Phonography, while they believed his motives to be thoroughly disinterested, desired him to think the same of theirs.

It became apparent, however, that the phonographic community was not altogether prepared for the changes which the Eleventh Edition introduced, but those who were favourable to the Tenth Edition found it no easy matter to teach it. Appeals were made to Isaac Pitman to continue to supply at least one of the instruction books in the Tenth Edition, but these requests were not acceded to. Yet in several quarters instruction in the Tenth Edition was persevered in, and teachers and professional writers found in the *Phonographic Reporter*, a monthly magazine lithographed in the Reporting Style by Mr. Reed, an able champion of the Phonography of their choice. The Eleventh Edition had the effect of bringing into existence a body styled the Phonographic Alliance, which was concerned in keeping the standard of Phonography unchanged for a definite period of time, and free from " spasmodic disturbances." Happily this strenuous controversy over the two Editions had no effect on the cordial personal relations of English phonographers with the Inventor of Phonography and with each other.

There was an Art Treasures Exhibition at Manchester in the summer of 1857, and among the various gatherings to which it gave rise was a meeting for the promotion of the Reading and Writing Reform, attended by Isaac Pitman. This was held in the same hall at the Mechanics' Institute in which he had first spoken to a Manchester audience sixteen years before, and his address is noteworthy because at the opening he reverently ascribed to the directing hand of Providence the invention of the art of Phonography, reminding his hearers of the " most certain " words of Shakspere—

> There's a divinity that shapes our ends,
> Rough-hew them how we will.

These lines, it will be remembered, for many years figured in the Introduction to the " Manual of Phonography," readers being exhorted that this truth " should ever inspire men with energy and perseverance to do something, however small, to rectify error and replace evil by good."

At this time Isaac Pitman sustained a domestic bereavement in the death of his wife, which occurred on the 19th August, 1857, after an illness extending over three years.

XIII

1857-1862

To the Spelling Reform, or Phonotypy, and the
Writing Reform, or Phonography, Isaac Pitman
added a third—the Reckoning Reform—at this
period. When very near the close of his life, he
was much gratified to find Herbert Spencer advocating a duodecimal method of reckoning similar
to that which he had proposed so long before, and
he then wrote : " I formulated a Reckoning
Reform on the basis of Twelve forty years ago
(1856), used it for three or four years, advocated
it in my *Phonetic Journal*, kept my accounts in
it, and paged the *Journal* in it. The phonetic
alphabet was then on the anvil, and as I could not
do justice to both reforms, I let the Reckoning
Reform slide. A goodly portion of the brain of the
English nation has now taken it up, and I hope
we shall hear no more of changing our money,
weights, and measures, which are mostly on a
twelve basis ; but instead of the intolerable confusion of altering the *value* and the *name* of every
coin, weight, and measure, we shall simply *change
our mode of writing them*, and introduce a few new

coins, measures, and weights, on the present basis of value, and give them Saxon names."

The proposal to reform our time-honoured methods of reckoning was as courageous as the attack on our spelling ; what might have come of the " Reckoning Reform " if it had been advocated with the same persistence as the Spelling Reform it is impossible to say. The fact must be recorded, however, that Isaac Pitman did not find many who were inclined to follow his example in the use of a duodecimal method of numeration. A brief summary of his proposals should, however, find a place here, and is therefore given below :—

Duodecimal Notation : Add two figures to the present scale for *ten* and *eleven*, thus :

1, 2, 3, 4, 5, 6, 7, 8, 9, ⌇ (ten), ⅀ (eleven), 10 (dozen).

Nomenclature : Units, Dozens, Grosses, Milliads ; no higher name is necessary. To express numbers above a dozen, say the names of the figures, and in writing the twelve notation, separate the three lowest figures by a point ; thus, 4.9 = four dozen and nine ; 7.3.2. = seven gross, three dozen, and two ; 584.6.3.1. = five-eight-four milliads, six gross, three dozen, and one.

Money : Penny, Shilling, Mark (twelve shillings), Banco (paper money = £7 4s., in place of the £5 note).

Weight : Pounds, with twelfth sub-divisions.

Liquid Measure : Pint, Quart, Gallon, Hogshead ; with fractions of a pint.

All calculations of the cost of articles would be performed in plain figures, or by " simple " instead of " compound " arithmetic.

Example : What is the cost of **36Z** (three-six-ten, or three gross, six dozen, and ten) yards of cloth at 2s. 4d. per yard ?

$$36Z$$
$$24$$

$$1234$$
$$718$$

$$83\mathcal{E}4$$

Answer : Eight Bancos, three Marks, eleven shillings, and four pence.

The Spelling Reform question at this time assumed an important place among the movements which were attracting a large measure of attention. Some influential public men had become interested in the Reform, and gave it personal and pecuniary assistance. From this period may be said to date the patronage and generous support of the Spelling Reform by Sir Walter Calverley Trevelyan (1797-1879), the sixth Baronet, of Nettlecombe Court, Taunton, and Wallington, Newcastle-on-Tyne, and of his friendship with Isaac Pitman. The Spelling Reform propaganda was from first to last a serious financial drain on the resources of its originator. The subscriptions of the members of the Phonetic Society probably only defrayed the cost of free literature, and the expenses of costly experiments in the production of phonetic type were met by special subscriptions and by the profits on the sales of the shorthand books. But these sources of income were insufficient, and Isaac Pitman found it necessary to procure loans from friends of the Reform, to whom interest at the rate of 5 per cent per annum was paid for the use of the money. The highest amount which the loans reached in the aggregate was £2,000. Sir Walter afforded substantial aid in this way; the last of his loans was repaid by Isaac Pitman in 1877. Apart from his help in the shape of loans, Sir Walter gave considerable sums to the movement. In 1858 the hon. Baronet accepted the Presidency of the Phonetic Society, which he filled until the time of his death.

In the year 1857 attention was specially called to the Spelling Reform movement by a generous offer on the part of Sir Walter C. Trevelyan, of two prizes of £100 and £40 respectively, " for the two best and approved essays on a reform in the spelling of the English language, by the introduction of a phonetic instead of the present unphonetic system." The essays were to include, " An historical account of the origin and growth of the present imperfect system of spelling ; an analysis of the system of articulate sounds ; and an exposition of those occurring in our language ; with a notice of the various modes in which it has been attempted to express these sounds graphically, and a suggestion for doing so, in which care should be taken that no letter should express more than one sound, that no sound should be expressed by more than one letter, and that as few new types as possible should be admitted." The competition was to be open to Great Britain and Ireland, British North America, and the United States. The adjudicators were Mr. A. J. Ellis, Dr. R. G. Latham, Professor Max-Müller, Isaac Pitman, and Sir Walter C. Trevelyan. Eighteen essays were received from various parts of England and America, but not one of them, Mr. Reed states, was adjudicated as meriting a prize, all the conditions of the offer not having been fulfilled. Several of the essays, however, were said to show much talent, and Sir Walter Trevelyan, as the offerer of the prizes, gave to the writer of one of the essays (Professor S. S. Haldeman, of Columbia, Pennsylvania, U.S.A.) the sum of £50, and a further sum of £50 on the author undertaking to revise, complete, and publish the essay. The Professor published his essay in a quarto volume of 148 pages. Sir Walter also gave £10 to the writers of four other essays, namely, the Rev. F. G. Fleay, vice-president of Culham Training College, Abingdon ; Mr. James Kerr, M.A., the Rev. R. Wells Whitford, and the Rev. Neil Livingston.

In association with the competition described above Isaac Pitman received a letter from Professor Max-Müller (1823-1900), which led to a life-long friendship with the famous occupant of the Chair of Comparative Philology at Oxford University. Professor Max-Müller's communication to Isaac Pitman was as follows :—

I was well acquainted with the strenuous exertions which you and some of your friends have been making in order to effect a reform in the present system of English Orthography. I possessed myself of several of your publications, and had derived much information from a book, first published, I believe, in your *Journal*, the " Alphabet of Nature," by Mr. Ellis. What I wrote to Sir W. Trevelyan was only to express my conviction, that though hitherto the reform of English spelling had not met with that success which one might have wished and expected, yet it was sure ultimately to effect the desired result ; and that I thought the encouragement which Sir Walter intended to give to this movement, by offering a prize for the best Essay on the Reform of English Spelling, very opportune and beneficial. My own line of studies has led me to pay some attention to the general subject of phonetics, and the origin and history of alphabetical writing, and I was very much interested in seeing how this science had been applied by you with so much ingenuity to the practical purpose of reforming the English system of spelling, and facilitating the method of learning to read and write.

Soon afterwards Professor Max-Müller delivered his well-known series of " Lectures on the Science of Language " at the Royal Institution (1861-3). In the first volume of the published lectures occurred a forcible plea for reformed spelling, and commendation of the Phonetic Reform. " I am far from underrating," Max-Müller said, " the difficulties that stand in the way of such a reform, and I am not so sanguine as to indulge in any hopes of seeing it carried for the next three or four generations. But I feel convinced of the truth and reasonableness of the principles upon which that reform rests." He had no doubt that our " effete and corrupt orthography " would go :

" Nations have before now changed their numerical figures, their letters, their chronology, their weights and measures ; and though Mr. Pitman may not live to see the results of his persevering and disinterested exertions, it requires no prophetic power to perceive that what at present is poohpoohed by the many will make its way in the end, unless met by arguments stronger than those hitherto levelled at the *Phonetic News*."

At this period, in addition to the works in the ordinary phonetic printing issued from the Phonetic Institute, Isaac Pitman printed for the British and Foreign Bible Society a number of works in Mikmak (a language spoken by a tribe of Indians in New Brunswick, Nova Scotia). These included the Book of Genesis, the Book of Psalms, St. Luke's Gospel, and the Acts of the

TᴀN ʋmskwes pơktʋmkiƀk Niksksm kisidơgʋp wƀsơk ƀk mƀkʋmigou,

2 Ꜹk mƀkʋmigou weskedek ƀk sigweƹk, ƀk bơgʋnitpƀk ƹkʋp wolkơgʋmigegʋ. Ꜹk Niksksm utçidjƀk'midj'l etlimadjƀsilib'nn ɯskitpƀktɯgʋ.

3 Ꜹk Niksksm ƹƹp : Wosadetç; tơkɯ wosadegʋp.

4 Ꜹk Niksksm nemidơgʋp wosadék ɯkʋlɯltʋnʋnʋ. Ꜹk Niksksm wedjitepkiss-dơgʋp wosadek bơgʋnitpƀk iktɯk.

5 Ꜹk Niksksm telɯiidʋgʋp wosadék nƀgwek, ƀk bơgʋnitpƀk telɯiidʋgʋp depkík. Tơkɯ welƀgɯp ƀk eskitpɯigɯp ʋmskwesƹwé nƀgwek.

FACSIMILE OF GENESIS i. 1-5, PRINTED IN MIKMAK.

Apostles.   The three other Gospels were printed by the missionary, the Rev. S. T. Rand.   The plan of teaching Indians to read by the phonetic alphabet was " a decided success."

A few words may be added here as to the progress of the Spelling Reform in America.   Mr. Andrews, in addition to his phonographic books, published a phonotypic reader.   Some years later a more vigorous impulse was given to the movement in the United States by the phonetic books and periodicals published by Mr. Elias Longley, of Cincinnati.   In later years, and down to the present day, American phoneticians have devoted considerable attention to Spelling Reform.

On 21st April, 1861, Isaac Pitman married his second wife, Miss Isabella Masters, of Bath, and the honeymoon was spent on the Continent.

XIV

A QUARTER OF A CENTURY OF PHONOGRAPHY— PRESENTATION TO THE INVENTOR

1862

In 1862 Pitmanic shorthand had been before the world for twenty-five years, and at this point we may with advantage review its position. There was one noticeable feature about Phonography which distinguished it from all other shorthand systems that had preceded it. A large and varied phonographic periodical press had appeared in Great Britain devoted to the art ; Australia had also its periodicals ; and there were, of course, many published in the United States. Such a number of journals could only flourish if the art were very extensively cultivated, and the information given in this chapter demonstrates that this was unquestionably the case. Mr. Reed is of opinion that at this time " the great majority of newspaper reporters throughout the country employed Phonography in their daily avocations." A proportion of the older hands, who had learnt shorthand before Phonography was invented, were non-phonographers, but the new method had done such good work that it could no longer be denounced as impracticable.

When the Inventor of Phonography visited Manchester in 1841, his system was criticized in a not altogether favourable way in the *Manchester Guardian,* but Mr. John Harland, the famous reporter, afterwards one of the proprietors of that paper, and himself a shorthand author, made handsome amends later on by his tribute to the philosophical and stenographic excellence of Phonography. " We believe," he wrote in the *Guardian,* " that it contains within itself the power of becoming superior to all, with the further improvements and augmentations which a careful revision on the part of its author and his pupils, in the course of a few years, will be able to give it." The prediction of 1843 had been amply fulfilled ; in 1857 when Isaac Pitman was invited to address a meeting at the Mechanics' Institution there, a resolution was passed recording the opinion of the gathering that Phonography was " the briefest and most legible system of shorthand," and in 1862 we find that all the reporters of the Manchester newspapers used Phonography. It was at this time, too, in Manchester, that Sir Edward W. Watkin, then Chairman of the Manchester, Sheffield, and Lincolnshire Railway Co. (now the Great Central), introduced the practice of dictating correspondence to shorthand writers, and classes were established by him, with Mr. Henry Pitman as instructor, who continued to teach the railway clerks Phonography for fifty years.

The practice initiated in Manchester was soon followed by other railway companies, and also in

commercial and legal offices, and Mr. Reed records
that " about this time advertisements began to
appear in the newspapers for assistants who could
render this kind of service." A new employment,
that of shorthand clerk, was created by Phonography, and Isaac Pitman did much to promote
it through his *Journal*. Even in the most con-
servative sphere of professional shorthand writing,
that of note-taking in the London law courts,
where son succeeded father, and the same shorthand had been practised for generations, fresh
practitioners writing the new system found their
way, and the excellent work they did led to the
softening of old prejudices against Phonography.
In America there was no daily newspaper which
did not employ phonographic reporters, and the
system had been subjected to a severe test in
scientific reporting by Dr. Stone, who took notes
of lectures by Agassiz, the distinguished professor
of natural history at Harvard, on comparative
embryology, with an exactitude which was most
remarkable.

In the early part of 1859 a movement was set
on foot in London for recognizing by a substantial
token of appreciation Isaac Pitman's unwearied
and disinterested labours for close upon a quarter
of a century in the promotion of the Reading and
Writing Reform. Although the output of phonographic and phonotypic books was very great, the
phonotypic branch of the movement was a heavy
drain on the resources of its originator and

principal promoter, and he had found it necessary, as we have seen, to borrow considerably to carry on the work. It was thought that a pecuniary gift would be acceptable, and accordingly a committee was formed, the Rev. C. H. E. Wyche being appointed chairman. Assurances of support were received from different parts of the country, and it was decided to consult the proposed recipient. Mr. Wyche therefore wrote the following letter :—

11 YORK PLACE, KENNINGTON, LONDON, S.,
12 Aug., 1859.

DEAR SIR,

I have been requested to communicate with you on a subject more agreeable than the little matters of business which usually call for a letter to you.

It seems that Phonographers in various parts of the country have come to the conclusion that the present is a fit time for testifying their appreciation of the beautiful Art for which they are indebted to you, as well as the estimation in which they hold your personal character and your unwearied labours in the Phonetic cause. They desire accordingly to begin raising a subscription for a Testimonial, and they wish to know whether you would accept such a recognition, provided, of course, it were offered in a form of which you could approve.

If I remember rightly, Phonographers of America did, some years ago, subscribe for such a purpose, but you refused to let their Testimonial take the form of a personal gift, and requested them to retain the money so raised as the nucleus of a Phonetic fund for the promotion of the Reform in the United States.

It occurred to my mind at that time that it would have been better had you accepted the offering, and devoted it yourself to this good purpose. I cannot help thinking that something of the kind might very properly be done now. It would be a proof that Phonographers, although divided on

some points, yet agree in the high value which they set upon
their Art, and in grateful feelings towards its Inventor ; and
it would be a practical proof to the American phoneticians
that many of the statements put forth in that country with
respect to yourself are without any real foundation.

It has been suggested that a Committee of London Phonographers should be formed to carry out this good intention,
and I have been asked to act as its Chairman, but before
proceeding in the matter I wish to know your opinion of it,—
whether such a Testimonial would be accepted by you ; and,
if so, as a secondary matter, in what form it would be most
acceptable.

I remain, very truly yours,

CYRIL H. E. WYCHE.

To Mr. Isaac Pitman, Bath.

Isaac Pitman's reply to this communication
showed a grateful appreciation of the kindly
proposal of his friends, and he described the letter
as " one of those rarely occurring events in life
in which we recognize the Angel of the Divine
Providence as soon as he is at our side." He
made it clear, however, that he should devote the
proposed testimonial to the cause to which he
had devoted his life. He proposed that the fund
should be used for building a Phonetic Institute—
a home suitable for the work in association with
Phonography and Phonotypy, and in which the
printing establishment of the Reform could be
housed. He considered that a suitable building
could be erected for £1,000. " I am not able
to build it myself," he said, " because to say
nothing of twenty-two years of personal labour,
I have given more than twice this sum to the

cause in various ways." His office in Parsonage Lane was most unsuitable for his work, and he drew a lugubrious picture of the discomforts of the place.

The Pitman Testimonial was at once promoted, and the Committee, with Sir Walter C. Trevelyan at their head, issued an appeal for subscriptions. The sum of about £350 was collected, and on 26th June, 1862, the presentation was made at a meeting convened for the purpose, held at the rooms of the Young Men's Christian Association, Aldersgate Street, London, at which the recipient of the testimonial attended, accompanied by Mrs. Pitman. As the amount raised was not sufficient to carry out Isaac Pitman's idea, the gift took the form of a cheque and a handsome marble timepiece, which bore the following inscription :—

Presented, with a purse of £350, to Isaac Pitman, the Inventor of Phonography, by many friends of the phonetic system, in token of their high appreciation of its many excellences, and of his untiring labours in its extension.

A good many speeches were made, and eloquent testimony borne to the personal esteem in which the Inventor of Phonography was held. The Rev. C. H. E. Wyche (Chairman) happily expressed the appreciation of phonographers of Isaac Pitman's untiring and unselfish labours in the dissemination of Phonography. Had he made his invention an article of merchandise, he would have been by that time a rich man—but then they would not have

met together to do him honour. He chose,
however, a different method, and had improved
his system and made it known as widely as possible
by publishing it at a price barely remunerative.
Their testimonial was presented to him as Inventor
of Phonography, but they did not forget his
labours, in association with Mr. Ellis, in the
invention of a system of phonetic spelling.
Resolutions in favour of the Writing and
Printing Reform were unanimously passed.

The reception given to Isaac Pitman, when he
rose to acknowledge the presentation, was most
enthusiastic, and evoked from him a sincere
expression of gratitude. His admirers were, however, hardly prepared for the remarkable disclaimer to which he saw fit to give expression, that
" he invented nothing and discovered nothing,"
that during a thoughtful walk in the neighbourhood of Paddington, he had come to the conclusion
that Phonography was a " usufruct "—" a fruit
of use "—and so forth. While it was, of course,
true that phonetic notation was no new thing,
and that the art of shorthand had been in vogue
more or less since the days of Cicero, it was equally
true that Isaac Pitman invented the system of
Phonography with which his name is associated.
The disclaimer was, indeed, not consistent with
his assertion—and very just assertion—from time
to time of the usual author's rights in the phonographic treatises he had written. This self-
abnegation, though not an unusual trait of Isaac

Pitman's character, and manifested on occasions like the present, was, to say the least, liable to be misunderstood. It is probable, however, that he desired to express a sentiment similar to that which inspired his Manchester speech of 1857.

The question as to what use he should make of the £350 presented to him led its recipient to discuss quite frankly his financial position in relation to Phonography and the Spelling Reform. "I feel," he said, "that I have no right to receive such a sum of money as £350 and appropriate it to my own purposes." Mr. Ellis was the only man besides himself who had spent a large sum of money on the Reform. But unlike Mr. Ellis, he had not a fortune at his command, and hence could only spend money as it came in from the sale of shorthand and other books. He then mentioned the amount of capital he had borrowed (£2,000) and explained how the money had gone in the improvement of the phonetic printing alphabet : "The alphabet which Mr. Ellis and myself had employed until 1851 was so defective that type-founders and printers would not look at it as a possible alphabet for representing the English language in books. Mr. Besley, the eminent type-founder, remonstrated somewhat sharply with me for thinking to overturn good-looking printing by bad. ' Your page,' said he, ' is covered with little hooks, and tails, and triangles.' I spared no labour and no expense in removing this obstacle to the general introduction of phonetic printing."

He had given his means so entirely to the movement that if he had not already spent on the phonetic alphabet the sum with which he was presented he should devote it to the Reform in some other way. What he eventually did with the money will be related later on. In the course of his long and interesting speech Isaac Pitman gave statistics of the sale of phonographic books during the past year, from which it appeared that there had been a total sale of 90,000 publications, although the demand had been low in consequence of the anticipated appearance of a new and improved edition of Phonography. Cheered by the progress made he added, " I return to Bath with a determination not to work so many hours as I have for twenty years, but to work with the same application of mind as of old. My hours of labour from the beginning of the Reform to about a year ago, were from six in the morning till ten in the evening, taking out three hours for meals and exercise. I have now made a change, and ' knock off ' at half-past six. I intend to continue to labour at this good work twelve and a half hours per day, and, with your kind co-operation, I think that will be sufficient to keep the Reform in motion, and realize, in the end, all that we desire."

In association with Isaac Pitman's allusion to his labours given above, Mr. Reed's observations at this gathering on his method of daily work are of particular interest. Mr. Reed said :—

Those who have witnessed Mr. Pitman's labours in that remarkable little spot called Parsonage Lane, descriptions of which some of you possibly may have read, must have been struck with admiration at the intensity of labour and of earnestness which he has exhibited. I could tell you if I had the time, of instances of it that I have myself observed. I have on more than one occasion partaken of Mr. Pitman's hospitality at Bath, and on the last occasion he was good enough to invite me to his house, he asked me to go with him to his office the next morning for the purpose of running over some proof-sheets of a work that was then going through the press,—an invitation that I gladly accepted, as I am at any time delighted to show him my willingness to render him any little services I can in the adaptation of the system to useful purposes. We retired to rest at eleven o'clock. Mr. Pitman asked me if he should call me the next morning. I thanked him, and requested him to be good enough to do so. It was then in the depth of winter. In the morning when I was fast asleep some raps came at my door, which after being repeated some few times awoke me. You must know that I am not one of the " rising " generation. I responded in a sleepy kind of way ; the door opened, and I saw Mr. Pitman's familiar features. He entered holding a light, and announced that it was actually five o'clock in the morning. I rose and was speedily dressed, but not in so short a time as Mr. Pitman takes. I joined him, and we took a walk of nearly a mile down a very steep hill on a cold December morning, under circumstances not the most comfortable for sensitive nerves, and at about ten minutes to six we were in front of his office in Parsonage Lane. At about six o'clock we were seated at his desk, by gaslight, of course, and for two hours we waded through some pages of the little book upon which Mr. Pitman was then at work. Having laboured for two hours, we returned just as it was getting daylight, ascended the steep hill leading to Lansdown Crescent, and found ourselves in excellent condition for breakfast. I have no doubt that if any

other visitor had called upon Mr. Pitman just before ten
o'clock that night, he would have found him still at his desk,
as absorbed as ever in the mysteries of the phonetic art.
This is, I believe, a fair specimen of Mr. Pitman's general
labours, under which any ordinary mortal would certainly
succumb. And when we see that all these labours are devoted
to a cause from which he himself derives little or no personal
benefit beyond a bare living, we shall all the more admire the
disinterestedness which is so conspicuous a characteristic of
the man.

XV

A CHARACTER SKETCH—ADDRESS TO THE BRITISH ASSOCIATION ON "BRIEF WRITING"

1862-1864

THERE appeared in September, 1862, in *Weldon's Register*, a popular periodical of that time, a character sketch of Isaac Pitman, written by Mr. William White, (author of a voluminous life of Swedenborg), who was associated with New Church publishing work, and whose name for some years figured on the title page of the phonographic text-books as publisher, in addition to Mr. Frederick Pitman. Mr. White had a very intimate knowledge of the Inventor of Phonography, and insight into his character. His graphic description of Isaac Pitman at work, when read along with the reminiscences quoted at the end of the last chapter, furnish a vivid picture both of the man and of his methods, which did not alter materially during the rest of his working life. Mr. White began by observing that the name of Isaac Pitman would not be found in " Men of the Time "—an omission that was made good in later years—and went on to observe that Isaac Pitman had effected a great work in his generation, but it had not become " the talk of the newspapers," and consequently many well-informed

men were ignorant of him and his schemes. This
assertion needs qualification, but at any rate it
afforded Mr. White the pretext for giving the
readers of the *Register* a lucid historical account
of the Reform (introductory to his personal sketch
of its Inventor), which furnished the basis of
several articles on the same subject published in
later years.

" If," wrote Mr. White, " we were asked to name
the most diligent and hard-working man we know,
it would be Isaac Pitman.   It is a treat to visit
his printing office in Bath.   Printing offices are
usually very dirty and untidy places ; but Mr.
Pitman's office, save for its furniture, might be a
lady's drawing-room.   Everything is in what, for
some unknown reason, is called ' apple-pie ' order.
In a large room sits Mr. Pitman himself, writing
an article, reading a proof, or answering a letter.
His correspondence is immense ; letters and papers
flow in upon him from every part of the world.
He attends to all himself.   Those who write to
him in ordinary handwriting he answers in longhand phonetic spelling, but the mass of his correspondence is in Phonography ; and the speed
and ease with which he writes enables him to get
through an amount of work which would else
seem fabulous.   We wish we could reproduce one
of Mr. Pitman's phonographic letters on this page.
Written on a scrap of ruled paper, half the size
of an ordinary page of note-paper, would be seen
a series of lines, circles, and dots, sharp and delicate
as if traced by a fairy, and containing as much
matter as an ordinary letter of four pages.   A
most courteous correspondent, he commences in

the ancient style, ' Isaac Pitman to Mr. ——, or
Mrs. ——, or Miss ——,' as it may be, and goes
on to say what is necessary in a free, kindly, and
concise style, closing his letter with the simple
word ' Farewell.'

" Letters in this way he writes off by the score,
without haste, and with an ease which fills one,
used to drudge with the pen in the customary
fashion, with pity for his own sad lot.   Mr. Pitman
carries into his printing office the *régime* of the
schoolmaster ;   he is a strict disciplinarian.   No
talking is allowed, beyond necessary questions
and orders, and the quiet is unbroken except by
the click of the types, or the packing of parcels
for the carrier or the post.   Seeing his set of
apprentices so sedulously and silently at work,
and the prim order which pervades the place, is
really tempting to one's mischievous propensities,
and stirs the desire to cry out, ' Boys, do let's
have a romp and tumble things about ! '   We have
sometimes amused ourselves with drawing com-
parisons between Isaac Pitman and John Wesley ;
and, did we believe in the transmigration of souls,
we might imagine that the soul of Wesley had left
its ' world parish ' to write shorthand, and persuade Englishmen to spell phonetically.   Unlike
Wesley, Pitman is tall, but, like him, he is spare
and muscular, with bright eyes, a keen face, and
rapid   motions.   Like   Wesley,   his   habits   are
regular, and almost ascetic.   He goes to bed early,
and rises early summer and winter, and may almost
invariably be found posted at his desk by six in the
morning.   Except for the progress of his work,
he seems to have no care in the world.   He sees
no company ;   he seldom dines from home, or pays
visits, and, first in his office in the morning, he is

last to leave it at night.   He delights in walking
exercise, and scampers over miles of country with
the same ease that his pen goes over paper.   Like
Wesley, he is very abstemious : wine, beer, or
spirits of any kind never pass his lips : nor fish,
flesh, nor fowl.   For years he has been a strict
vegetarian ; and, but for a cold now and then, he
has enjoyed perfect health.   As if his shorthand
and phonetic printing were not enough to task
all his powers, he preaches twice each Sunday in
a little chapel, at Twerton, a village a short way
from Bath.   Like Wesley, he has no love for
money save for its uses in promoting his ends.
His personal wants are few and simple, and every
penny beyond what is required for them is devoted
to the phonetic propaganda.   Like Wesley he has
a governing and despotic temper.   In all things
he takes his own way.   He hears the advice of a
disciple in the blandest and most candid spirit.
The disciple thinks, surely never was there a man
more pliable than this.   But if he observes carefully, he will discover he has made no progress.
Somehow, he will find that Pitman has not changed
his mind, and has rejected his disciple's advice,
but yet so kindly that the rejection gives no pain,
but almost pleasure.   His alterations in Phonotypy and Phonography have usually been proposed
in the face of strong opposition ; but he has always
carried them.   Consciously or unconsciously he
makes up his mind as to what ought to be done,
and though he undergoes much palaver with all
the appearance of being affected by it, he ends in
executing his programme to the final letter.
Alternately he is accused of fickleness and obstinacy : of fickleness, because when he sees, or
fancies he sees, a possible improvement, he will

pull down any amount of building to make room for it ; and of obstinacy, because what he thinks right he does, whatever be the outcry."

In some comments on the above extract Isaac Pitman mentioned that his ministrations to a New Church congregation in the village of Twerton had been discontinued, and that he was temporarily taking the services at the New Church, Henry Street, Bath, the minister, Mr. James Keene, being indisposed. As to the application to himself of the term " despot," he remarked, " I feel sure that Mr. White used the word in no harsh sense, as implying the love of rule for its own sake, but simply the love of order, use, and beauty."

The annual meeting of the British Association for the Advancement of Science was held at Newcastle-on-Tyne in 1863, under the presidency of Sir William (afterwards Lord Armstrong) who, among other topics, referred in his address to the waste of time and labour attendant on the use of the common longhand, and threw out suggestions in the following terms :—

The facility now given to the transmission of intelligence and the interchange of thought is one of the most remarkable features of the present age. Cheap and rapid postage to all parts of the world ; paper and printing reduced to the lowest possible cost ; electric telegraphs between nation and nation, town and town, and now even (thanks to the beautiful inventions of Professor Wheatstone) between house and house,—all contribute to aid that commerce of ideas by which wealth and knowledge are augmented. But while so much facility is given to mental communication by new measures and new inventions, the fundamental art of expressing thought by written symbols remains as imperfect now as it has been for centuries past. It seems strange that while we actually possess a system of shorthand by which words can be recorded as rapidly as they can be spoken, we should persist in writing a slow and laborious longhand. It is intelligible that grown-up persons who have acquired the present conventional art of writing should be reluctant to incur the labour of mastering a better system ; but there can be no reason why the rising generation should not be instructed in a method of writing more in accordance with the activity of mind which now prevails. Even without going so far as to adopt for ordinary use a complete system of stenography, which it is not easy to acquire, we might greatly abridge the time and labour of writing by the recognition of a few simple signs to express the syllables which are of most frequent occurrence in our language. Our words are in a great measure made up of such syllables as *com, con, tion, ing, able, ain, ent, est, ance*, etc. These we are now obliged to write out over and over again, as if time and labour expended in what may be termed visual speech were of no importance. Neither has our written character the advantage of distinctness to recommend it.

An utterance so notable on the importance of shorthand, and a recognition so generous of the merits of Phonography, was greatly appreciated by all phonographic practitioners, and not least by their leader. It suggested to Isaac Pitman the idea of offering a paper on the subject for the forthcoming meeting of the British Association in his own city. His offer was accepted, and a paper with the title " Brief Writing " was prepared to be read before the Section of Economics and Statistics on 20th September, 1864. But, as is not infrequently the case, there were more papers down for reading than could be delivered in the time available, so that Isaac Pitman's had perforce to be " taken as read." Copies were handed to all present, and the paper was duly included in the published Transactions of the British Association. It was afterwards issued in separate pamphlet form, and as it contained a full description and explanation of the art, it brought Phonography under the notice of many who would not have taken an interest in it had it not been introduced to them under the ægis of the British Association. In the course of his paper Isaac Pitman showed the insufficiency of longhand abbreviations, and made some observations on the respective legibility of longhand and shorthand which merit reproduction. He pointed out the insufficiency of any mere longhand abbreviations such as those suggested by Sir William Armstrong, and stated his objections to their introduction.

" The game," he wrote, " is not worth the candle. All can abbreviate if they like, yet only reporters and lawyers do it. If the game were worth the candle, we should all soon fall into the same contractions, but the truth is we do not want them. Abbreviations were formerly in extensive use, when fewer people wrote, but now they have all gone out, except the Latin *et* for *and*, in the form of ' & '—that is, the letter *e* written across *t* ; the downstroke of ' &,' which represents *t*, being written first. With most people who spend but a small portion of their time in writing, abbreviations are not worth the effort of mind necessary in keeping up two habits of writing the same word. On some occasions it is necessary, or at least advisable, to write every word fully, and if the hand were accustomed in its ordinary style to abbreviate some words, it would hesitate when called upon to write the same words in another manner. No one can write fluently, either in longhand or shorthand, whose hand thinks, so to speak, how it shall form the words. It must form them without thinking, and leave all thinking to the brain. In the quotation which I have just read from Sir Wm. Armstrong, consisting of 346 words, and containing 1,626 letters, there would be but 47 letters saved by the adoption of the abbreviations therein recommended ; that is, for the loss of power through occasional hesitation in the act of writing, there would be a gain of 3 per cent. If we were to adopt, in addition, all the abbreviations which reporters use in transcribing their notes for the press, writing a slanting stroke / for *the*, & for *and*, *o* for *of*, *wh* for *which*, *t* for *that*, etc., the saving would be 8 per cent additional. This saving of 11 per cent is of considerable importance to men who spend many hours each day in writing, but it is not sufficient to commend the system for general adoption. Longhand is still too long, and we must recur to the alphabet as the proper subject of abbreviation."

Referring to Sir William's suggestion that some of the longhand letters should be more clearly distinguished from others, Mr. Pitman said : " His objection lies against the *n*, *u* classes of letters. Of the first kind we have *m*, *n*, *r*, *v* ; and of the second *i*, *n*, *u*, *w*, and portions of other letters. The use of *r*, in preference to *n*, increases the legibility of a rapid style of penmanship. The evil complained of lies in the alphabet—in the numerous strokes we have to scribble, to get down one word. Men accustomed to dispatch in other things cannot endure a tedious style of writing ; they hurry through their work, and spoil it, forgetting that whatever is written has to be read. Writing-masters distinguish the curves that form the *n, u* classes of letters, as over-curves (*n*) and under-curves (*u*). Swift writers generally make only under-curves, because this is an easier action of the hand than the over-curve, thus mingling all these letters of both classes in an undistinguishable mass of under-curves ; but surely everyone who has time for longhand writing, should consider himself, in justice to the reader, bound to distinguish *n* from *u, m* from *ni, ui, in,* etc. ; and be especially careful to dot the letters *i* and *j.* The want of these distinctive points is one of the most serious impediments in the reading of bad manuscript. I find that I can decipher writing made up of under-curves if the dots or jots be placed over *i* and *j ;* but writing that consists of undercurves only, where these dots are omitted, is hopelessly illegible. As a bad servant is said to be ' the greatest plague of life ' domestic, so bad writing may be called the greatest plague of literary and commercial life. Not infrequently I receive letters, the signatures of which I am utterly unable to decipher. In such cases I cut out the name, gum it on my reply, and hand over the puzzle to the post-office. The letter finds its way by virtue of the other portions of the address. Shorthand signatures are very rarely illegible. Phonetic shorthand is much more legible than longhand, supposing both styles to be written with equal rapidity, but whether the penman or our cumbrous alphabet is to be blamed for making a mess of such words as *minimum, ammunition,* there is no proposition before us for changing the forms of any of these letters ; and whoever may propose new forms must make his script letters harmonize with the roman and italic printing letters ; for italic type is simply script letters disconnected, and roman type, except in the two letters ' a, g,' is merely italic made upright."

In the year 1864 the Royal Society of Arts held its first annual examination in shorthand. Mr. Frederick Pitman was the first examiner, and the following notification appeared in the Society's syllabus : " Candidates beginning the study of shorthand are recommended to adopt Phonography."

The first adaptation of Isaac Pitman's system of Phonography to any foreign language made its appearance in 1864, when Señor Guillermo Parody published his adaptation of the art to the Spanish language under the patronage of the Argentine Government, which established a hall for the teaching of Spanish Phonography in the National College, and promoted the use of the art in reporting the proceedings of Congress, in which it has been successfully practised ever since.

A slight carriage accident on 16th March, 1864, for a time incapacitated Isaac Pitman, and the shorthand supplement to his *Journal* was suspended for some weeks. This was the year of the Shakspere Tercentenary Celebrations, and the

Inventor of Phonography not only took a great interest in the civic honours which were paid to the national poet at Bath, but through the medium of his *Journal* on the memorable 23rd April circulated the play of " The Tempest " in reformed spelling.

XVI

PHONOGRAPHIC AUTHORSHIP—TESTIMONY IN THE JUSTICIARY COURT AT EDINBURGH—ADDRESS AT MANCHESTER

1865-1872

THE period of seven years between the dates given above was with Isaac Pitman one of prolific work in phonographic authorship and transfer writing, which resulted in many valuable and interesting additions to the literature of the system, and of improvements in existing works. Opposition to the changes introduced in the Tenth and Eleventh Editions no longer seriously hindered the progress of Phonography, and the antagonism to the improvements did not now affect its fortunes to any appreciable extent. There had been considerable changes in the text-books since Mr. Reed took his historic stand on the Tenth Edition, and it was not easy to teach either the Ninth or Tenth Editions of Phonography by modifications of their rules. To assist in the continued teaching of the Tenth Edition, Mr. Reed brought out a little book of exercises in 1871, of which Isaac Pitman expressed strong disapproval. The work had little, if any, effect in checking the teaching of Phonography by the new books, but it had the unfortunate result of estranging for a time the two friends, though happily in later years the friendship was re-established as firmly as ever.

With regard to the improvements introduced into the system from time to time, Isaac Pitman never had the intention or desire—as he certainly had not the power—to coerce any writer of his system to adopt the alterations. For example, in September, 1871, he wrote thus : " A change in the manner of writing Phonography is no slight matter to a reporter. We do not wonder then that Mr. Reed does not alter his manner of writing some few words that differ in his style and ours ; and that reporters engaged on the Press generally have not adopted the few improvements that have from time to time been made in the system. To do so would imply a kind of indiscretion." But apart from those who used the system professionally, it was Isaac Pitman's desire that future learners of Phonography should have the benefit of such improvements in it as its more extensive use showed to be practicable or desirable. The growth of the literature of the system, however, caused some reluctance on the part of his brother, Mr. Frederick Pitman, to adopt the new forms for *kw* and *skw*, which were introduced in 1869. It was not, in fact, till two years later that he used these improvements in the magazines controlled by himself. But fortunately for the system and its practitioners, from the period at which we have arrived, and onward, no further organic changes were made. To the Spelling

Reform movement the same remarks apply generally. There was experiment and consultation
with the Phonetic Society, and this resulted in the
introduction of a limited number of improved
phonotypic forms which rendered the phonetic
printing alphabet far more useful, acceptable, and
presentable than it had ever been before.

At this time Isaac Pitman was engaged on the
production of two phonographic works of reference
which involved a vast amount of labour and
application. The first of these was a new edition
(the third) of the " Phonographic Dictionary,"
a lithographed work consisting of 336 crown 8vo
pages, containing shorthand outlines for all the
principal words in the English language, together
with the longhand spelling of each. A companion
work was also taken in hand which materially
assisted in the reading of doubtful unvocalized
shorthand outlines. This laborious undertaking
is described by Mr. Reed as follows :—

" About this date (1867) we find Isaac Pitman
bringing out a new shorthand book, the preparation of which involved an immense amount of
labour. It is, in its way, a marvel of industry,
and required almost as much patience as the
collation of the marginal references in Bagster's
Bible. Some twelve years previously Isaac
Pitman had carefully written out all the words
in the ' Shorthand Dictionary ' not exceeding
in outline three consonant strokes (and in Phonography very few ordinary words require more),
and had them cut up and sorted according to the

Phonetic Alphabet. From this extensive list all the words containing the same consonants were classified, first according to their forms, and secondly according to their position as determined by the principal vowel. The list was designed to bring before the reporter all the words occurring under any particular combination of consonants as to the meaning of which he might be doubtful in his work of transcription ; thus under *p-s-tion* he would see *apposition, opposition, possession, (com)position ;* and under *p, t, r, n, pattern* (written by *pt, rn*), *patron (p, irn), upturn (p, t, rn).* He would thus be shown the best way of differentiating these words either by position or outline, the system admitting, to a greater extent than any other, of two or more varieties of form for the same consonants, thus rendering the insertion of vowels almost superfluous. The weight of the MS. of this work is 16 lb. It was prepared by writing the words in shorthand, with the consonants in longhand underneath, on thin card. The words were then cut up, sorted into basins, as to their first consonant, then as to the second, and again as to the third, etc., in accordance with the Phonetic Alphabet, and pasted in a folio blank book. From this a fair copy was made, and published in a lithographed edition, 1867, under the title of ' The Reporter's Assistant.' In a second edition the shorthand outlines were printed from metal types."

It is a striking indication of the extent to which Phonography was cultivated at this period that the business of producing literature in phonographic characters may be said to have been added to the literary industries of the country, and the widespread popularity of the art was demonstrated by the great number of periodicals and books which made their appearance from this date onward. Isaac Pitman's own work was, however, never excelled by any of those who engaged in this method of production. As supplements to his *Journal* he issued from week to week portions of standard literature in lithographed shorthand, so that in time subscribers became possessed of complete volumes executed by the Inventor of Phonography in the highest style of phonographic penmanship, which were, with many thousands of writers of the system, treasured possessions. There were produced in this way by Isaac Pitman the Holy Bible (1867), the Book of Common Prayer (1869), Macaulay's Biographies (1868) also his Essays (1870), Gulliver's Travels (1871), " Paradise Lost " (1871), and a large number of other works, among which were some written by an assistant (Mr. J. R. Lloyd), who was at that time engaged at the Phonetic Institute. Of other workers in the same field the most prolific was Mr. James Butterworth, of South Shields, who set up his own lithographic press, and for many years produced a vast number of books, and also monthly periodicals. All the transfers were written by Mr. Butterworth, and some of the periodicals were edited by him, while Mr. Frederick Pitman was the editor of others, the most popular of these being the *Shorthand Magazine*, founded by Mr.

FACSIMILE OF ISAAC PITMAN'S LITHOGRAPHED SHORTHAND
FROM THE 1870 EDITION OF MACAULAY'S BIOGRAPHIES

ISAAC PITMAN
(1868 *age* 55)

F. Pitman in 1866, and edited by him until his death.

The following anecdote associated with Isaac Pitman's work as a transfer writer may be appropriately quoted here : " One afternoon, while busy as usual at his desk in a quiet corner of his office, engaged in writing one of those beautiful lithographic transfers which the earlier generation of phonographers know so well, a clumsy young clerk, in reaching for something from a shelf above the already snow-white head of Isaac Pitman, managed to knock down a book from the shelf right upon the delicate work beneath. That work was spoiled and had to be done again. The only trace of annoyance observable on the countenance of the veteran shorthand writer was a momentary access of colour, which passed off as rapidly as it came. Not one word of anger or reproach was uttered, and this very fact, no doubt, made the awkward young fellow feel more repentant than he otherwise might have been."

Since 1861 Isaac Pitman had permitted himself certain relaxations from the Spartan discipline he had followed in earlier years. He felt it consistent with his duty to the Reform to leave his desk at the Institute early in the evening, instead of toiling on till a late hour, but as he continued winter and summer to begin work at 6 a.m., his working day was still by no means a short one. From the date above mentioned he also began to take an annual holiday. It was in association with one of these that he inserted a personal explanation in the *Journal*, which is of some biographical note, as throwing light on his methods of work at this period. Someone had written an article entitled, " Objections to Phonotypy," and he took a proof with him on his summer holiday of a month at the seaside. To a notice accounting for its non-publication, he added a further explanation of the reason which led him to publish in the shorthand portion of the *Journal* during 1867 a reproduction of a work once highly popular among Evangelical Christians—" The Dairyman's Daughter." The issue had created some surprise, Mr. Reed records, because hitherto religious works reproduced in this way had usually been associated with the Swedenborgian views of the Inventor of Phonography.

When the time came for this holiday, Isaac Pitman says, " We had been unable to get a single day ahead with our lithographic labours for the *Journal*. We therefore took our lithographing tools with us, sat down at Sandown, in the Isle of Wight, and in a month did seven of the *Journal* transfers. This gave us an opportunity of taking a fortnight's holiday, and yet have one transfer ahead for the first week after our return to Bath. During this fortnight's travelling about the island, and enjoying its lovely scenery, there was no disposition to entertain arguments for or against Phonotypy. This little bit of personal history brings us to ' The Dairyman's Daughter.'

" Six of the seven transfers spoken of were the last six of the ' Phonographic Vocabulary.' It was necessary to do one more transfer before leaving Sandown, to secure the punctual appearance of the *Journal*. The question to be decided was, What shall we take for the subject ? The ' Vicar of Wakefield ' we considered too long for that brief emergency. Had we been at home the ' Reporter's Assistant,' now being issued, would have been commenced ; but to do it away from the Phonetic Institute was impossible. Being in the very centre of the interesting spot where the scene of Leigh Richmond's narrative is laid, Sandown being only two miles from Brading, his residence, two miles from Ashey Down, his ' lovely mount of observation,' and four miles from Arreton, which contains the grave of Elizabeth Wallbridge ; and knowing how sincerely a vast multitude cherished the kind of religious sentiment (considered as distinct from life and doctrine) which is embalmed in this book, we though it would be a gratification to such of them as read the *Phonetic Journal* to have the book in shorthand. While admiring the author's piety, and his tact in the composition of the work, we inwardly protested, as we wrote, against many of the sentiments. . . . We had a strong desire in transcribing the book, to write a Supplementary Note to it . . . . but time, which stays not in its course, hurried us on in our ordinary sphere of duty. We trust this apology will be accepted by those who have reasonable objections to Leigh Richmond's book ; and as for our Evangelical readers, they will thank us for giving them this favourite book in shorthand."

At this period public attention was called to a
phonetic system entitled " Visible Speech," the
invention of Alexander Melville Bell (1819-1905),
the author of a shorthand system known as
" Steno-Phonography," which was noticed by
Isaac Pitman in no unfriendly spirit when it first
appeared in 1852, but which—although it had
the advantage of appearing in the early editions
of " Cassell's Popular Educator " under circumstances already described—did not secure any
considerable number of practitioners. In 1866
Mr. Bell read a paper on " Visible Speech " before
the Society of Arts. " No explanation," Mr. Reed
says, " was given of the symbols employed by
Mr. Bell, who contented himself with explaining
the theory on which his alphabet was founded—
namely, the use of signs which pictorially represented the arrangement of the vocal organs required
to produce the various sounds of the language.
By this method it was stated that all possible
shades of elementary sounds could be accurately
represented. Isaac Pitman was naturally interested
in Mr. Bell's invention, and reprinted his paper
in the *Phonetic Journal*. He also offered to contribute to the cost of casting types to illustrate
the new system, and invited Mr. Bell to make use
of the *Journal* as a means of illustrating and
promulgating his scheme. The offer was not
accepted. Mr. Bell desired a Government subsidy
before revealing the secret. This, however, was
not forthcoming ; and the author of the system

subsequently published it on his own account. It
was a much more ambitious attempt than Isaac
Pitman's, and was designed as a mode of expressing
every sound that could be uttered by the human
voice, and that by a comparatively small number
of symbols, having no resemblance whatever to
the letters of the ordinary alphabet. But it was
not at all adapted to the common purpose of reading and writing, and no practical result followed
the publication."

When resident at Edinburgh Mr. Melville Bell
had associated himself with Isaac Pitman's work
as a member of the British Phonetic Council.
In later years he proceeded to Canada and subsequently to Washington, D.C. ; he was the joint
compiler with his brother of the well-known " Bell's
Standard Elocutionist," and his son, Mr. Graham
Bell, was the inventor of the telephone.

In the early part of 1868 a summons of unusual
character reached Isaac Pitman, in the form of a
citation to appear as a witness for the Crown at
Edinburgh, at the trial of a well-known phonographic lecturer on indictments charging him with
" falsehood, fraud, and wilful imposition " (*anglice*
" false pretences "). The case related to jewellery
and other property of about eight hundred pounds
in value. After a postponement, the trial was
fixed for 8th June, and in obedience to the citation
Isaac Pitman left Bath on the 4th, and reached
Edinburgh the following morning. " The time
being near our usual summer holiday," he writes,

" we took wife and family [his two sons, Alfred, b.
1862, and Ernest, b. 1864] for the purpose of spend-
ing some time in Scotland after the trial.   Our
appearance in the witness box was the first experience of this kind during a life of fifty-five years,
and we certainly felt, on being sworn, the religious
solemnity that should always accompany the
administration of an oath for furthering the ends
of justice."   After two long wearisome days of
waiting " we were called, soon after the proceedings
commenced on the third day, to enter the court.
The sight was exceedingly impressive," and he
proceeds to give a general description of the
interior of the Justiciary Court, and of the
solemn administration of the oath by the Lord
Justice-Clerk.

The testimony Isaac Pitman was called to give
related to the authorship of two letters in
Phonography, which purported to be written by
New York and Boston merchants respectively to
the accused as to his financial status.   These the
Procurator-Fiscal sought to prove through the
evidence of Isaac Pitman, and of a member of the
Scotsman staff (Mr. Thomas Paul) to be forgeries
written by the accused.   Isaac Pitman's testimony
is worthy of reproduction here, because it is the
first occasion on which a phonographic expert
gave evidence as such in a court of justice.   He
was, he deposed, by profession a shorthand
author, and had been known as such for thirty-
one years.   Through correspondence he had known

the accused for twenty years. He had received many letters from him, all in shorthand, except the direction—" There was no necessity for longhand," he continued, " the other being plainer. Handwriting could be more easily and certainly identified in shorthand than in longhand. In longhand you have one shape for each letter except *r* and *s*, but in our system of shorthand we have five or six letters, each with two or three, sometimes four shapes. This variety of shapes for these few letters gives such a choice of what we call consonantal outlines for words that almost every writer has a style of his own, which can be known by his choice of outlines. I am able to distinguish shorthand writing with more certainty than longhand." From numerous communications from the individual who was undergoing his trial, he had thoroughly familiarized himself with his shorthand, and he affirmed positively that the " New York " and " Boston " letters were in the handwriting of the accused, and similar to the entries in a diary found in his possession.

There was a long cross-examination on shorthand details, conducted by the accused, because his counsel were not acquainted with Phonography. The curious fact was elicited that the " New York " letter was written in the new style of Phonography, while the " Boston " letter was written in the old (or Ninth Edition). The point the accused sought to establish apparently was that the last named letter was written by one who had acquired what

was called the Graham system. " I am aware,"
Isaac Pitman said, " that a Mr. Graham has
adopted my system of Phonography in America
and called it his own."   " Would it not be
extremely difficult," he was asked, " for the same
hand to trace these letters in the different styles
without occasionally mistaking the styles ? "
" Not at all," was the reply. As a matter of fact
vowels were very sparingly used in the two letters,
and there was no writing in position. Isaac
Pitman's opinions were strongly supported by
the independent evidence of Mr. Paul, and no
witnesses were called by the defence to refute
their testimony.

The trial, which evoked unusual interest in
Scotland, resulted in a conviction and sentence.
Great sympathy was felt for the innocent wife
and child of the convicted man. Isaac Pitman
actively interested himself on their behalf, and
collected through an appeal in his *Journal* a sum
of money for their immediate necessities, and in
later years took a kindly interest in their welfare.

Before he returned to Bath, the Inventor of
Phonography visited Manchester, and one of the
most successful phonographic meetings ever held
took place in the Manchester Town Hall on the
14th July, 1868. The weather was intensely hot,
but the attendance was very large, and Isaac
Pitman, who was accompanied by Mrs. Pitman,
was accorded a most enthusiastic reception.
Professor Greenbank was in the chair, and a

remarkable feature of the preliminary proceedings was the reading by Mr. Henry Pitman—who had organized the meeting—of letters from many notable men expressing their appreciation of Phonography and the Spelling Reform, including one from the Rev. Dr. Parker (afterwards Pastor of the City Temple), who wrote in shorthand that he had practised Phonography for twenty years, and could " honestly recommend its study to all who wish to acquire a simple, philosophic, and perfect system of shorthand." The principal resolution in favour of Phonography and the Spelling Reform was moved by Dr. Pankhurst, a well-known barrister, and embodied a cordial Manchester greeting to Isaac Pitman, and a recommendation to parents and teachers to place the time-saving art within the reach of every boy and girl under their authority. Isaac Pitman's address was of an interesting autobiographical character, and much of what he then said has been quoted or otherwise embodied in the pages of this Life. An able address was also delivered by Mr. Edward Jones, head master of the Hibernian Schools, Liverpool, and a prominent spelling reformer. He was related to Isaac Pitman, whose sister Melissa was Mr. Jones's first wife.

For about seventeen years there resided in Bath a gentleman of good birth and education named Francis Foster Barham (1808-1871), a relative of the author of the " Ingoldsby Legends." He had lived in London till his thirty-seventh

year, and had attempted to establish himself as a
solicitor there, but apparently with indifferent
success, due chiefly to his strong propensity for
literary pursuits and theological studies. On
leaving London he settled in Clifton, and when
forty-six and in failing health, he removed to
Bath, where he spent the remainder of his days.
During his residence in Bath a great friendship
sprung up between Mr. Barham and Isaac Pitman.
Mr. Barham was a most laborious and voluminous
writer on theological and ecclesiastical subjects,
but he is now remembered for his efforts to establish
a new, and as he conceived, more spiritual phase
of religion, under the title of Alism (or Godliness)
in association with which he published propagandist literature, and styled himself " Alist
Francis Barham "—" that he might thus constantly be reminded of the nearness of God."
During his declining years Mr. Barham produced
a " Rhymed Harmony of the Gospels," and when
he died Isaac Pitman became his literary executor.

The Barham library was bequeathed to local
institutions, and was in due course distributed.
The literary remains of the deceased consisted of
a hundredweight of closely written manuscript
in the form of prose, verse, and dramatic compositions.   Isaac Pitman conceived it to be his duty
to his friend's memory that he should rescue
some portion of this great mass of literary matter
from oblivion.   He devoted eight months to its
thorough examination, and selected from it such

pieces as appeared most worthy of inclusion in the projected volume. " A Memorial of Francis Barham " made its first appearance serially in 1872, as a supplement to the *Phonetic Journal.* It was the largest book ever issued in phonetic spelling, being a closely printed crown 8vo work of nearly five hundred pages. The " Rhymed Harmony " of the Gospels and Barham's translations of the poetical books of the Bible had appeared in the same fashion during 1870-1. Much of Mr. Barham's work, and especially his " Harmony," was edited by Isaac Pitman. His friendship for the " Alist " and desire to honour his memory led him to publish a good deal of matter of doubtful value ; but as we have no desire to do an injustice to Mr. Barham's memory, it should be recorded here that in early life one of his dramas, entitled " Socrates," was read and spoken of with much admiration by Macready, although the great tragedian considered that it must remain " a dramatic poem and not be an acted play."

A few other activities of Isaac Pitman in the period covered by this chapter call for notice here. In 1866 he lithographed the entire Bible in shorthand, and it was issued serially as a supplement presented to the purchasers of the *Journal.* A second issue of the Bible in this form was begun, and the New Testament having been completed, the Old Testament was taken in hand and executed as far as 2 Kings xviii. 25, when serial publication was discontinued with the *Phonetic Journal* of 28th September, 1872. Probably through pressure of other duties Isaac Pitman's hand at this time seemed to have lost something of its cunning. He therefore decided to suspend the task of completing this edition of the Shorthand Bible till a more convenient opportunity. For reasons which will be related in due course, he was unfortunately never able to resume his labours in the production of the exquisite lithographed shorthand literature which had become justly famous.

Towards the close of the sixties Isaac Pitman waged a vigorous war against a custom which was for many years his *bête noire,* namely, the paid postal teaching of Phonography. The only kind of postal tuition which the Inventor of Phonography would tolerate was that of a gratuitous description, but someone had the temerity to point out that the early editions of the " Penny Plate " contained this legend : " Any persons may receive lessons from the Author by post at 1s. each, to be paid in advance." Isaac Pitman's reply was that soon after this announcement was printed he crossed it out and substituted " gratuitously." For a long time, under this self-denying ordinance, he laboured at the correction of all phonographic exercises sent to him, till the work was delegated to the Phonetic Society. But it never seemed to strike him that the phonographic teacher was doing nothing immoral in asking people

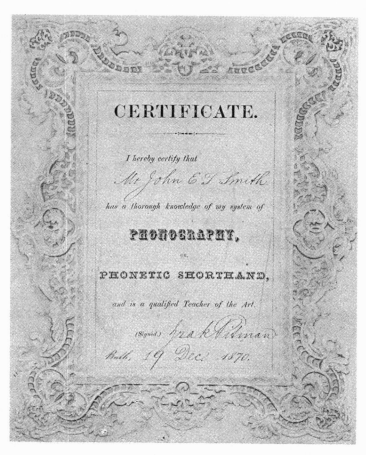

CERTIFICATE ISSUED TO MEMBERS OF THE PHONETIC
SOCIETY FROM ABOUT 1870 TO 1879

THE FOURTH PHONETIC INSTITUTE, KINGSTON BUILDINGS,
ABBEY CHURCHYARD, BATH

who were perfectly well able to pay for his services to remunerate him for his time and skill, in exactly the same way as they would any other expert teacher in the arts or sciences. It is significant of the position which Phonography had won for itself at this period, that arrangements were made by the leading encyclopædias for fully exhibiting the system in their pages, an enterprise in which Isaac Pitman gladly co-operated.

XVII

SHORTHAND PRINTED FROM MOVABLE TYPE—
THE FOURTH INSTITUTE

1873-1875

FROM an early time in the history of his shorthand
system Isaac Pitman had directed his attention
to the possibility of printing shorthand from
movable metal characters. Originally the phonographic alphabet and the characters required for
the rules and illustrations had been produced for
the instruction books of the system in the form of
woodcuts, but in 1847 it was found possible to
use metal type for this purpose, which was in
every respect preferable. A shorthand fount was
cast by Messrs. V. and J. Figgins, the London
type-founders, in which separate shorthand types
were produced for the consonants and vowels, of
which the following are specimens :—

For an outline containing several consonants the
character was engraved separately on a metal
" blank." A great many experiments were made
by Isaac Pitman's staff at the Phonetic Institute
with a view to the employment of metal types by
which shorthand outlines could be built up, but
it was found impracticable to adopt this method,

except in the case of simple words with upright
or horizontal straight consonant forms, such as :

.| *eat*, |- *toe*,   _._ *ache*,   _._ *cow*,

where two types, for a consonant and vowel
respectively, could be placed together to represent
a word. This method had, as we have indicated,
been in use for a quarter of a century, and no
development was now found possible on these
lines. But it was, as it had always been, practicable to engrave each outline on a separate " blank "
of metal of a suitable width, and this method was
introduced in 1873 for the production of shorthand reading matter. A story or a speech was
taken, and the words or phrases it contained were
engraved in shorthand on separate " blanks " of
metal. The characters were set up by the compositor like ordinary type, and punctuated with
the marks used in letterpress type of the same
size (pica). When the page had been stereotyped,
the shorthand type was available for resetting.

A number of wooden trays divided into com-
partments by strips of wood were obtained—
similar to the " cases " with " boxes " used by the
ordinary compositor in the printing office. In
these " cases " the outlines are distributed in a
similar style to the letterpress type, but with two
important distinctions. The " boxes "—which
are all of similar size—are labelled, dictionary
fashion, so that the shorthand outline for any
particular word or phrase can be readily found ;

and a shorthand " type " instead of being dropped
into its " box," as in letterpress, is carefully placed
in its particular compartment with the face
upward, so that a word can be readily found among
twenty or more " cuts " in the same box, which
are allied to it in the common spelling.   In setting
up every fresh story or speech in shorthand, words
are encountered for which no type is found in the
" cases."   The forms for these words are engraved,
and in due course added to the existing stock.
This method of producing shorthand reading
matter from movable metal type characters,
which Isaac Pitman at this time initiated, is
absolutely unique.

Key.—Who, that is much in the habit of writing, has not often wished
for some means of expressing by two or three dashes of the pen, that
which, as things are, it requires such an expenditure of time and labour
to commit to paper ? Our present mode of communication must be felt
to be cumbersome in the last degree ; unworthy of these days of invention ; we require some means of bringing the operations of the mind
and of the hand into closer correspondence.—*English Review.*

SPECIMEN OF PITMAN'S SHORTHAND (REPORTING STYLE)
PRINTED FROM METAL TYPE CHARACTERS

On the 4th January, 1873, appeared the first number of a new series of the *Phonetic Journal.* This was an important departure in connection with that periodical, and one which to a very remarkable extent promoted the cultivation of Phonography in succeeding years. The price was reduced from three pence to one penny, and the small circulation of one thousand weekly was speedily quadrupled, and as the years passed it increased from twenty to thirty times the total weekly circulation of the *Journal* prior to 1873. Supplements in lithographed shorthand and phonotypy were discontinued, but shorthand reading was provided in the shape of two pages of matter every week, printed from engraved characters by the method described above. As time went on, more pages were devoted to the weekly shorthand instalments, which became an increasingly popular feature.

A singular rumour was rather prevalent in phonographic circles in the early seventies, to the effect that Isaac Pitman was not quite in his right mind. The Inventor of Phonography made at this time no appearances at phonographic gatherings ; the art no longer aroused enthusiasm for its novelty, it had settled down into a business, and the phonographic " festivals " and similar social gatherings of earlier years had no successors. As a consequence comparatively few of those of the younger generation who employed the phonographic art had come into personal contact with

its originator. Legends about Isaac Pitman's
untiring habits of work and simple life were freely
circulated, and it was thought that he was devoting
himself to the promotion of Spelling Reform with
a perseverance and an expenditure of his private
means that was considered Quixotic. But these
were unsubstantial grounds for the apocryphal
story about his mental state. One of those who
saw fit to disseminate this rumour rather extensively—although he did not originate it—was the
Rev. William James Ball, B.A., of Harrogate,
a member of a well-known Irish family, and a
retired missionary of the Church Missionary
Society. Between 1869 and 1871 Isaac Pitman
and Mr. Ball were in frequent correspondence.
In his retirement Mr. Ball had taken up the study
and teaching of Phonography with much ardour,
and had developed some proposals of a comprehensive nature for what he considered to be
improvements in the system, which he had discussed at great length with its Inventor. This
had gone on for some years, until at last Mr. Ball
thought the time had arrived for the publication
from the Phonetic Institute of a treatise to be
entitled, " Ball's Standard Phonography." He
appears to have been, to use his own words,
" greatly pained " when he found that Isaac
Pitman had no intention of doing anything of the
kind, and he accused the latter of having " broken
faith " with him, and was especially aggrieved to
find his (Mr. Ball's) postal teaching very strongly

denounced. This seemed so extraordinary to the ex-missionary that he wrote, " some of my correspondents have come to the conclusion that Mr. Pitman cannot be in his right mind."

In his phonographic work Mr. Ball succeeded in securing the approval and support of a considerable number of friends and pupils in all parts of the United Kingdom, and on the 12th February, 1873, he was presented at Dr. Heigham's Harrogate College with a purse of gold and a handsome timepiece as testimony to his valuable services rendered to the cause of Phonography in promoting " one style for all, and one style for ever." A great deal was made of a letter of Isaac Pitman's to Mr. Ball in 1869, in which, in the freedom of friendly correspondence, he observed that Mr. Ball's style of Phonography came to him with a new freshness ; that he delighted in it like a person who learned the system for the first time ; and that Mr. Ball had fixed " the outlines of those words which have been wandering about for years on the face of the phonographic earth without a home," and so forth. When invited to subscribe to the testimonial, Isaac Pitman vigorously declined to recognise Mr. Ball's " improvements," and on being reminded that his correspondence had placed him entirely in Mr. Ball's power, promptly replied that he would himself publish the whole correspondence in lithographed shorthand. But as he was soon afterwards engaged in a project to be described later in this chapter, the subject ceased to be a burning one in a few months after the presentation, and this intention was never carried out.

Could Isaac Pitman have foreseen the use to which his unstudied letters to Mr. Ball would have been put, he would probably not have expressed himself in such indiscreet terms about his correspondent's efforts. In the advertisement columns of the *Journal* the Harrogate phonographer's proposals were discussed with considerable warmth by various correspondents. Mr. Ball desired to introduce some absolute rules for writing initial and final *l* and *r*, and advocated position writing to an extent which Isaac Pitman and the majority of practical phonographers considered unnecessary. The previously unused outline ⌒ (upward *r* and *m*) " some of us have adopted," Isaac Pitman wrote, through " Mr. Ball's phonographic perception," but the writing of that gentleman's own name with *b* and downward *l* ⟩ *Ball* (as compared with ⌄ in the text books) exhibited a phonographic " principle " which, with some others, Isaac Pitman affirmed he had " tried and found wanting." Such " hard and fast " rules, had they been adopted, might have proved seriously detrimental to the practical usefulness of Phonography.

The large top room in Parsonage Lane, Bath, reached by " a dreary staircase of fifty steps," which had been occupied for eighteen years as the Phonetic Institute, was at that time one of

the most unsatisfactory places which could have
been found in the elegant city of Bath for the
labours of a man of Isaac Pitman's temperament,
to whom unsavoury and evil surroundings were
peculiarly repellant, while the place itself was
extremely uncomfortable, and unsuitable for a
Phonetic Institute. As his lease of these undesirable premises expired in 1873, Isaac Pitman
felt that the time was appropriate to carry into
effect his long cherished idea of building a national
institute to be devoted to the Phonetic Reform.
Accordingly, in the month of April, he laid
before phonographers a " Proposal for the
Building of a Phonetic Institute at Bath." The
opening paragraph of this appeal read as follows :—

   " ' Phonography,' a new system of Shorthand,
based upon the sounds of the English language ;—
' Phonotypy,' a new style of printing words as
they are pronounced ;—and the place at Bath
where the phonetic books are produced, known
as the ' Phonetic Institute ' ;—are words familiar
to tens of thousands of people in every part of
the world where the English language is spoken.
The great value of Phonography in saving time
in writing, and the exceeding importance of
Phonotypy as an easy means of teaching children
to read ordinary books, are now widely acknowledged.   I propose to call the attention of Phonographers and Spelling Reformers, and of all who
are interested in the education of the people, to
the inadequacy of the premises where the phonetic
books are produced."

Following this came an account of the short-
comings of the existing Institute, with the observation that " the Phonetic Reform has now outgrown
the means of producing books which this wretched
place affords." Only hand presses could be used
there, and machinery and steam power were now
necessary to produce the books demanded by the
public. There was the *Journal*, which since its
reduction in price had shown a healthy tendency
to rapidly increase its circulation, while of the
phonographic instruction books and books printed
entirely in shorthand, some 80,000, were now
sold every year, and the sale was constantly rising,
to say nothing of the Spelling Reform and its
demands on the limited capacities of the Institute.
It was Isaac Pitman's original idea to build an
Institute, and for this purpose a site was selected
on the Manvers Estate, and the appeal for funds
included a ground plan of this and an invitation
to any architect who sympathized with the
" Writing and Spelling Reform " to help it
forward by supplying a suitable design of the
proposed Institute. Embodied in the appeal
was a passage of autobiographical interest, the
statements contained in which have been often
quoted.

" I should not mention," Isaac Pitman wrote,
" the following facts in my personal history in any
other connection than the present : they seem to
be appropriate here. From the year 1837, when
Phonography was invented, to the year 1843,

when I gave up my private day school in order to live for and by the Writing and Spelling Reform, I occupied all my spare time before and after school hours, in extending Phonography through the post, and by travelling and lecturing during the holidays. In this period I gained nothing by my system of shorthand, but spent all the proceeds of my books in extending their circulation. From 1843 to 1861, I laboured at the cause from six o'clock in the morning till ten at night, and literally never took a day's holiday, or felt that I wanted one ; and I worked on till 1864 without the assistance of a clerk or foreman. During this period my income from the sale of phonetic books, after paying the heavy expenses connected with the perfecting and extension of ' Phonetic Printing,' did not exceed £80 per annum for the first ten years, £100 for the next five years, and £150 for the next three years. During the first of these periods I was twice assessed for the income-tax. I appealed, and proved that my income was under £100. The commissioners appeared surprised that I should carry on an extensive business for the benefit of posterity. From 1861 to the present time my income from Phonography has been sufficient for the expenses of my increased family, but not more. If phonographers think that this labour, extending over the best part of a life, has been productive of pleasure and profit to them, and to the world at large, they have now an opportunity of placing me in a position to carry on the work of the Reading, Writing, and Spelling Reform more effectually. That which is done promptly is generally done well. Let us all labour in the eye of the motto—The Future is greater than the Past."

Fourteen years before this an attempt had been made to raise a thousand pounds to build a Phonetic Institute, and in three years £350 was raised and presented to Isaac Pitman, as already recorded. The project was regarded as a "testimonial" to him, and he consequently took no part in its promotion. By steering clear of the ideal of a personal testimonial, and by the united efforts of all working for the Reform, Isaac Pitman expressed the confident belief that *this* attempt to build a Phonetic Institute would not prove a failure. Such was the personal influence of the Inventor of Phonography, and so persuasive and untiring were his efforts in a movement of this description, that he was a host in himself ; he had, moreover, at the Institute the needful equipment for bringing the appeal under the notice of everyone in the country who was likely to prove a helper.

The response to this appeal was immediate and cheering. The amount collected in 1862 headed the first subscription list, and was followed by a contribution of £100 from Sir Walter C. Trevelyan, and smaller amounts from over seventy other contributors. From week to week additional subscriptions, accompanied by encouraging letters, flowed in, and the Rev. W. J. Ball wrote from Harrogate expressing his high approval of the project and his intention to do what he could to promote it—a magnanimous utterance after the recent controversy. Among those who took an interest in the project was Mr. H. J. Palmer, then unknown to fame, but destined in later years to become a journalist of distinction as the Editor of the *Yorkshire Post*. Mr. Palmer had come to Bath for the first time in his life in the Spring of this year, to visit the Inventor of Phonography, and he found it hard to realize that " the most universal system of stenography extant " emanated from " a wretched top floor tenement." He afterwards read Isaac Pitman's " Proposal " to remedy this state of affairs when viewing the city from Beechen Cliff, and mentally resolved to help. Words of cheer and additions to the fund came later on from many well-known people throughout the United Kingdom. Mr. John Coltman, of Newcastle-on-Tyne, who was a zealous spelling reformer, contributed £100. In India, Australia, and Canada, there were many subscribers, and when the last list was published, at the end of 1876, the total amounted to £1,326.

While the anxieties attendant on his endeavour to secure new premises were pressing hardly upon him in the early days of 1874, Isaac Pitman met with an accident which kept him from his work for ten weeks, five of which were spent in bed. It was his habit to take a Turkish bath every week, and on 28th February he burnt his right hand and part of his body very severely while in the hottest room. He made an excellent recovery, but was much grieved at the unavoidable hindrance to the completion of the transfer writing of the Shorthand Bible, to which he had pledged himself.

From the pressure of other duties this work was never again resumed.

For a time the question of a site for the proposed Institute was a source of considerable anxiety to Isaac Pitman, as negotiations in different quarters proved ineffectual. Fourteen months had passed since the fund was opened, when " a ray of light and hope " dawned on him from an unexpected quarter. An announcement was made that Earl Manvers proposed to dispose of his extensive property at Bath, and on 28th and 29th May, 1874, there took place one of the largest sales of property ever held in that city. The houses were situated between the Abbey Church and the Great Western Railway Station, and the sale realized a total of something like £44,000. The property included a number of large buildings which formed part of the Abbey Churchyard, occupied chiefly by important business concerns, and Isaac Pitman purchased a block containing two large houses known as Nos. 6 and 7 Kingston Buildings, at the low price of £600. He was thus provided with a structure in a suitable position, which could be converted into a Phonetic Institute without the heavy cost of building a new Institute, which could not have been erected of the size required under an outlay of £3,000.

Writing directly after the purchase of the houses, Isaac Pitman said that, " By expending about £500 upon them, they may be made into a commodious and beautiful Institute, or printing office, in the very heart of the city, in what may be called the south side of the ' St. Paul's Churchyard ' of Bath. The block of buildings, five storeys high, faces the north, and has seven windows, at uniform distances, on each floor. At present nine of them are blocked up,—a reminiscence of the hateful window-tax. No. 6 being a corner house, facing Church street on the west, has also windows on that side, and No. 7 is lighted both front and back. . . . The extent of floor space in the new building will be 1,000 ft. on each floor, giving a total of 5,000 ft. This is the space we proposed to obtain in a new building 100 ft. long and 50 ft. broad. We have arranged with the present tenants to take possession at the end of this month (June). The alterations, it is supposed, may be completed in three months, and the next three months would suffice to get the Institute into working order— to place a boiler, engine, and printing machine on the basement, and the different departments of the business in the several rooms above, with the necessary fixtures and furniture. Our friends proposed not only to build a Phonetic Institute for the promotion of the Writing and Printing Reform, but also to put in it a small steam-engine and a machine for printing the *Phonetic Journal*, on which there is no profit that could be appropriated to this purpose."

At the end of 1874 the premises in Kingston Buildings, after being for six months in the hands of the builders and carpenters, were in a sufficiently advanced state of completion to admit of occupation as the fourth Phonetic Institute. The removal of the printing plant and stock of books and paper from the top room in Parsonage Lane to the new premises in the Abbey Churchyard, though the distance was not great, was a laborious undertaking, and the interference with Isaac Pitman's usual orderly routine of answering innumerable correspondents who wrote to him about the many enterprises in which they were mutually interested was considerable ; there is a touch of pathos in his appeals to his many friends for their patience with him under these distracting conditions. " We have been compelled," he wrote, " to leave many letters unanswered, and they must remain so until we get fairly at work in the new Institute." But when, with his staff of eighteen workers, he was in occupation for the first time of the building which the generosity of the phonographic world enabled him to call his own, all was not, alas, plain sailing. His printing machinery propelled by steam power led to protests from neighbours on each side, and promised developments were delayed by this cause, as will be gathered from the following communication addressed to phonographers by Isaac Pitman on the 8th May, 1875 :—

" The friends of Phonetic Spelling who see this *Journal* have sympathized with us in our trials for the past six months with respect to the labour we have undergone, the great expense we have incurred, and the annoyances to which we have been subjected, in our attempt to introduce into the Phonetic Institute a steam-engine and printing machine. These troubles have arisen from two sources, first the difficulty of getting our machine to work at all, through our having been deceived in the purchase of an engine and boiler that eventually proved not worth the cost of erection ; and, secondly, after we had had a new boiler and engine made, the machine was pronounced a ' nuisance ' to our neighbours. We removed it to another part of the building to pacify the neighbour on one side, and then found that its sound could just be heard by the neighbour on the other side, who is much more exacting in his demands. . . . We shall now have to print a *Journal* of eight pages at a hand-press, as formerly, till something shall turn up, either here or in some other premises, whereby we can employ steam power, and it will not be voted a legal nuisance. We regret to have to say that it is utterly impossible for us to print 10,000 copies of this *Journal*, containing sixteen pages, at a hand-press in the time in which it must be produced. If the circulation should suffer in consequence, we must bide our time till we have the means of issuing sixteen pages. But one, or at the utmost two, columns will be given to advertisements, and these will be inserted *Times* fashion, without ' display.' "

During these troubles, Mr. William Lewis, proprietor of the *Bath Herald*, hospitably placed his machines at Isaac Pitman's service, and thus enabled him to print the *Journal* with comparatively little inconvenience till matters were put right at the Institute.

There was considerable discussion during 1875 relative to the re-organization of the Phonetic

Society, which was initiated by a pamphlet written by Mr. J. C. Moor, a North of England phonographer, who suggested a " constitution " which in his opinion could assume a national character. Many phonographers joined in the discussion, including the Hon. Ion Keith-Falconer (second son of the ninth Earl of Kintore), at that time an undergraduate at Trinity College, Cambridge, who took an important part in shorthand affairs in later years. He now advocated that " The Phonetic Society should consist only of those who are perfectly able and competent to assist others in learning the art." Mr. Timothy M. Healy, destined to become a famous Irish M.P., took a keen interest in Phonography and the Spelling Reform, and also in the re-organization of the Society. During this year he visited Isaac Pitman at Bath, and for the man and for his life work has ever since manifested a cordial appreciation. The change in the constitution of the Phonetic Society effected as the result of a prolonged discussion was slight, but useful so far as it went. The number of classes of members was reduced from four to two, the " learners' class " and the class for those who approved of but did not write Phonography being abolished. For the future the classes for members were as under :—

" Class 1. Members who write Phonetic Shorthand, and engage to correct the Exercises of Students through the post gratuitously."

Ðe Fonetik Sosjeti

1873

FACSIMILE OF ISAAC PITMAN'S LITHOGRAPHED LETTER TO
MEMBERS OF THE PHONETIC SOCIETY

HAZELWOOD, WARMINSTER ROAD, BATH

" Class 2. Members who write Phonetic Short-hand, but are prevented by their other engage-ments from correcting exercises through the post."

Each candidate had to submit a specimen of Phonography attested as his own unaided work, and the card of membership issued to those who were admitted now testified that they were qualified as teachers of Phonography.

XVIII

MAX-MÜLLER AND THE SPELLING REFORM—
A PROPOSED ROYAL COMMISSION

1876-1879

THE year 1876 was with Isaac Pitman a time of
many activities and interests, and vigorous effort
in various directions. His special work for Phonography consisted in the production of a new
edition (the fourth) of the " Phonetic Shorthand
Dictionary," which was now for the first time
produced with the phonographic characters
engraved in metal. Each character had at its
side the longhand spelling of the word, with the
pronunciation in phonotypy in parenthesis, accompanied by the meaning in ordinary longhand.
The three earlier editions were lithographed, and
this useful work had been for considerable periods
" out of print " ; phonographers therefore welcomed the new form, which admitted of further
impressions being made from the type as required.
Isaac Pitman had contemplated the publication
of a small dictionary by the engraved method
seven years before, in connection with which an
attempt was made to produce certain outlines
in accordance with the Rev. W. J. Ball's ideas
for writing final *r* and initial and final *l*. But it
was found that awkward outlines were the result,
and as a consequence the enterprise was given up.

What this style of writing was like may be seen in the earlier portion of " Macaulay's Essays," lithographed by Isaac Pitman and published in 1870 ; the outlines were not, he declared, " to be depended on." In this year appeared the first adaptation of Phonography to the Welsh language, the work of the Rev. R. H. Morgan, M.A. (1852-1899), a minister of the Welsh Calvinistic Methodist body. The Inventor of Phonography actively co-operated, and the work was produced under his supervision at the Phonetic Institute, and published at Wrexham.

Amid the labours of this year Isaac Pitman found diversion in attending some of the " Spelling Bees " which were a popular form of public literary competition at this time. Spelling contests had not been unknown in England long before 1875, but in that year some ingenious American hit on the phrase " Spelling Bee," a designation which created for the competitions a wide popularity for some years on both sides of the Atlantic. As directing attention to the inconsistencies of English spelling, and thus indirectly helping forward the movement for orthographic reform, Isaac Pitman welcomed the " Bees," and published in his *Journal* during 1876 annotated reports of some of the more interesting of these events.

There was a meeting of supporters of the Reading, Writing, and Spelling Reform held at Manchester on 26th October, 1876, for the purpose of hearing from Isaac Pitman a statement of its condition and prospects. The chair was taken by Dr. Samuel Crompton, an old Spelling Reformer, and the author of a work entitled " Medical Reporting, or Case-taking," published in 1847, which enjoyed the distinction of being the second work printed in phonotypy. The principal resolution was proposed by Mr. John Eglington Bailey, F.S.A., a well-known phonographer and an able writer on shorthand history, and was seconded by Mr. J. A. Parker, who had been shorthand writer to the Supreme Court of Judicature of India. Mr. Parker had recollections of the early days of hte Reform, and of Isaac Pitman's work in Bath. He testified from what he had seen of his efforts, " from earliest dawn of light to the time when the stars were shining " in the perfection of the phonetic printing alphabet and the dissemination of Phonography. This work he found was being carried on with the same unconquerable application at that time as when he first became acquainted with the Inventor of Phonography twenty-two years before.

Isaac Pitman in his speech in reply mentioned incidentally the objects for which he had visited Manchester, namely, in support of the anti-tobacco movement and vegetarianism respectively. When the friends of Spelling Reform heard of his contemplated visit, they thought the occasion a favourable one for hearing from his lips an account of the Reform and its present prospects. One characteristic passage of his speech deserves quotation. Someone had talked, he said, of obstacles and difficulties : "I really have not seen or felt any. I have done nothing from the beginning but simply pursued my course of work for a right, true, and good idea. I have paid no attention to opponents, except, occasionally, to meet their objections as well as I could. I have not felt any opposing powers at work against me, except the dead weight of a long-established custom, but have gone on promulgating the truths and the uses of phonetic shorthand in the first instance; and after seven years of this kind of labour . . . phonetic printing was commenced." At the date of this meeting propagandist work had assumed great dimensions, and the total output of printed matter from the new Phonetic Institute was half a ton per week. For the production and wide circulation of Spelling Reform tracts, Mr. John Coltman, of Newcastle-on-Tyne, at this time gave a sum of £300.

It was a source of extreme gratification to Isaac Pitman when the *Fortnightly Review* appeared for April, 1876, with an article by Professor Max-Müller on the Spelling Reform. "This remarkable paper," he rightly anticipated, would "make a sensation in the literary world, which is wont to look upon the Spelling Reform as the most Quixotic of all the professed reforms of the day. In his attack on the old spelling, with its absurdities and its evil effects, and in his defence of true or phonetic spelling, Max-Müller goes to work like a Teuton." This is absolutely true; and the utterance of the great philologist remains the most striking statement of the case for Spelling Reform which has appeared in the English language.

Max-Müller wrote : " What I like in Mr. Pitman's system of spelling is exactly what I know has been found fault with by others, namely, that he does not attempt to refine too much, and to express in writing those endless shades of pronunciation, which may be of the greatest interest to the student of acoustics, or of phonetics, as applied to the study of living dialects, but which, for practical as well as for scientific philological purposes, must be entirely ignored. Writing was never intended to photograph spoken languages : it was meant to indicate, not to paint, sounds. If Voltaire says, ' L'écriture c'est la peinture de la voix,' he is right ; but when he goes on to say, ' plus elle est ressemblante, meilleur elle est,' I am not certain that, as in a picture of a landscape, so in a picture of the voice, pre-Raphaelite minuteness may not destroy the very object of the picture. Language deals in broad colours, and writing ought to follow the example of language, which, though it allows an endless variety of pronunciation, restricts itself for its own purpose, for the purpose of expressing thought in all its modifications, to a very limited number of typical vowels and consonants. Out of the large number of sounds, for instance, which have been catalogued from the various English dialects, those only can be recognized as constituent elements of the language which in, and by, their difference from each other convey a difference of meaning. Of such pregnant and thought-conveying vowels, English possesses no more than twelve. Whatever the minor shades of vowel sounds in English dialects may be, they do not enrich the language, as such ; that is, they do not enable the speaker to convey more minute shades of thought than the twelve typical single vowels. . . ."

" The real state of the case is this : No one defends the present system of spelling ; everyone admits the serious injury which it inflicts on national education. Everybody admits the practical advantages of phonetic spelling, but after that all exclaim that a reform of spelling, whether partial or complete, is impossible. Whether it is impossible or not, I gladly leave to men of the world to decide. As a scholar, as a student of the history of language, I simply maintain that in every written language a reform of spelling is, sooner or later, inevitable. No doubt the evil day may be put off. I have little doubt that it will be put off for many generations, and that a real reform will probably not be carried except concurrently with a violent social convulsion. Only let the question be argued fairly. Let facts have some weight, and let it not be supposed by men of the world that those who defend the principles of the *Phonetic News* are only teetotallers and vegetarians, who have never learned how to spell. If I have spoken strongly in support of Mr. Pitman's system, it is not because on all points I consider it superior to the systems prepared by other reformers, particularly by Messrs. Ellis and Jones, who have devised schemes of phonetic spelling that dispense with any new types ; but chiefly because it has been tested so largely, and has stood the test well."

THE PHONETIC ALPHABET.

*The phonetic letters in the first column are pronounced
like the italic letters in the words that follow. The last
column contains the names of the letters.*

CONSONANTS.

Explodents.

P   p.....*rope*.....pee
B   b.....*robe* ....bee
T   t ....fa*te*.......tee
D   d ....fa*de*.....dee
Є   ɡ ....e*tch* ...chay
J   j .....e*dge*.....jay
K   k ... lee*k*.....kay
G   g ....lea*gue*..gay

Continuants.

F   f.....sa*fe*....... ef
V   v....sa*ve*......vee
Ƭ   *ţ*....brea*th*.. ith
Ɖ   *đ*...brea*the*..thee
S   s....hi*ss*......ess
Z   z....hi*s*.......zee
Σ   ʃ.....vi*ci*ous...ish
Ӡ   ʒ.....vi*si*on..zhee

Nasals.

M   m...see*m* ...em
N   n...see*n*.......en
Ŋ   ŋ...si*ng*......ing

Liquids.

L   l....fa*ll*........el
R   r....*r*a*r*e......ar

Coalescents.

W   w....*w*et..... way
Y   y....*y*et......yay

Aspirate.

H   h...*h*ay... aitch

VOWELS.
Lingual.

A   a......*a*m, f*a*r..at
Ɒ   ɒ......*a*lms....ah
E   e......*e*ll,f*e*ru..et
Ɛ   ɛ..... *a*le,*ai*r..eh
I   i...... *i*ll........it
Ɨ   i......*ee*l,f*ear*..ee

Labial.

O   o..... *o*n, *o*r...ot
Ꝍ   ꙍ......*a*ll..... aw
Ɤ   ɤ......*u*p, c*u*r..ut
Ơ   σ.....*o*pe,*o*re.. oh
U   u......f*u*ll....ŏŏt
Ꙍ   ꙑ...f*oo*d, p*oo*r..ōō

DIPHTHONGS: ei,   ou,   iu,   ai,   oi.
as heard in   b*y*,   n*ow*,   n*ew*,   *ay* (yes),   b*oy*.

With the above alphabet Max-Müller declared that English could be " written rationally

and read easily." The passage from Max-
Müller's article on pp. 206-7 is reproduced
below in phonotypy in accordance with the
alphabet.

Whot ei leik in Mr Pitman'z sistem ov speliŋ iz ek-
zaktli whot ei nố haz bịn found fɷlt wiɖ bei ʀɖerz, nɛmli,
ɖat hị dʒz not atempt tu refein tụ mʒç, and tu ekspres
in reitiŋ ɖɷz endles ʃɛdz ov pronʒnsiɛʃon, whiç mɛ bị ov
ɖe grɛtest interest tu ɖe stiudent ov akoustiks, ɷr ov
fɷnetiks, az apleid tu ɖe stʒdi ov liviŋ deialekts, bʒt
whiç, for praktikal az wel az for seientifik filolojikal
pʒrposez, mʒst bị enteirli ignɷrd. Reitiŋ woz never
intended tu fɷtograf spɷken laŋgwejez : it woz ment tu
indikɛt, not tu pɛnt, soundz. If Voltaire sez, " L'ecri-
ture c'est la peinture de la voix," hị iz reit ; bʒt when
hị gɷz on tu sɛ, "plus elle est ressemblante, meilleur
elle est," ei am not serten ɖat, az in a piktiur ov a land-
skɛp. sɷ in a piktiur ov ɖe vois, prị-Rʒfɛleit miniutnes
mɛ not destroi ɖe veri objekt ov ɖe piktiur. Laŋgwej
ɑịlz in brɷd kʒlorz, and reitiŋ ɷt tu folɷ ɖe ekzampel ov
laŋgwej, whiç ɖɷ it alouz an endles vareieti ov pronʒnsiɛʃon, restrikts itself for its ɷn pʒrpos, for ɖe pʒrpos ov
ekspresiŋ ɟɷt in ɷl its modifikɛʃonz, tu a veri limited
nʒmber ov tipikal vouelz and konsonants. Out ov ɖe
larj nʒmber ov soundz, for instans, whiç hav bịn kata-
logd from ɖe veriʒs Iŋgliʃ deialekts, ɖɷz ɷnli kan bị
rekogneizd az konstitiuent elements ov ɖe laŋgwej whiç
in, and bei, ɖɛr diferens from ịç ʒɖer konvế a diferens ov
mịniŋ. Ov ʒʒç pregnant and ɟɷt-konvɛiŋ vouelz, Iŋgliʃ
pozếsez nɷ mɷr ɖan twelv. Whotever ɖe meinor ʃɛdz
ov vouel soundz in Iŋgliʃ deialekts mɛ bị, ɖɛ dụ not en-
riç ɖe laŋgwej, az ʒʒç, ɖát iz, ɖɛ dụ not enɛbel· ɖe spịker
tu konvế mɷr miniút ʃɛdz ov ɟɷt ɖan ɖe twelv tipikal
siŋgel vouelz.

Max-Müller's paper was re-printed by Isaac Pitman with some additional matter incorporated by its author, including an account of Mr. Jones's project for improving the existing orthography without the addition of new letters to the alphabet. His only doubt about this scheme, Max-Müller said, was whether " a small measure of reform would be carried more easily than a complete reform." He also directed attention to Dr. J. W. Martin's narrative of the successful experiments in teaching reading by phonetic books carried out under the doctor's supervision in the Infant National School of Portlaw, co. Waterford. Mr. Ellis's system, referred to by Max-Müller, was a method of using the letters of the common alphabet, which the inventor thus described : " My Glossic was invented for the purpose of writing all our dialects in one alphabet." It was not primarily an educational instrument.

Within a few months of the publication of Max-Müller's article, the Spelling Reform question was brought before the country in a fashion which afforded Isaac Pitman reasonable grounds for anticipating that at last his unwearied labours were to be rewarded ; that at least an inquiry would be made by the Government of the day into the practicability of improving English orthography. But unfortunately there are three great obstacles to reform. One of these is the fact that there is no official body whose function it is to make those improvements in the English language and its representation which the lapse of time demands. The second obstacle is the great diversity of projects for improving our spelling which are put forward by reformers, who have never agreed on any single scheme. Isaac Pitman, however, in spite of the approval of Max-Müller of full phonotypy, was not so wedded to his own scheme but that he was prepared to agree to an instalment of reform from whatever quarter it came, and he showed his sincerity by exhibiting in his *Journal* methods devised by himself and others for improving English spelling with the minimum of change in the shape of new letters, or, in fact, without new letters at all. The third obstacle to reform is the immense dead weight of vested interest opposition, from the Universities downward, and on the part of all engaged in the production or sale of periodicals and books. In association with the occurrences described below, Isaac Pitman on 1st January, 1877, addressed a manifesto on the Spelling question to all the School Boards in England and Wales. The episodes of this period mark the zenith of the Spelling Reform movement in England ; Mr. Reed was a participator in and the historian of them, and has ably summarized what then took place in the following passages :—

" In the London School Board a movement was inaugurated by Dr. Gladstone, Dr. Angus, and other spelling reformers. Great dissatisfaction had been expressed at the results obtained in

Board Schools in regard to the teaching of reading and spelling, and attention was directed to the subject at various meetings of the Board. A proposal was made for a memorial to the Government requesting the appointment of a Royal Commission, and a circular was sent to the School Boards throughout the country requesting their opinion as to the propriety of such a step. The majority of the 277 Boards appealed to were against the proposal, but 100 were in its favour— a remarkable evidence of the extent to which the Spelling Reform had gained adherents among the educationists of the country. Notwithstanding the adverse replies of the majority of the country School Boards, the London School Board, on the 14th March, 1877, passed a resolution, proposed by Dr. Gladstone, for the nomination of a Select Committee to draw up a memorial for the appointment of a Royal Commission. The Committee met in due course, and drew up a memorial, which was adopted at a meeting of the School Board on the 25th of July. In this memorial it was recommended that the Government should be moved to issue a Royal Commission for considering the best method of reforming and simplifying English spelling. It was urged that the results of primary education in England and Wales were far from being satisfactory, and that several of Her Majesty's Inspectors had attributed this poor success in a great measure to the difficulties caused by our present unsystematic spelling. Many eminent scholars, many of the leading philologists of England and America, and the National Union of Elementary Teachers, had all affirmed the necessity of some change. . . . This memorial was signed by J. H. Gladstone, Chairman of the Committee, Joseph Angus, and John Rodgers.

" In the same year, 1877, an important Conference was held at the Rooms of the Society of Arts, London, on the 29th May, on the subject of Spelling Reform, the Rev. A. H. Sayce, Professor of Philology, Oxford, presiding. The primary object of the Conference was to support the request of the London School Board for the appointment of a Royal Commission to inquire into the subject of English Spelling. It was stated by Mr. Edward Jones, the hon. secretary, that the idea of such a Commission had been mooted ten years previously by Mr. Russell Martineau, at a meeting of the Philological Society, and had been supported by the Rev. J. Rice Byrne, M.A., one of Her Majesty's Inspectors of Schools, and that from that time the idea had gained general acceptance with the Society of Arts and other educational institutions. Among the letters read at the Conference was one from the Right Hon. Robert Lowe, which appeared to be a reply to a question put by Max-Müller—' Is there no statesman in England sufficiently proof against ridicule to call the attention of Parliament to what is a growing national misfortune ? ' ' I am not afraid of ridicule,' said Mr. Lowe, ' and I have a strong opinion on the spelling question. . . . There are, I am informed, 39 [40] sounds in the English language. There are 24 letters. I think that each letter should represent one sound, that 15 [16] new letters should be added, so that there be a letter for every sound, and that every one should write as he speaks.' [1] The Bishop of

---

[1] There appeared in *Punch* of 9th June, 1877, under the

Exeter also wrote expressing sympathy with the movement, but suggesting that there should be a minimum of change with no new characters, and only the introduction of a few diacritical marks.''

One of the earliest speakers at the Conference was Isaac Pitman, who began his remarks by observing : '' Nothing that can occur this day can possibly afford me more gratification than the letter of Mr. Lowe, which our Hon. Secretary has just read. I feared there was not a man among the 650 members of the House of Commons that would lead us on to victory ; but Mr. Lowe is the man ; and without meaning any disrespect to Bishop Temple, I must say that Mr. Lowe's letter, when weighed against the letter of the Bishop of Exeter, makes the latter kick the beam instantly. You will observe that there are two distinct opinions expressed in those letters. The Bishop of Exeter says: ' Introduce no new letters, but use diacritic marks ' : we should want fifteen marked letters. I will venture to say that the Bishop has never written a single page with the diacritic marks which he thinks might do. Mr. Lowe, on the other hand, takes the common-sense view of the question, and says that as there are fifteen

---

quotation from Mr. Lowe's letter given above, a poetic protest against reformed spelling which concluded thus :—

'' They (the Muses) must leave old England, with regret,
If Lowe lays hands upon her alphabet ;
And far from the Adelphi make their dwelling,
If Pitman sets his spell upon her spelling.''

sounds without representative signs, they must have them as a matter of course. I shall not say a single word on behalf of any particular alphabet —the question of signs for the sounds is tabooed for the day. All that we have to do to-day is to state our case—to show the reason for the Spelling Reform movement, and back up the London School Board in their application to Government for a Royal Commission of inquiry ; and I certainly think that our Government will be unable to refuse the application."

The particular topic on which Isaac Pitman was invited to speak for ten minutes was " The loss of time caused by the current spelling," and he proceeded to show with abundant illustrations, for which he was never at a loss in his public addresses, that time was wasted in learning to read, to spell, and to write. Other speakers at the meeting included Sir Charles Reed (the Chairman of the London School Board) ; Dr. Gladstone ; Signor Tito Pagliardini (an Italian scholar who with pen and voice advocated English spelling reform) ; the Rev. John Curwen (of Tonic Sol-fa fame) ; and Mr. William Storr (of *The Times* reporting staff, an old phonographer and friend of the inventor of the art, and a strong spelling reformer).

" These were not (to again quote Mr. Reed) the only public proceedings in connection with the Spelling Reform movement in 1877 ; for at a meeting of the Social Science Association, held in

London, on the 5th February that year, papers
on the subject were read by Mr. E. Jones and Mr.
W. Storr. These proceedings were reported at
considerable length in the newspapers of the day,
and many leaders and magazine articles were devoted to the subject. Many of the leading newspapers spoke favourably of the movement, and
even *The Times* went so far as to recommend that
children should be, at any rate, taught to read
and write in the first three standards on ' the easy
phonetic plan.'

" It was not until early in the following year,
1878, that the Spelling Reform question in connection with Board School teaching was brought
before the Government. On the 18th of January,
the Lord President of the Council (the Duke of
Richmond and Gordon) and Viscount Sandon
received a deputation at the Privy Council from
the London and many other School Boards,
and another from the Society of Arts. The depu-
tations consisted of about a hundred gentlemen
from different parts of the country, and representing various educational bodies. Mr. Pitman, his
brother Frederick, Mr. Ellis, Sir Charles Reed,
Dr. Gladstone, Mr. Rathbone, M.P. (representing
the School Board), and Mr. Richard, M.P. (who
expressed the bewilderment of the Welsh people
on the subject of English spelling) were among the
company present. The various speakers were
listened to with great attention, and the Lord
President promised, in the stereotyped form, but
with great courtesy, that he would lay before the
Cabinet the views that had been communicated
to him. Nothing further came of the matter.
No Royal Commission was appointed ; but the
subject had been thoroughly ventilated, and a

great deal done to clear the ground for future action in the same direction.

" The presentation of the memorial to the Lord President was soon followed (in 1879) by the formation of the Spelling Reform Association in London, under auspices which seemed to promise a successful result. Mr. Pitman, of course, joined its ranks, and occasionally assisted in its deliberations. Among the other well-known men who allied themselves with the Society were Lord Tennyson, Professor Max-Müller, Professor Sayce, Dr. J. H. Gladstone, Mr. A. J. Ellis, Charles Darwin, Dr. R. G. Latham, Professor Skeat, Mr. Westlake, Q.C., Dr. Charles Mackay, Professor Candy, M.A., Rev. John Rodgers, Dr. Hunter, etc.

" It is not necessary to write the history of the Spelling Reform Association in connection with the biography of Isaac Pitman ; but it cannot be passed over. Its career, which promised to be a brilliant one, was short and unsatisfactory. During the first year or two of its existence it was the means of drawing a good deal of attention to the question of a reformed orthography. It published a number of pamphlets and leaflets, and held a few public meetings at which addresses were delivered by men of great distinction. But its efforts were a good deal frittered away in academic discussions on the minutiæ of Phonetics, instead of being directed to more practical work. As in the case of most reforms, great differences of opinion existed as to the precise manner in which phonetic spelling should be carried out ; and notwithstanding the appointment of endless sub-committees with the view of reconciling these differences, no definite line of action was taken ; and, after a few years of fitful and spasmodic

effort, the Association collapsed. Though several
attempts were made to galvanize it into renewed
activity they were wholly unsuccessful."

The appearance of a letter in *The Times* over
the signature of Eizak Pitman, dated from the
" Fonetik Institiut, Bath," and spelled " fonetikali " as was, he explained, his custom, led to some
facetious observations in *Punch* of 15th February,
1879, which remarked of the letter that—

It is mainly a commendation of Vegetarianism and Teetotal-
ism, which he, being now " siksti-feiv yeerz of aij," has
practised for the last forty years.   He testifies that :—

" Theez forti yearz have been spent in kontineus laibor in
konekshon with the invenshon and propagashon ov mei sistem
ov fonetik shorthand and fonetik spelling, korrespondens, and
the editoarial deutiz ov mei weekli jurnal."

His " weekli jurnal " is of course the *Fonetik Nuz*, still alive
and kicking, as the People say—kicking against etymology and
common sense.   Its longevity seems even more wonderful than
its editor's survival of his " forti yeerz " regimen to the " aij "
of " siksti-feiv."   His circulation has been maintained on that
regimen, but what can have supported that of his paper ?

Spelling Bees have for some time dropped out of vogue, or
else a " Fonetik " Spelling Bee might answer Mr. PITMAN's
purpose of propagating his peculiar orthography.   He would
not, of course, be deterred from that expedient by any remark
which might possibly be made that he had a Spelling Bee in his
bonnet.

Punch seemed oblivious of the many things
which had happened in association with phonetic
spelling since Mr. Ellis's periodical appeared for the
last time thirty years before ; and that the widely
circulated *Phonetic Journal* should have so entirely

escaped its notice was certainly remarkable. Isaac
Pitman's brief comment on *Punch's* humour was
as follows : " On the publication of this article, a

AN EVERGREEN VEGETARIAN

*(Reproduced by special permission of the Proprietors of
" Punch.")*

friend of the Spelling Reform sent a copy of the
Phonetic Journal to the editor of *Punch*, with the
sensible recommendation that he should keep
abreast of the times."

Through the death of Sir Walter C. Trevelyan in 1879, at the advanced age of eighty-two, Isaac Pitman lost a friend who had with singular disinterestedness given valued support at a time when the Reform movement most needed it, and who had been for twenty years the President of the Phonetic Society. Professor Max-Müller was invited to fill the position rendered vacant by the death of Sir Walter, and readily consented to do so. At this time a slight change was made in the constitution of the Society, and the statement that members were qualified to teach was removed from the certificate of membership. Isaac Pitman paid a visit to Oxford as the guest of Professor Max-Müller in 1876, and was keenly interested in all that his host showed him of the ancient University.

The four hundredth anniversary of the introduction of printing into England by William Caxton was marked by an exhibition at South Kensington in the summer of 1877, to which Isaac Pitman obtained permission to send phonotypic literature for distribution, and as this included an illustrated life of Caxton in reformed spelling, there was a considerable demand for the novelty. In this year also he received a visit at Bath from Professor J. D. Everitt, of Queen's College, Belfast, who had invented a system of shorthand in the early fifties, first circulated privately and in 1877 published in the ordinary way.

At this time Isaac Pitman made a change in his

residence. After living in various parts of Bath, since leaving Lansdown Terrace in 1858, he had for a considerable time made his home at No. 3 Darlington Place, Bathwick. Not far distant from this, he, in 1879, built a house in the Warminster Road. He named his residence after the school conducted by Sir Rowland Hill, and his father, Mr. T. Wright Hill, near Birmingham, known as Hazelwood. Writing on the subject of his new abode Isaac Pitman observed : " The situation gives one of the finest views in this beautiful part of Somersetshire. There is seen at a glance a large portion of Bath, built on the side of a hill, a stretch of hilly country in front, with a valley in the centre, and the river Avon, the Kennet and Avon Canal, and the Great Western Railway, running up another valley to the right, that of the Avon. The city portion, when lighted at night, has the effect of a grand illumination. The name ' Hazelwood ' was chosen to perpetuate the memory of the fact that the profits of Phonography furnished the means of building it, and that Sir Rowland Hill's ' Penny Post ' made Phonography popular. To make the name somewhat appropriate, a row of hazel trees has been planted by the garden wall on the left side of the house."

XIX

MANY SCHEMES OF SPELLING REFORM AND " THREE
RULES "—PUBLIC APPEARANCES—ACTION IN THE
HIGH COURT—AMEN CORNER

1880-1886

In the early eighties the spelling reformer was
very much abroad. Nearly every reformer who
addressed the public had his own particular scheme
for supplanting the existing spelling, and was
firmly convinced of its superiority to all others.
There were fifty orthographic schemes under the
consideration of the English Spelling Reform
Association, and in 1880 Isaac Pitman published
specimens of twenty-seven of these which he was
able to exhibit with his available type. Nothing
could have shown more clearly that while the
reformers were attacking a common foe, each was
armed with a different weapon. This idea was
cleverly expressed in a poetical parody (annotated)
which attracted a good deal of attention at this
time, and was read with amusement by all
interested in Spelling Reform. It ran as follows :—

GRAPHOPHONOMACHIA :

THE BATTLE OF THE SIGNS AND SOUNDS

In deep recesses of a sunless vale
Hides a huge monster, miscall'd Orthograph,
(But Malefido is his rightful name)
Horrid, inform, unsighted. Many a peer,

Who sits, where Archibald [1] is King, supreme,
At that round table nigh the Strand, i' th' Court
Where all his Knights assemble, oft has urged
Against the giant's force a mad career
And come back worsted home. For mighty spells,
Coin'd in the gloom of wizard gramarye,
Guard the abysmal cavern where he bides.
Weapons twiform'd, and things that change their shape,
While gazers stand aghast with wonderment,
Are hurl'd against the rash invading foes,
Who seek to pierce the dark Cimmerian mist,
Where Malefido hides him : and behind
Briarean Custom stretches polyp arms
To hurl the enemy back. Yet none the less
The crippled monster bleeds at many a wound.
First patriarchal Isaac [2] smote him hard
With missiles forged in shapes unknown to men,
Like the weird talismans in Egypt found,
Graven uncouth, or those mysterious signs
On Babel's arrow-headed cylinders.
But ere brave Isaac pierced the giant's cave
To thrust him to the heart, a digraph-shower
As thick as Vallombrosa's autumn leaves
Hurl'd him back breathless. Then his puissant peer,
Strong Alexander [3] seized, the two-fork'd forms,
Gather'd them, shaped them, polish'd them anew,
And with his own darts smote the giant down.
Again uprising, Malefido urged
Myriads of Mutes to beat the invader back
With soundless death. So Alexander fail'd.
Next a Welsh Knight [4] devised a magic charm,
To lead the Mutes by many a devious path,

---

[1] Archibald H. Sayce, President of the Spelling Reform Association.

[2] Isaac Pitman, originator of the Spelling Reform.

[3] Alexander J. Ellis, contriver of a Glossic, Digraph system.

[4] E. Jones, advocate of the use of *e* as modifier to indicate long vowels.

So that they err'd unwitting how they went,
And smote their parent.   He invoked his gods :
They sent him aid : the witch Perplexity
Assail'd the Welshman in the rear : who call'd
His countrymen to help him.   One [1] like-named,
One of strange weapons, passing small, but keen,
That drive men crazy with their eerie looks :
Along with him a little sharp-tooth't thing [2]
That skipt now here, now there ; but always bit,
Whether he skipt on this side or on that ;
So these two plagued the monster, robb'd his sleep,
And made him frenzied with incessant pricks :
But fail'd i' th' main achievement.   Next came one
Of honey'd name, [3] with quilted doublet arm'd,
Who had good aim, but weapons all too weak.
So these all fail'd : they did their best devoir
And yet they fail'd.   But last came one transform'd
With spells of gramarye like the monster's own ;
A form of wonder like to half a man, [4]
(But none could tell which half), now head, now tail,
Now either-sided, always half a man,
Dress'd in queer armour dotted o'er with *ohs :*
He waited not to skirmish at the mouth,
But rush'd into the cave, dived in the mist,
And with new weird enchantments mazed the fiend.
But whether he will in the quest succeed,
Or whether he will hobble limping home,
None knoweth ; but, deep hidden in the mist,

---

[1] W. R. Evans, deviser of tear-shaped and tadpole-shaped modifiers for the same purpose; Evan and John are etymologically identical.

[2] F. G. Flea, or Fleay, proposer of a partial immediate reform as introductory to a perfect system.

[3] H. Sweet, author of a scheme which requires doubled letters for long vowels.

[4] A. J. Ellis in a new character, as a " Dimidian " reformer. In this spelling *Rome* appears as " Roam," but the *Romans* as " *Roh*munz " ; hence the allusion to " *ohs.*"

Doubtless he fighteth ; and a crowd of men,
Poets and scholars, stand a little off
And shout, " God speed him ! " but they give small help
Meanwhile one waiteth, like a motley fool, [1]
And gathers the spent weapons in a heap,
And sorts them wisely, for he bides his time,
Forging proof armour, weaving common spells ;
Common, yet mighty : for he deems the knights,
Each one too trustful to his own device,
Fail'd therefore. And he spies the monster's ways,
Watches his thrusts, and marks his change of shape,
Biding his time. Yet he perchance may fail,
Though he has waited now a score of years,
And valour loses oft where patience wins.

PHRENETICUS.

Most of the newspapers and reviews of the day
gave expression at this time to opinions on
Spelling Reform, usually of a hostile character.
The *Spectator* denounced the movement in vigorous
fashion, thus : " We look upon Mr. Pitman, of
Bath, and his adherents as guilty of as flat
burglary as ever frightened Dogberry. Nothing
has ever astonished us more than the fact that the
foremost philologist in England, Professor Max-
Müller, should find it in his heart to thrust the
ægis of his great name and authority in front of
this forgetive felony." Isaac Pitman replied to
this accusation in a style of reformed orthography
he had now introduced under the title of the
" First Stage of the Spelling Reform," which did

---

[1] F. G. Fleay, in another form, and it is to be hoped in his last
avatar before his final interment in a four-cross road.

not involve the addition of new types to the existing Romanic alphabet, but could be used by cutting down one letter (p) to form a character to represent the vowel sound ŭ. His rejoinder to the *Spectator* was as follows :—

" On reading this akiuzashon peepel wil be led tu inkweir intu the natiur ov the ' bɒrglari,' and the ' feloni ' with hwich we ar charjd ; and hwen they feind that we ar simpli sɒpleiing the defishensiz ov our alfabet, and ' puting things tu reits ' in the use ov leterz, az meni ov them az lɒv truth and utiliti more than their own eaze, wil aid us in the wɒrk."

There was promulgated about this time in the United States by the American Spelling Reform Association and the American Philological Society a set of " Five Rules " for the improvement of English spelling without the addition of new signs. These rules were approved and adopted in several influential quarters, and ran as follows :—

RULE 1.—Omit *a* from the digraph *ea* when pronounced as *e* short, as in *hed, helth*, etc.

RULE 2.—Omit silent *e* after a short vowel, as in *hav, giv, liv, definit, forbad*, etc.

RULE 3.—Write *f* for *ph* in such words as *alfabet, fantom, camfor, filosofi, telegraf*, etc.

RULE 4.—When a word ends with a double letter, omit the last, as in *shal, wil, clif*, etc.

RULE 5.—Change *ed* final into *t* when it has the sound of *t*, as in *lasht, imprest, fixt*, etc.

In a letter addressed to the English Spelling Reform Association dated 22nd May, 1882, Isaac Pitman remarked : " The ' Five Rules ' of our American friends do not give a satisfactory style of spelling for three reasons. 1. They do not affect more than thirty-four words in a column of *The Times* Parliamentary debates, or one word in seventy. 2. The rule to omit final *e* after a short vowel cannot be applied in the case of the letter *o*, as in *love, come ;* for the omission of the final *e* would turn these words into *lov, kom.* 3. The fourth rule is too general. If *all, fall,* lose the second *l*, the words will be mispronounced as *al* (alley), *fal* (fallow), and so with eleven words of this kind." He recommended in preference a bolder and easier style of spelling, namely, the use of the old alphabet phonetically as far as it can be thus applied, and explained the method by which he considered certain consonants and *u* should be dealt with.

The " Five Rules " in the hands of Isaac Pitman were experimented with and revised till in the end a set of directions was evolved in which little or no resemblance to the original " rules " could be traced. At one time he enlarged these instructions to " Six Rules " and later on, towards the close of his life, he reduced them to " Three Rules," as under :

THE THREE RULES OF THE SPELLING REFORM

RULE 1.—Reject *c, q, x* as redundant ; use the other consonants for the sounds usually associated with them ;

and supply the deficiency of twelve other letters by these digraphs :—

ch,	'th,	th,	sh,	zh,	ng.	aa,	ai,	ee ;	au,	oa,	oo.
*ch*eap,	*th*in,	*th*en,	wi*sh*,	vi*s*ion,	si*ng*.	p*a*lm,	p*a*l*e*,	p*ee*l ;	p*a*ll,	p*o*le,	p*oo*l.

Write *ay* for the second vowel, and *aw* for the fourth, *at the end of a word ;* as *pay, law.*

RULE 2.—*A, e, o, u, ending a syllable* (except at the end of a word ; as, *sofa*), represent a *long* vowel ; as in *fa-vour, fe-ver, ho-li, tru-li.*

RULE 3.—*A, e, i, o, u,* in *close* syllables (and *a* at the end of a word), represent the short sounds in *pat, pet, pit, pot, put.* Use *ŭ* for *u* when it is pronounced as in *but.*

Write the Diphthongs thus : *ei,* b*y* ; *ou,* n*ow* ; *iu,* n*ew* (*yu* initial) ; *ái,* K*ai*ser ; *oi,* c*oy.*

NOTE.—In the First Stage concede to custom *I* instead of *ei* for the first personal pronoun ; *n* for *ng* when followed by *k* or *g,* as *bank* (bangk), *anger* (ang-ger) ; *father, piano-foarté, pianist* (*for* faather, piaano-forté, piaanist). When the letters of a digraph represent separate values insert a (·) between them as *short·hand* (not *shor·thand*), *be·ing* (not *by·ing*). Proper names and their adjectives, addresses, and the titles of books, should not be altered at present.

After the introduction of the " First Stage," the bulk of Isaac Pitman's Spelling Reform publications were printed in this style, and no longer in full Phonotypy. The enlarged alphabet, which had been the object of experiments conducted at vast expense for forty years, and in which a library of literature had been printed now fell almost into disuse, in favour of a more practicable scheme of reformed spelling through the medium of the existing Roman alphabet. In the advocacy of this method of spelling Isaac Pitman engaged with the same persistence that he had before shown in the cause of reform with an enlarged alphabet. Phonotypy, considering the amount of attention which it at one time received, has left very few vestiges of its existence in English literature and orthography. An interesting trace of it is to be found in the great " Oxford English Dictionary," which Dr. Murray began to issue in 1884. In this work he has adopted in the representation of pronunciation the phonotypes ∫ (sh), ʒ (zh), and ŋ (ng) from the phonotypy of Isaac Pitman and Alexander J. Ellis. Of the labours of these phoneticians in several directions Dr. Murray had spoken approvingly in his Presidential Address to the Philological Society in 1880, but he then expressed the opinion that until the general principles of phonology are understood by men of education, no complete or systematic scheme of Spelling Reform has the least chance of being adopted, though he wished it were otherwise. The Spelling Reform might have occupied a different position to-day could it have secured in the eighties the active support of William Ewart Gladstone. Unfortunately this was not possible. Mr. Gladstone, however, sympathised with the movement. In a letter to Mr. Henry Pitman he wrote, " If I were younger and had some things off my hands, I would gladly take hold of this reform." [1] But in our own time there are signs that phonetic science is becoming more generally cultivated among those interested in education than was the case when Dr. Murray spoke over a quarter of a century ago. Isaac Pitman's disinterested efforts to introduce a better alphabet than the present have not therefore been wholly futile ; they have, at any rate, prepared the way for practical improvements in English spelling in the future.

Several addresses were delivered at this time, which were reported at considerable length in the

---

[1] The following letter on Spelling Reform was addressed by Mr. Gladstone to Mr. E. Jones fourteen years before :—

HAWARDEN CASTLE, CHESTER,
27th June, 1874.

Sir,—There is much that might be done with advantage in the reform of spelling as to the English language ; but the main thing is, that whatever may be proposed should be proposed with the weight of great authority to back it. The best plan, if proposed without such backing, will in my opinion only tend to promote confusion. I should advise those who are interested—and very justly interested in this question—to busy themselves not so much with considering what should be done as with considering in what way opinion can be brought to bear on the matter, and some organ framed to inquire what should be proposed. It is not in my power to offer to give any time under present circumstances to the undertaking which I recommend, and in which I should gladly have found myself able to join.

I remain, your very faithful servant,
W. E. GLADSTONE.

E. JONES, ESQ.

newspapers. Isaac Pitman visited Bristol on 8th November, 1880, and addressed a large gathering at the Young Men's Christian Association, in St. James's Square, on " Phonography and the Spelling Reform." Mr. Mark Whitwell, Chairman of the School Board, a member of the City Council, and from his exertions for the welfare of the young known as " The Children's Friend," presided. Mr. Whitwell was an old phonographer. He had taken up another system in 1841, but abandoned it for Phonography in 1843, and had since made much use of the art, which he recommended to all young men. Mr. Whitwell had not long before been instrumental in introducing Phonography in the curriculum of Queen Elizabeth's Hospital for Boys, a famous Bristol educational foundation.

The appearance in *The Times* in the early days of 1881 of a letter from Mr. James Griffin, himself a publisher, complaining of the high price (31s. 6d.) at which Lord Beaconsfield's new novel " Endymion " was published, and suggesting that it could have been issued at the popular price of half-a-crown, and have thus secured a sale of half a million, elicited the following observations from Isaac Pitman : " The principle contended for by Mr. Griffin has been followed in the phonographic and phonotypic publications from the commencement, and the result is that the sale of the shorthand books in England is above 100,000 a year, that the price is sufficiently remunerative to the author, and that eight hundredweight of phonetically printed books in shorthand and phonotypy are sent from the Phonetic Institute every week in the year." A year later the output of phonographic and phonotypic literature had risen to half a ton weekly. In 1882 Isaac Pitman published an adaptation of his system to the French language, of which Mr. Reed was the author. The Inventor of Phonography visited Rome in 1883, and while there gave considerable help to Signor Giuseppe Francini in his translation and adaptation of the Pitmanic system to Italian.

About the end of 1881 a new association was started in London under the name of the Shorthand Society, for the study and discussion of the art of stenography in all its phases. The first President, Mr. Cornelius Walford (1827-1885), by profession an actuary, was of literary and antiquarian tastes, the author of "A Statistical Review of the Literature of Shorthand," and a phonographer. The Shorthand Society consisted of writers of various systems, and its transactions included many valuable papers, which were published for some years in the *Phonetic Journal*. Before this Society Isaac Pitman on 28th June, 1884, delivered an address on "The Science of Shorthand." The question had, he said, been raised whether there was a science of shorthand, and this query he answered with an emphatic affirmative. There were truths, laws, and facts connected with shorthand, about which knowledge could be gained.

While the old school of shorthand dealt with the letters of the known alphabet, the new, or phonetic school, was concerned in the sounds of speech and the signs available to represent them. In constructing Phonography Isaac Pitman introduced the scientific method which he here describes, and as we have seen, founded his system entirely on the science of phonetics. Among the members of the Society he was addressing were several who had invented systems of shorthand, and outside that body there were other contemporary inventors. All these had developed their methods in accordance with their individual applications of the truths of phonetic science. They thus formed a new school of shorthand inventors, and, though perhaps they did not acknowledge it, were influenced by the success with which Isaac Pitman had utilized the phonetic principle. In this address to the Shorthand Society he showed how greatly the success of Phonography as a philosophical and practical system of writing was due to his use of three simple geometrical signs—a right line, and a curve bending to the right or left—in the construction of a phonetic shorthand alphabet in obedience to the principle of writing sounds of a like nature by signs of a like nature. The address is valuable as a contribution to the history of Phonography, because it demonstrates that in the construction of the system its inventor developed this scientific principle in a practical manner, and that to his successful effort to discover the "alphabet of nature," his system owes its great popularity. For some years Isaac Pitman was one of the Vice-Presidents of the Shorthand Society.

There were several International Exhibitions held at South Kensington in successive years at this time and at one of these, the International Health Exhibition of 1884, there was an Educational Section which was placed in the Gallery of the Albert Hall. Although the space which was allotted was inadequate for the display he desired to make, Isaac Pitman exhibited his principal shorthand works, and arranged for an attendant and a supply of free literature on shorthand and spelling reform. The display proved of considerable interest to the many thousands who visited the Exhibition, and there was a good demand for literature. Just before the Exhibition closed, Isaac Pitman received official notification that his Phonography had received the only award made for shorthand. The letter of the Joint Secretaries was in the following terms :—

" We are instructed to inform you that the Jury Commission, acting on the reports of the International Juries, appointed by H.R.H. the Prince of Wales, have awarded you a Silver Medal in Class 48."

For the third time in his life Isaac Pitman visited Edinburgh, where he delivered an address at the opening of the twelfth session of the Scottish

Phonographic Association on 1st October, 1884. He had first visited the city in 1841 when his shorthand method was in its infancy. The young inventor was then unknown to fame, and his system was comparatively untried. But very early in the history of Phonography Scotland had become convinced of the value of the art and of its practical utility, and as a result it had been for many years extensively taught and practised in the North, in some respects perhaps more successfully than in England, and the Scottish Phonographic Association, established in 1874, had grown to a large, influential, and flourishing society for the propagation of the art. From this society Isaac Pitman received an enthusiastic welcome, the place of meeting was thronged, and great numbers were unable to obtain admission. The Lord Provost, Sir George Harrison, presided, and was influentially supported. His Lordship was much impressed by the enthusiasm displayed. It showed, he said, that Scotchmen and Scotch women retained the love of knowledge which had characterized them for centuries, and he was gratified to find them taking advantage of the opportunity to honour Isaac Pitman for what he had done " to increase the sum of human knowledge."

The contrast between his first and his third visit to Edinburgh had profoundly impressed Isaac Pitman. When he visited the city as a young man forty-three years before, and " the first

seeds of the phonetic reform were deposited," his
publications were few and insignificant; " Now,"
he continued, " I dispose of a million phonetic
books and *Phonetic Journals* every year, and about
half a million of phonetic tracts." To him this
was a source of " devout thankfulness to the
Source of all good." " It is hardly necessary,"
he went on, " that I should say to this meeting of
phonographers that I regard the phonetic educational movement in the light of a holy crusade
against ignorance. In this age of railways and
tramways, and exhibitions, and the Suez canal,
and the Mersey and Severn tunnels, and a dozen
more good things projected, it cannot be that
people will go on writing with the stammering
pen of longhand, when they may write with the
fluent phonographic pen, with all the rapidity of
speech, and with more than the ease of speech."
As to spelling : " All the efforts of teachers and
committees of School Boards are baffled by our
barbarous and inconsistent spelling, which ' no
fellow ' can master, except some of the teachers,
and some writers for the Press, editors, proof-
readers, and compositors. Only a portion of the
writers for the Press are what are called good
spellers. There is a chorus of lamentation from
the Inspectors that the reading taught in the
Board Schools is non-intelligent. The Inspectors
say that the children read in a senseless manner.
They pronounce the words, but in such a way that
a listener cannot understand what is read. The

main cause of this is that they have been taught to read and spell mechanically, and by 'cram,' without the use of their reasoning powers. The memory alone has been exercised, and not the judgment." In replying to a hearty vote of thanks Isaac Pitman expressed himself amazed and delighted at the manner in which Phonography had been received by the public of Scotland. Two years later, in 1886, an exhibit of Phonography attracted much attention at the Edinburgh International Exhibition, where it was awarded the highest distinction—a gold medal.

A short time after his visit to the North, Isaac Pitman appeared in the Queen's Bench Division of the High Court of Justice as the plaintiff in " Pitman v. Hine," an action for the alleged infringement of copyright of several of his phonographic instruction books. The action was tried before Mr. Justice (afterwards Lord Justice) Mathew, without a jury, in the Court of Queen's Bench (No. 9) on 4th, 5th, and 6th November, 1884. The counsel for the plaintiff were Mr. Arthur Charles, Q.C. (afterwards Mr. Justice Charles) and Mr. Shortt (instructed by Mr. E. B. Titley, of Bath), and the defendant's counsel was Mr. R. T. Wright. The hearing of witnesses occupied two days, and on the morning of the third his lordship delivered judgment. Not only was the case for the plaintiff presented with much ability—which was the more notable from the

fact that counsel were unacquainted with Phonography, but the case for the defendant was
conducted with marked skill throughout.

The principal witness was the plaintiff in the
case, and his appearance in the witness-box excited
much interest. A number of shorthand writers
who had used the Pitman system professionally
for years, but had never seen its inventor, took
the opportunity of attending the Court, while a
good many other phonographers who were interested in the art in various ways followed the
proceedings with much interest. A blackboard
was placed in position between the witness-box
and the Bench, and by its aid the Inventor of
Phonography illustrated his evidence, and as
his work was followed with close interest by
Bench, Bar, and a considerable gathering of
practical phonographers, the appearance of the
Court was strongly reminiscent of a large shorthand
class. The point which it was sought to establish
on behalf of the plaintiff was that defendant's
work, entitled " Contracted Outlines," had rules
which were identical in their effect with those
contained in the books of which the plaintiff was
the author. Isaac Pitman's evidence was given
with great clearness, and under a long and searching
cross-examination he was perfectly calm and
collected, emerging from the ordeal with his case
strengthened rather than otherwise. Several
expert witnesses had been retained for the plaintiff,
of whom three were called, namely, the Hon. Ion

Keith-Falconer, who had about this time written the article on " Shorthand " for the Ninth Edition of the " Encyclopædia Britannica," and Mr. Reed and Mr. Thomas Hill, both well-known as professional shorthand writers in the High Court and elsewhere. The defendant claimed that his rules were his original work, that they taught advanced and new principles, and were not copied from the books of the plaintiff.

In the course of a lengthy judgment Mr. Justice Mathew decided that the evidence led to the " irresistible conclusion that the defendant had been copying the plaintiff's book ; and the only reason why he can say he has not done it is that he has illustrated the plaintiff's system by different words from those that the plaintiff has used."

His lordship concluded :—

The defendant felt his way very carefully in commencing his publication. He published first a small pamphlet, which was printed [chromographed], and against that the plaintiff protested, but he thought it a small matter, and he probably hesitated (either from his own good sense, or from the excellent advice he may have had) about commencing a Chancery suit in reference to that. The defendant, emboldened perhaps by the plaintiff's neglect, at a certain interval afterwards printed [lithographed] what he had previously put forward in a different form, and then again the plaintiff protested. In the year 1880, when this publication was brought to his knowledge, he protested against it and pointed out once more that it was an infringement of his copyright, but he took no proceedings. Again the defendant made a further experiment, that expanded work No. 2, and the work the subject of the present proceedings. He expanded the " Contracted Outlines " from 600 to 1,000, and then once more the plaintiff

protested. He did allow unquestionably nearly a year to
go by, and then, when the defendant had sent him a copy
of his book requesting that he would insert an advertisement
of it in the *Journal*, of which the plaintiff was the publisher,
the plaintiff determined to bring the matter to an end, and
a correspondence commenced, which certainly in the first
instance exhibited proper feeling on the part of the defendant ;
and the plaintiff would be justified in expecting from that
correspondence that the matter might be amicably settled.
The correspondence went on for a considerable time, until it
was clear that the defendant would not admit what the
plaintiff considered his rights in the matter, and then these
proceedings were commenced.   Now it certainly throws a
flood of light upon the plaintiff's conduct in the matter, as
we have been informed, in the course of the proceedings, that
the defendant is defending this action *in forma pauperis*.
It is perfectly evident that a plaintiff would hesitate a long
time before he would attack a man who could not pay damages.
Subsequently he was driven to take the course he has taken.
Now it is said, " You ought to give the plaintiff damages ;
you ought not to give him an injunction."   That would be
denying him all remedy, for the defendant is a man who
cannot pay damages.   What is proposed is, that the defendant
should be suffered to go on to publish this work, which I hold
to be an infringement of the plaintiff's copyright, the plaintiff
being at liberty to sue him from time to time for damages,
which he would never recover.   If ever there was a case in
which the powers of the Court ought to be exercised, as asked
by the plaintiff, it seems to me that this is that case.   I therefore grant the injunction asked for by the plaintiff.   I direct
the copies of his book now in the defendant's possession either
to be given up to the plaintiff, or such an arrangement to be
come to between the parties as would preclude the possibility
of the work being further published.   I further give a formal
direction that the plaintiff shall have his costs at any time
should the defendant be in a position to pay him.

Though Isaac Pitman's name was so well-known
to writers of his system of shorthand through his

many publications, the phonographers of London had for a very long time had no opportunity of seeing and hearing him on the platform, and the announcement that he would lecture at Exeter Hall on the 3rd October, 1885, under the auspices of the Young Men's Christian Association, on " Shorthand, with a Peep at the Reading, Writing, and Spelling Reform," created considerable interest in the ranks of phonographers in the Metropolis. Mr. John Bell presided over the gathering, which was held in the Lower Hall—the same place in which Isaac Pitman had spoken thirty-four years before—and when the veteran Inventor of Phonography appeared on the platform the hall was crowded in every part, and large numbers were unable to obtain admission. " Among those assembled," we are told, " were many well-known in the shorthand and literary circles of the Metropolis ; a goodly proportion of phonographers, a slight sprinkling of ladies, whose presence attested to the growing interest taken in Phonography by the fair sex, and here and there were seen the white hairs of age. The rest of the audience consisted of young men of the student class." The *Christian World* noted that the lecturer, though seventy-two years of age, was hale and hearty in appearance, and spoke for over an hour with ease and vigour. A storm of applause greeted him on rising.

" Not quite knowing," Mr. Reed says, " the kind of assembly he was addressing—whether it

consisted chiefly of phonographers who had come
out of curiosity to see him, or of the outside public
who desired to be instructed—he called for a show
of hands from those who were acquainted with
Phonography, and discovered, perhaps to his
surprise, that the large majority of his hearers
were already his disciples. This, as he remarked,
enabled him the better and the sooner to get in
touch with them, and rendered needless any such
minute explanation of the system as he might
otherwise have given. He rather dwelt on the
principles underlying the construction of his
alphabet ; and (the traditions of Exeter Hall
notwithstanding) he could not refrain from throwing in a small modicum of Swedenborgian philo-
sophy and applying it to his subject. The mascu-
line and feminine element, said by the Swedish
seer to pervade all things in nature, he applied
to the consonants and vowels respectively ; and
in the pairing of the consonants themselves, as
shown in the arrangement of the phonographic
symbols, he found another illustration of the same
all-pervading dualism. The ' reading reform '
was also advocated with the lecturer's accustomed
earnestness and energy ; and some striking illustrations were given of the inadequacy of the
common spelling to convey the sounds of the
words represented."

A considerable impulse was given to the formation of Shorthand Writers' Associations throughout the country by the issue in 1885 for the first

time of Shorthand Speed Certificates from the Phonetic Institute. These testimonies to practical skill were issued from Bath in co-operation with examining committees appointed by the local associations, and the granting of certificates had a most beneficial effect on the promotion of useful efficiency in shorthand writing throughout the country.

Isaac Pitman's two sons, Mr. Alfred Pitman and Mr. Ernest Pitman, who were educated at Bath College, had for some time assisted their father in his work at the Phonetic Institute. In his New Year's address to the Phonetic Society in 1886, the Inventor of Phonography made the brief but interesting announcement that " The present occasion seems an appropriate one for informing phonographers and the public that I have now associated with me in the phonetic business my two sons, and that the title of the firm will in future be ' Isaac Pitman & Sons.' " An auspicious event marked the opening of the career of the new firm— Isaac Pitman's " Phonographic Teacher," the most popular shorthand book published in the English language, this year reached its First Million.

On 21st November, 1886, Mr. Frederick Pitman, the youngest brother of the Inventor of Phonography, and his London publisher at No. 20 Paternoster Row, died at the early age of fifty-eight. His services to the wingèd art were considerable, not only as teacher but as author of books dealing with the practical uses of shorthand, and as editor of various lithographed phonographic periodicals, which for many years enjoyed a wide popularity. It was decided that the firm of Isaac Pitman & Sons should for the future have their own London publishing house, and the end of the year saw them in occupation of their present premises, No. 1 Amen Corner, London, E.C.

XX

1887-1889

THE celebration of the Jubilee of Phonography in 1887 was one of the most important events in the life of Isaac Pitman, and in the history of his system of shorthand. Its unique character attracted great attention, not only in this country but in distant parts of the world. No other stenographic author in our own or any other land had ever before been the central figure in a commemoration of this description. To himself personally the event formed the introduction to a remarkable series of honours, while the impulse the Jubilee gave to the teaching, the study, and the practice of Phonography, as well as to its recognition as an educational subject, was not only immediate but permanent and far reaching. It is probable that until the Jubilee Isaac Pitman did not fully realise the value which the English-speaking world set 'on his work as a shorthand inventor. For years past his chief aim in life had been to bring about Spelling Reform, and his efforts in this direction would, he again and again urged, be helped forward by teaching Phonography —regarding the art merely as a means to a greater end. He was now to have overwhelming testimony that the art was valued by vast numbers of people not interested in orthographic reform, as among the most important of modern time-saving inventions in association with the art of writing.

Very early in the preceding year the attention of phonographers was directed to the advisability of celebrating the Jubilee of Phonography. After the matter had been discussed in phonographic circles, it was brought before the Council of the Shorthand Society by Mr. Reed, on the 3rd March, 1886, when the following resolution was passed : " That this Council having heard from Mr. T. A. Reed a statement as to the proposed Jubilee of Phonography, in 1887, and a public recognition of Mr. Pitman's labours, desire to express their entire sympathy with the object, and request Mr. Reed to represent them on any committee that may be formed with a view to its promotion." The Shorthand Society, it will be remembered, was a body containing those writing various systems of shorthand, and one of its most distinguished members, John Westby-Gibson, LL.D., an indefatigable investigator in shorthand history and bibliography, had discovered that the date of the Jubilee practically coincided with the three hundredth anniversary of the beginning of modern shorthand in England by Timothy Bright, in the reign of Queen Elizabeth. He therefore proposed that the celebration of 1887 should assume a double character, namely, the Jubilee of Phonography and the Tercentenary of Bright's system. The proposal met with approval, and at the same meeting of the Council of the Shorthand Society at which the above resolution was passed, it was further agreed on the proposition of Dr. Westby-Gibson, seconded by Mr. Reed, " That it is desirable that advantage should be taken of the Phonographic Jubilee of 1887 to hold in London an international gathering of shorthand writers of all systems, in celebration of the Tercentenary of the origination of modern shorthand by Dr. Timothy Bright, 1587." The actual date of Bright's first published book was 1588, but as he was using the system in 1586, the celebration was made to fall in 1887 in order to coincide with the Phonographic Jubilee. These projects were brought under the notice of Isaac Pitman by Mr. Reed, and the correspondence included the following characteristic letter from the Inventor of Phonography :—

" Bath, 30 March, 86.

" Isaac Pitman to Thomas Allen Reed.

" You have removed the only objection I felt to the vigorous prosecution of the Jubilee of Phonography, and its advocacy in the *Phonetic Journal,* by suggesting that whatever sum be raised as a thank-offering should be utilized for the extension of Phonography. This has my hearty approval.

" I am happy to say I need no addition to the income I derive from the copyright of Phonography. But I think a better appropriation of the funds will be found than the institution of prizes for the best and swiftest writers. This would seem to involve the holding of the championship gold medal for the year. Think what labour and anxiety would attend the examination of several hundreds or thousands of specimens of writing, and after a decision had been come to nobody would be a ' pin ' the better, not even the winners.

" If it is a defect in my mental constitution to be without ' emulation ' [or jealousy], one of ' the works of the flesh ' (Gal. v. 20), I suppose I must bear it with all contentment, but I confess that I never, as a boy or a man, felt a wish to rival or outstrip another, but only to excel my former self.

" But we need not now consider *this* part of the Jubilee. I shall be glad to assist in any way I can, with the *Journal* at my back. Farewell."

Soon after Isaac Pitman wrote the letter quoted above, public announcement was made of the objects of the proposed celebration. The General Committee which had undertaken its promotion included many personages of distinction, as well as the leading representatives of the stenographic profession in this country, on the Continent, and in America, with Mr. Reed as Chairman and Treasurer, and Dr. Westby-Gibson as Hon. Secretary. The gathering was designated " The International Shorthand Congress, London, 1887," and it was the first of this series of meetings. There were two sections of the Congress : (1)

FACSIMILE OF SHORTHAND LETTER ON THE JUBILEE
CELEBRATION FROM ISAAC PITMAN TO MR. REED
(*For Key see page* 247)

ISAAC PITMAN, 1887 (AGE 74)
From a Marble Bust by Thomas Brock, R. A

The Phonographic Jubilee. (2) The Tercentenary of Modern Shorthand, in the shape of a conference to discuss the history and development
of shorthand; its principles and modes of application ; and its position, interests, and prospects.
It became apparent at an early date that there
was a wide divergence of opinion as to the respective claims of the two branches of the proposed
Commemoration, and there seemed at one time
a probability that this conflict of views might
result in a split among the supporters of the
movement. The wise tactfulness of Mr. Reed,
however, happily prevented this, and a method of
working was agreed upon which gave satisfaction
to all parties, and resulted in the entire success of
the Congress. This welcome result was achieved
by the appointment of two executive committees.
One of these was the Phonographic Executive
Committee, with Mr. Reed as Chairman ; and the
other was the Tercentenary Executive Committee,
with Mr. W. H. Gurney-Salter as Chairman. The
first of these committees consisted, with one
exception, of phonographers only. The second
was presided over by the head of the Gurney
system, and consisted of well-known writers of
various methods of shorthand, including several
phonographers. To the last named committee
was entrusted the arrangements connected with
that portion of the programme which dealt with
matters of general interest to shorthand writers
of all systems, and to a great extent the general

arrangements. A satisfactory agreement was come to as to the allocation of any surplus funds after the payment of expenses, and the Jubilee Committee decided that their share should be devoted to some method of perpetuating Isaac Pitman's name and services—his wishes to be consulted in the matter.

The Congress was held in the Geological Museum, Jermyn Street, London, lent for the purpose by the Lords of the Council. The proceedings extended from Monday, 26th September, to Saturday, 1st October. Five days were devoted to various functions of the Congress and to the discussion of subjects of general interest to all shorthand writers, while Wednesday, 28th September, was specially set apart for the phonographic celebration.

Great distinction was given to the opening of the Congress by the inaugural speech delivered by the Earl of Rosebery, K.G., who had accepted the office of President. His Lordship humorously observed that nobody had ever suspected him of knowing anything about shorthand. He had read that between the system of Willis in 1602, and Pitman in 1837, there were 201 systems, while since that date there had been 281 more, and he felt that it was almost a relief to feel that one was absolutely ignorant of all of these systems. In the course of an interesting comparison between the reporting at the commencement of the eighteenth century and in the nineteenth century respectively, he showed conclusively that it was the century in which he was speaking that had witnessed the real triumph of shorthand. But apart from reporting, he held shorthand to be of immense service in the administration of the country. " I believe," he said, " our first economy must lie in the direction of a much greater employment of shorthand." Then all our growing lads must understand that an almost indispensable condition of a commercial education is a knowledge of shorthand. It must be understood, too, that to all those who aspire to secretarial and clerical posts a knowledge of shorthand is at least equally indispensable, and that " in the days when women are loudly and justly calling for increased and enlarged employment, shorthand offers them a pursuit which they are eminently qualified to excel in." Without doubt this practical appreciation of the advantages of shorthand greatly promoted the wider use of the art which has come about in the present day.

In the same speech the Earl of Rosebery made a felicitous reference to Isaac Pitman as " the venerated father of one system of shorthand," and this suggested the slightly altered form of " Father of Phonography," which his admirers began to apply to Isaac Pitman soon afterwards. Lord Rosebery was so much interested in Isaac Pitman that he received him at the Hotel Metropole for the purpose of expressing to him personally his appreciation of the value of his work. In

the course of their conversation Lord Rosebery
remarked on the distinct way in which the veteran
shorthand author spoke, observing that it was
in pleasing contrast to the mumbling utterances
only too common. " I have frequently to com-
plain," Lord Rosebery said, " of people bringing
out their words in such a slovenly and obscure
manner, or so rapidly, that it is quite an effort
to understand what they say." In reply Isaac
Pitman was able to say " I have, from my youth
up, studied to speak distinctly." His Lordship
further remarked that he observed that his visitor
most carefully articulated every syllable of the
words he uttered, and to this Isaac Pitman
replied, " Yes, my lord, that is the result of my
phonetic system."

During the week the Congress discussed Parliamentary Reporting, the History and Literature
of Shorthand, Legal and Official Shorthand Reporting, Shorthand in Education, and the Principles
and Structures of Systems. The proceedings
were reported at considerable length in the daily
newspapers from *The Times* downwards, and
those who had not hitherto paid any special heed
to the art of shorthand and the work of reporting,
were led in many instances to take a keen practical
interest in the Pitmanic system, which was brought
so prominently to the front by its practitioners
during the Congress. A valuable feature of the
Congress was an international exhibition of shorthand books and manuscripts, held at St. James's

Hall Restaurant, Piccadilly, London, W., which was collected and arranged on behalf of the Exhibition Committee by Messrs. E. Pocknell, F. H. Valpy, and H. Richter. No such collection of books representative of shorthand literature of Great Britain and the principal Continental nations had ever been exhibited before or since, and the Chronological Collections of English systems exhibited the progress of English shorthand authorship from 1588 to the year of the Congress. From his library at the Phonetic Institute, Bath, Isaac Pitman lent a large number of rare works of early shorthand authors, as well as many extremely interesting exhibits illustrative of the development of Phonography. A valuable catalogue of much bibliographical interest was issued by the Exhibition Committee, which included an account of the British Museum exhibition held at this time in the King's Library, contributed by Dr. Westby-Gibson.

The phonographic celebration of Wednesday, 28th September, is not likely to be forgotten so long as any interest is felt in Isaac Pitman and his system of brief writing. The central figure in the day's proceedings contributed two papers at different times in the day and delivered a speech in the evening, all three utterances being characterized by the straightforward, cheery optimism, good sense, and modesty in speaking of his own achievements, which marked Isaac Pitman's public utterances. Dr. J. H. Gladstone presided

at the morning conference.   There had been some
current misconceptions, and so he was careful to
explain that they were not celebrating the Jubilee
of shorthand and phonetic writing, but " the
Jubilee of the first publication by Isaac Pitman
of his particular system, a phonetic system
applied to shorthand, which he termed Phonography."   He " devised a thorough English alphabet, capable of being applied to all the sounds of
the English tongue, and in that way was able to
start the very rational and simple style of shorthand which so many of us practise."   Another
advantage which had not been insisted upon so
much was " that the alphabet of Isaac Pitman
affords the best means we possess of writing down
the pronunciation of any new word."   Dr. Gladstone spoke from experience; he had at that time
used Phonography for more than forty years.
Isaac Pitman's contribution to this gathering
was a paper entitled " The Spelling Reform and
How to Get It," which elicited a brisk discussion.
At the afternoon sitting he read a paper entitled
" The Genesis of Phonography," from which we
have quoted somewhat fully in a preceding
chapter (page 36).

Of the evening gathering in the Theatre, which
was the most interesting event of the day, Mr.
Reed (who took a leading part in it) has left a
pleasant and vivid description, which is substantially reproduced here, with some added facts,
and with an additional passage from Mr. Reed's

speech of especial interest as exhibiting the very reasonable view he took of Isaac Pitman's labours for the improvement of his system. " The Theatre," Mr. Reed tells us, " was crowded with phonographers from all parts of the country, as well as the writers of other systems at home and abroad, who desired to join in the congratulations to be offered to the venerable guest of the evening. It had every appearance of a pleasant family gathering, with a few welcome visitors who had dropped in to offer their felicitations. Isaac Pitman was accompanied by Mrs. Pitman and his two sons, Alfred and Ernest, his brother Henry, from Manchester, two of his sisters, Miss Rose Pitman and Mrs. Webster, and his nephews, Harry, Guilbert, and Clarence, sons of Mr. Joseph Pitman. Dr. J. H. Gladstone was among the visitors ; and Mr. Brock, the sculptor, was present throughout the proceedings, and received many a compliment on the successful and highly satisfactory completion of his marble bust, which was on the platform ready for the process of unveiling."

Mr. Reed was chosen to make the presentation, and it was with particular satisfaction that he announced that many persons besides phonographers, and many writers of other systems, had gladly joined in the effort to do honour to the Inventor of Phonography. Since " Stenographic Sound-Hand " was produced, the Pitmanic system had become familiar to hundreds of thousands of writers. " Whatever little differences of opinion,"

Mr. Reed went on to observe, " may have existed among phonographers on small matters of detail, there is but one opinion among those who, like myself, have had the advantage of knowing Isaac Pitman personally, as to his intense desire to leave behind him the very best stenographic instrument that his wit could devise. I have known him, while a book has been in the process of printing, cancel the printed pages at a considerable pecuniary loss, and begin afresh in order that he might incorporate in the work some suggestion that he had received for its improvement." After this illustration of Isaac Pitman's painstaking care as an author—a by no means infrequent occurrence at the Phonetic Institute— Mr. Reed called attention to his services to the community, and concluded thus : " I have now to discharge what is perhaps the pleasantest duty that has ever devolved upon me, that of asking you to accept for your family from the phonographers of Great Britain and Ireland this marble bust. It will be to them a constant reminder of the regard and affection entertained towards you by those who have known best how to appreciate your labours ; and it will, at the same time, be an acceptable legacy to posterity. Not that it is needed to secure you a place in the recollection of your countrymen. Your *work*, far better than even Mr. Brock's faithful chisel, will keep alive your memory in the future ; but all the more will those who fill our places in the coming years be grateful to us for having preserved to them the lineaments of a man to whom they are so deeply indebted for the services he has rendered and the example he has set."

Amid enthusiastic applause the bust was then unveiled. It is by general consent admitted to be a faithful likeness and an admirable specimen of Mr. Brock's art. The bust was exhibited at the Royal Academy in 1888.

Addresses were then presented from the phonographers of South Australia, of New South Wales, and of Carlisle ; an album had been sent from Italy, and it was announced that a medal from the United States was promised. Personal congratulations were sent from the stenographers of Russia, and the venerable Dr. Michaelis, one of the official shorthand writers in the Upper Chamber of Berlin, telegraphed his congratulations.

In rising to respond, Isaac Pitman was greeted with a storm of cheers. He said : " Mr. Chairman, and my dear and affectionate friends : There is a passage in the Divine Word that has rested upon my mind for a month or two as one that I could use on the present occasion. It is a Divine inquiry submitted to us to institute a kind of self-introspection or self-examination. It runs thus : ' Seekest thou great things for thyself ? ' If we put that question to our hearts, I think there are very few of us who can say that we do not. The inquiry is followed by a positive command from the Maker of the Universe, ' Seek them not.'

I have quoted this portion of the Divine Word
for the purpose of saying that, consciously, this
passage has been my guide from my youth up.
To-night instead of feeling that I am a kind of
Roman citizen, and that you have placed a civic
crown upon my brow, I rather feel in the condition
of a criminal arraigned before this Court on the
charge of having sought great things for myself.
I fancy to myself somehow that our venerable
chairman (Mr. Reed) is the judge. If he were but
bewigged, which would well become him, he would
be an admirable judge—a very Portia. And my
friends upon the front row seem to me to be the
jury—the grand jury ; and the seats behind filled
with the public, are the audience : and now I
stand before you in some sense as a criminal
arraigned before the world for having sought great
things for myself ; and I must from my heart declare
myself ' Not guilty.' If you, in your clemency,
come to the same conclusion, I shall go from this
meeting a happy man.   And then to turn to this
bust, a doubt is suggested to my mind somehow,
and I cannot get rid of it.   I have some hesitation
in deciding which is the man and which is the
image. I must really appeal to Mr. Brock. (Mr.
Brock answered with a smile.) I think this
(pointing to the bust) must be the man, such as
he ought to be for purity and beauty, and this
(pointing to himself) the imperfect image. I
only wonder how my friend Mr. Brock could have
made such an image from such a subject."   Then,

passing from himself to his subject, he narrated, as an illustration of what can be accomplished by writing, and the astonishment it creates among those unaccustomed to it, the familiar story of the missionary Williams and the " speaking chip," which did excellent service as an introductory paragraph in the addresses of the young phonographic lecturers in the early days of the crusade. " My object in life," he added, " has been to make the presentation of thought as simple of execution, and as visible to the eye, as possible. Fifty years are a long time in the life of a man, and I have prosecuted my labours for that length of time, and though I cannot say that we have got in Phonography the best shorthand outline for every word, I do maintain that we are not very far from it. I think that the only thing that remains to be done is, to select any words that are not facile and beautiful in form, easy of execution by the reporter's hand, consider them, and put them in the best possible form, and then we shall have completed our work." Having alluded to the many indications of the daily increase in the popularity of Phonography, Mr. Pitman glanced at the question of the Spelling Reform, and then again assumed the rôle of a prisoner arraigned at the bar of justice and awaiting the verdict. Mr. Reed thus finding himself suddenly invested with judicial functions, submitted the case to the audience as the only jury capable of deciding it. A hearty burst of cheers and laughter followed, which the Chairman interpreted to mean a verdict of " Not guilty," adding, according to the customary formula, that the self-arraigned prisoner " left the court without a stain upon his character." This little interlude ended, Mr. Pitman said : " Well, my friends, I accept these beautiful gifts, including the bust, with the deepest and most affectionate gratitude of which my nature is capable. They shall be a stimulus to me to work on in the same line, but, if possible, with increased diligence and faithfulness." Mr. Ernest Pitman also, for the family, returned thanks " for the cordial way in which phonographers had shown their appreciation of his father's labours in the shorthand world."

On behalf of the foreign visitors, Dr. Dreinhöfer moved a congratulatory resolution, which was seconded by Dr. Gladstone, and supported by Mr. Crump, Q.C. ; Dr. Gantter, a representative of the Gabelsberger system, in Germany ; Dr. Weber, who represented the French stenographers ; Mr. W. H. Gurney-Salter ; Mr. J. C. Moor, of Sunderland ; Mr. J. B. Lawson, of Edinburgh ; and Professor Bridge, of the " Chatauqua University," who spoke in behalf of the phonographers of America.

The social side of the Congress included a dinner held on Tuesday, 27th September, at the Holborn Restaurant, over which Sir Charles Russell, Q.C., M.P. (afterwards Lord Chief Justice and Lord Russell of Killowen), presided with great acceptability. In the speeches many interesting observations were made relative to Parliamentary and legal reporting. The toast of "Success to the Shorthand Congress," was proposed by the Chairman in most felicitous terms. In dealing with the objects of the Congress, he indicated that it might lead " to the establishment of something like a permanent guild of shorthand writers, by which they may create for themselves a local habitation and focus point and centre." The toast was acknowledged by Mr. Reed. The toast of " The Judicial Bench and the Legal Profession " was responded to by Mr. F. O. Crump, Q.C., who stated that he had learned Pitman's system when a college student for taking down the lectures, and had throughout his career made considerable use of it. Mr. Crump made many interesting allusions to his employment of shorthand since he had been at the Bar, and mentioned that in the preparation of his well-known work on the Law of Marine Insurance he had been able to use his shorthand ability to the best advantage. Mr. Crump was an old friend of Mr. Reed's, and his graceful allusion to their early associations evoked an outburst of applause. The toast of " Shorthand Inventors " was proposed by Mr. Theodore R. Wright, who coupled with it " the name of the gentleman who certainly is better known throughout the four quarters of the globe than any other shorthand inventor," he referred to his old friend, Isaac Pitman.

In the opening words of his reply Isaac Pitman
made some remarks which were not altogether
understood, and were, as will be shown, elucidated
by himself later on. " As a personal matter,"
he said, " my love of shorthand is entirely with
respect to its uses to society ; and I may honestly
say, not in pride nor in depreciation of the subject,
that I have not an atom of love for shorthand as
an art for its own sake. It is only for its use."
As a superior medium of writing to the ordinary
longhand he advocated its introduction as part
of the ordinary curriculum of our schools. The
two points in the construction of a good system
of shorthand were, in his opinion, in the first place
a simple alphabet scientifically arranged, and in
the second place a good and extensive system of
abbreviations to adapt it to the requirements of
the reporter. In the generally practised system
of Phonography he ventured to think they had
those two conditions. " I hope," he added,
" that for the few remaining years of my life
I shall devote myself to the propagation of
that system, and in connection with it to the
simplification of the spelling of the English
language."

At a subsequent date, in his own *Journal*,
Isaac Pitman explained the statement in his
speech which had caused some surprise, that he
loved shorthand only for its use. His meaning
was that compared with the study of the spiritual
affections of man (as revealed through Swedenborg)

shorthand, viewed historically or practically, did not engage his affections. " Yet," he said, " I spend ten hours of a day in extending the system which I have been enabled to present to the world. . . . I have done this from a deep conviction of the utility of the art to English-speaking people, that is, from a love of use. This and the consequent Spelling Reform is my life-work, and I enjoy it intensely, but the enjoyment arises from the fulfilment of duty, and not from considering the thousand stenographic and ortho-graphic details on which it is necessary to decide, nor in prosecuting archæological studies in the ancient systems of shorthand. I never felt a greater relief from an irksome task than when I had finished reading and reviewing the systems of shorthand published previously to Phonography in 1845, in my ' History of Shorthand.' " [1]

The Shorthand Congress was honoured with an invitation to lunch with the Lord Mayor of London, Sir Reginald Hanson, at the Mansion House, and on Friday, 30th September, a company of about two hundred were the guests of his

---

[1] Isaac Pitman was about this time preparing the third edition of his " History of Shorthand," which was revised and enlarged, with valuable tables of alphabets specially lithographed. Notices were given of nearly 250 systems, and in the preparation of this edition Isaac Pitman had the valued assistance of Mr. Alexander Paterson.

Lordship in the Egyptian Hall. The cordial reception accorded to the members of the Congress and the graceful speech of the Lord Mayor in proposing the toast of the afternoon delighted all present. His Lordship had just before taken an interest in the shorthand work of the students of the City of London School, and he now mentioned that the name of Isaac Pitman was the first ever heard by him as a boy in connection with the art of shorthand. Whatever difference of opinion there might be with regard to the various systems, there was, the Lord Mayor observed, no difference of opinion at all that Isaac Pitman was the most eminent living English inventor. " It is a pleasure to me as Lord Mayor," he continued, " to welcome him here, and to say that to him and to those who are representatives of the art of shorthand we owe very much ; and we believe that in times to come we shall owe them still more, not merely from the commercial point of view, but from the general point of view of the increase of knowledge throughout the civilized world." These encouraging sentiments were acknowledged by Isaac Pitman and other gentlemen who had taken a leading part in the Tercentenary proceedings.

The Congress was brought to a successful conclusion on 1st October, but this narrative of Isaac Pitman's personal association with it would be incomplete without a reference to two very important works which his firm published in connection with it.   One of these is the " Transactions of the International Shorthand Congress, 1887." a closely printed book of 460 pages, containing a complete record of the speeches delivered and papers read at the Congress, with an appendix of 48 pages giving a catalogue of the shorthand exhibition.   Another work of permanent value to all interested in the history of shorthand was " The Bibliography of Shorthand," by John Westby-Gibson, LL.D., issued just before the Congress opened.   On the invitation of Isaac Pitman, Dr. Westby-Gibson visited Bath, and was able in a week's research in the library at the Phonetic Institute to make the phonographic portion of his work much more complete than it otherwise would have been.

The proceedings in London did not represent by any means the only commemoration of the Phonographic Jubilee and the Tercentenary. Manchester, which has been the home of many distinguished shorthand authors and practitioners, and is associated with important events in the history and development of Phonography, had celebrations worthy of itself and of the occasion. The first gathering, a public conference on the present position of Phonography, was held in the Mayor's Parlour at the Town Hall, on 29th August.   His Worship the Mayor (Alderman J. J. Harwood) who occupied the chair, gave an address on the association of Manchester with the art of shorthand, and mentioned incidentally

the interesting fact that he was acquainted with
the first edition of Phonography. " I remember,"
he said, " making very good use of the book."
On the following evening, the 30th August, a
public meeting was held, presided over by Sir
Edward W. Watkin, M.P., who gave a practical
account of his pioneer work in utilizing the art
for the dictation of correspondence in the offices
of the railways with which he was associated. It
was their custom, he remarked, when they engaged
a young man as clerk, to compel him to learn
shorthand, and Mr. Henry Pitman had been their
first teacher. " I am bound to say," he went on,
" that the Pitman system of shorthand has been
to those by whom I am here, and have been
elsewhere surrounded an unmixed blessing." Sir
Edward was thinking of many connected with
railway work to whom phonographic ability had
been of the utmost service. Isaac Pitman gave
a comprehensive address on Phonography and the
Spelling Reform. A number of able speeches by
other gentlemen testified to the interest of Manchester in these subjects. The Committee, with
Mr. W. E. A. Axon as Chairman, and Mr. A. W.
Croxton as Hon. Secretary, had in fact arranged
two highly successful meetings. Advantage was
taken by the Executive of the Vegetarian Society
of Isaac Pitman's presence in Manchester to
entertain him at a banquet.

The national commemoration of the Jubilee of
Phonography was followed by celebrations in

the City of Bath.   The first of these took place
in connection with the New Church in Henry
Street, and was held very appropriately on the
15th November, 1887, the anniversary of the first
publication of Phonography.   For nearly half-a-
century Isaac Pitman had been a most active
member of the Church, and he was at this time
its honoured President.   That his own people
should rejoice with him and congratulate him
on this auspicious occasion was very fitting.
There was, the minister (the Rev. J. Martin),
observed, an irrepressible desire among the New
Church friends to express their " wealth of affection and personal regard " for their fellow worker.
An address by Isaac Pitman on the origin and
progress of the Writing and Spelling Reform was
followed by a congratulatory resolution proposed
by Mr. William Harbutt, which expressed the
hope " that his life will be prolonged to see the
desire of his heart carried out to a far greater
extent."   A presentation was then made of a
beautiful miniature portrait of Isaac Pitman on
ivory, by Mrs. Harbutt (exhibited at the Royal
Academy in the following year).   Greatly touched
by the affection which the gift represented, and
the regard shown for him by those to whom he
was best known, Isaac Pitman expressed his
gratitude in a few fervent words and handed the
portrait to Mrs. Pitman, observing that whatever
wisdom he had, or common sense, tact, or business
capacity, were really the treasures of his wife,

and that beautiful and expressive likeness he presented to her.

The gold medal struck in America to commemorate the Jubilee of Phonography reached Isaac Pitman in February, 1888. The fund to provide it had been raised through the efforts of Mr. E. N. Miner, editor and proprietor of the *Phonographic World*, New York, and accompanying it was an address which indicated the high value set on Isaac Pitman's invention in the United States, as follows :—

But very few of the number who, in America, are now practising the art which your patient study of the principles that should govern the creation of written language enabled you to present to the world, know the early history of your work. Before your text-books were printed, shorthand writing was looked upon as a mystery, and the man who could, by its use, reproduce the utterances of a speaker, was a phenomenon of dexterity, and was regarded as little less than a nine days' wonder. And there was reason for the belief. Those who have compared the lessened lengths of forms in Phonography with the cumbrous outlines of the systems of Gurney, Taylor, Harding, Byrom, Gould, and others, marvel much that with them the requisite skill could be acquired to successfully report words uttered with the rapidity of colloquial speech. " Stenographic Sound-Hand," as given by you to the world a half century since, was the prophecy and promise of a new revelation in the art that was realised in 1848. For Phonography was a system of shorthand founded on scientific principles and unfolded in systematic arrangement and analogic harmony. It was the first in which the simplest signs were employed ; the first in which cognate sounds were represented by cognate signs ; the first in which those elementary sounds admitting of classification in groups were represented by groups of analogous symbols ; the first in which

THE AMERICAN GOLD MEDAL TO COMMEMORATE THE JUBILEE
OF PHONOGRAPHY, PRESENTED TO ISAAC PITMAN

THE FIFTH PHONETIC INSTITUTE, LOWER BRISTOL ROAD, BATH

the attempt was made to give circles, hooks, and loops distinct offices for efficient service in the stenographic art. By it the language was for the first time successfully presented in shorthand on a phonetic basis, and one who could read it could hardly fail to know the spoken words.

But the medal which you now have is not a tribute to your inventive genius alone. The evolution of a new idea is but half the work. It is not alone the inventor who accomplishes great purposes. As much credit is due to him who brings the improvement before the world with strength of purpose to command attention. And when the inventor and adapter combines persistence with creative talent to the extent that the world recognizes the truth of his statements and acts upon them, then more than double credit is due. In America, in nearly every commercial house, corporation, and public journal, in our commercial and manufacturing centres, in our Courts of law and equity, and in deliberative bodies ; indeed, in every place where much writing is done, the stenographer is a needed adjunct, and his presence was made possible by your work. Phonography came to us unheralded to meet a then unvoiced demand. With a status secured it created a further demand for its application in spheres of usefulness for which scarce any had thought it available.

With few exceptions, American writers who have presented the system have frankly acknowledged their indebtedness to you as its discoverer and inventor. In so doing they have but followed the lead of the distinguished pioneers, Stephen Pearl Andrews and Augustus F. Boyle, who, in their text-books published forty years ago, used these words :

" A system of writing, to be perfect, should have one uniform method of representing every sound of the voice that is uttered in speaking, and which is obviously distinct. In the next place, it is desirable for practical purposes to obtain the greatest possible brevity, and therefore the characters or letters by which these sounds are represented, should be the simplest in their form that can be found. And in the third place, in order to facilitate the learning and use of them, they ought to be selected and arranged in strict correspondence with the nature and order of the sounds which they represent ; thus, sounds which are related to each other by similitude of organic formation, should be represented by signs having in their forms a corresponding resemblance ; in other words, the best system of writing will be (1) true ; (2) brief ; and (3) analogical. These properties are admirably combined in the system of phonetic shorthand—the production of the genius and labours of Isaac Pitman."

It only remains for us to wish you health, happiness, and prosperity during the remainder of your career on earth, and that your life may be spared as long as existence shall be a pleasure to yourself and add to the happiness of others.

We are, respectfully yours,

EDWARD F. UNDERHILL,
ELIZA B. BURNZ,   *Committee.*
JAMES E. MUNSON,

There was a celebration of the Phonographic Jubilee by the Canadian Shorthand Society at Toronto on 12th August, 1889, when Mr. Thomas McGillicuddy delivered a eulogy on Isaac Pitman and unveiled a cast of the Jubilee bust.

The citizens of Bath did not allow this interesting event in the life of one who resided in their midst to pass without adding their congratulations, and promoting a suitable memorial of the occasion. This celebration took place a little later in point of time than those already recorded, but the great National Jubilee of Queen Victoria—the influence of which was felt in the London celebrations—had to be reckoned with. The committee which promoted the project was largely representative of the Bath Literary and Scientific Institution, with Mr. (afterwards Sir Jerom) Murch as Treasurer, and Messrs. Frederick Shum and William Tyte as Hon. Secretaries. On 22nd February, 1889, a large company of friends and subscribers met at the Bath Guildhall, under the presidency of the Mayor (Dr. H. W. Freeman), to present Isaac Pitman with a replica of the bust by Mr. Brock. His Worship, in opening the proceedings, observed that by his invention of Phonography Isaac Pitman had built up for himself a unique and lasting monument. He had travelled in America, and the fact that he was a fellow-citizen of Isaac Pitman's had gained him admission in societies in New York, and other cities, to which he would not otherwise have been admitted.

Mr. Murch, a master of graceful oratory, made the presentation. He pointed to the fact that although Isaac Pitman's career among them had been quiet and unobtrusive, yet it had really been marked by extraordinary and even world-wide usefulness. In every part of the world where the English language was spoken his system was used, lessening labour and quickening intelligence. In an age like the present, when success is valued far too much as bringing the means of luxury and self-indulgence, it was allowable to admire simplicity of life and perseverance of work. It was understood that Isaac Pitman would hand the bust to the Royal Literary and Scientific Institution, and alluding to this Mr. Murch concluded his speech thus : " We are glad to know that it will find a congenial home within those walls where we have so often met you.[1] We hope it will be generally thought that the sculptor has shown his accustomed skill and increased his well-known reputation. We believe that to your fellow-citizens, to the young especially, it will be a valuable memorial of one who, through a long and useful life, has gained their sincere respect, and set an admirable example of intelligent, benevolent perseverance. May you still be blessed with health and strength for many years to continue that example, to share the well-earned pleasures of old age with those who are near and dear to you — ' honour, love, obedience, troops of friends,' and to benefit mankind by hastening the time when knowledge shall cover the earth as waters cover the channels of the deep."

In his speech in response, Isaac Pitman said : " If I were a Stoic, a neat sentence of thanks might suffice for acknowledging this beautiful gift. But I am not a Stoic. I am indeed deeply moved by the kindness of the friends who have subscribed to this testimonial. I am especially indebted to Mr. Tyte, who originated the subscription, and to Mr. Murch, who completed it. Whatever of honour there may be in this presentation, I refer it not to myself, but render it to the Lord, to whom alone all honour belongs. The

---

[1] The speaker's allusion is to the fact that Isaac Pitman was a member of and regular attendant at the meetings of the Literary and Philosophical Association at the Institute, before whose members he read several papers on Phonography, the Spelling Reform, and Elocution.

Literary Institution has kindly offered to accept the bust, and to place it in the Reading Room, and I have much pleasure in asking Mr. Murch, as the representative of the Institution, to accept it. I like to think of English literature under the form of a vast temple, with a portico supported on two pillars, on one of which is inscribed the single word ' Letters,' and on the other ' Numbers.' The temple is adorned with the statues of the men, English and American, who have made the literature, the science, and the art, that now illumine, beautify, and bless the world. No one is permitted to pass the portico of this temple who is ignorant of letters and numbers, and their combinations. These little marks, ' a, b, c,' and ' 1, 2, 3,' that seem in themselves to have no more meaning than the marks of birds' feet in the snow, are really the foundation of our civilization. There can be but little trade and commerce, and no literature, without these seemingly insignificant signs. In the use of figures we are consistent, but in the use of letters we are inconsistent." Some observations in advocacy of Spelling Reform closed the speech.

All things have an end, and the final celebration of the Jubilee of Phonography has now to be recorded. The Jubilee Committee, after three years of arduous but successful work, commemorated the completion of their labours by a dinner held at the Holborn Restaurant on the 7th March, 1889, when Isaac Pitman was presented with a

gold medal struck in commemoration of the
Jubilee. The gathering was presided over by
one who described himself as " the youngest
recruit in the phonographic army," Viscount Bury

" FUN IN SCIENCE."

This was the title which Isaac Pitman gave to the above
humorous drawing by Lord Bury, to which he attached a description containing the following : " The faces of the above happy
pair are outlined by the two principal classes of phonographic
letters, the man's face by the surds *p*, *t*, *ch*, *k*, and the breaths *f*,
th, *s*, *sh*, which are male sounds—mere consonant contacts,
without voice or affection ; and the woman's face being formed
by the affectionate *vocal* surds and continuants.   On the neck of
the woman lie the vocal or affectionate nasals, liquids, and
coalescents ; and between the sturdy male and the smiling female
lies the aspirate *h*, waiting for the first of the six vowels beneath
to give utterance to ' Ha ! ha ! ha ! formed for each other ! ' "

(afterwards seventh Earl of Albemarle). His lordship had been abroad in South America at the time of the Jubilee, but reading the account of the proceedings, in *The Times* on his return to England, he procured the necessary phonographic books and began their mastery. They introduced him to a study which he characterized as " fascinating," and in eight weeks he was writing shorthand with considerable facility. His lordship placed himself in personal communication with the Inventor of Phonography, who was, of course, rejoiced to render him assistance in the mastery of the art. Lord Bury had some acquaintance with older systems of shorthand, having long previously had a knowledge of one of these imparted to him by Sir John Bowring ; he had also had lessons in Lewis's system. " Fifty years ago," he said, " Isaac Pitman found shorthand in a very chaotic condition, and a man who, out of such elements, could evolve a system which was brief, rapid, legible, and easily acquired, and which had so quickly taken the foremost place among shorthand methods, must be a remarkable man. But he has done more than that ; for by his indomitable energy he has brought his system to such a position that the little seedling which he sowed fifty years ago is now spreading its branches over the civilized world."

In accepting with profound gratitude this final mark of the esteem of his disciples, Isaac Pitman mentioned incidentally that his system could not have achieved the success it had done had he not been content to live somewhat the life of a recluse. Without steady work at his desk it would have been impossible for him to have evolved the simple yet comprehensive system which was now making the compass of the world. He mentioned with gratification the recent success of Phonography in a far-off land. Mr. A. Tacchi, the Private Secretary to the Queen of Madagascar, who reported the speeches of the House of Representatives in that country, had just published an adaptation of the Pitmanic system to the Malagasy language. He also noted the appearance of a Dutch adaptation of Phonography, by F. De Haan, first published in 1887.

Another announcement of much interest was made by Isaac Pitman on this occasion, namely, that on that day, he and his sons, with their staff, had entered on the occupation of a new Phonetic Institute. The premises in the Abbey Churchyard, which had been occupied for fifteen years, had latterly proved inadequate to the accommodation of the increasing staff, and accordingly a new Institute—the fifth—was built a little over a mile from the centre of Bath, and in the parish of Twerton-on-Avon. The new Institute was planned and constructed in a style most suitable for the complete production of books and periodicals, and the architect was Mr. W. J. Wilcox, of Bath. The opening was celebrated by a tea and entertainment to the staff and friends, to the number of two hundred, and Isaac Pitman, who presided, in his address to his employees urged them to cultivate a taste for reading, and stated that in order to encourage this he had established a free lending library in association with the Institute.

In spite of the many demands on his time and attention which have been described in this chapter, Isaac Pitman was able to make other public appearances. For the second time within his experience the British Association visited Bath in the year 1888, and on this occasion a paper by himself with the title " Economy in Education and in Writing," was accepted. It was delivered in Section F on the 11th September, and its reader urged with unusual freshness and force the saving of time in teaching to read which would follow from the adoption of phonetic spelling, and the saving of time in writing which would follow from the general use of Phonography. The speeches were almost entirely favourable to the arguments which had been placed before the section in the paper.

An address on " Literary Reform, and Economy of Time in Writing," was delivered by Isaac Pitman on 16th September, 1889, in the Lecture Theatre of the Midland Institute at Birmingham. The audience numbered considerably over one thousand, and many were unable to find seats. " There is something peculiarly fascinating," wrote the *Birmingham Daily Mail*, " in the contemplation of the career of this remarkable

man.   It is a life that gives the world a new idea
of everlasting energy.   Fifty-two years ago Isaac
Pitman was engaged in thinking out and develop-
ing the system of shorthand with which his name
will ever be associated, and to-day finds him
just as busily occupied with a much more daring
project, nothing less in fact than a sweeping
revision of [the orthography of] the English
language." But the *Mail* was fain to admit
that to a very large extent Isaac Pitman had
argument on his side.

The harmony which had prevailed among the
writers of various systems of shorthand during
the Tercentenary proceedings of 1887 was rudely
shattered in the following year. Certain proposals in association with the periodical issued by
the Shorthand Society led to some altogether
unfounded allegations being made against Isaac
Pitman at the annual meeting of that body on
the 30th June, 1888, when by a *coup d'état* the
control of the Society was secured by certain
anti-phonographers.   So far as he was concerned,
Isaac Pitman had no difficulty in demonstrating
that the charges levelled against him were
chimerical, and he resigned his membership.   His
example was at once followed by nearly all the
phonographic members of the Society, which
some years afterwards came to an end.

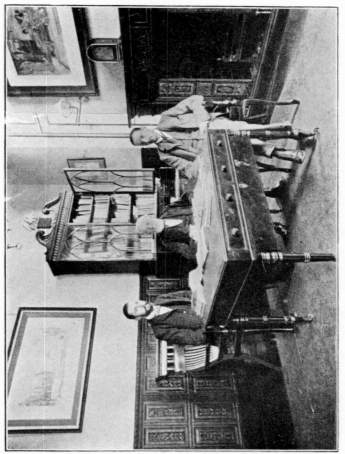

MR. ALFRED PITMAN   MR. ERNEST PITMAN

ISAAC PITMAN AND SONS

(*At the Phonetic Institute, Bath, 1889*)

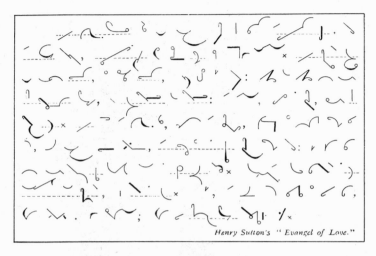

Henry Sutton's " Evangel of Love."

SPECIMEN OF PHONOGRAPHY PRODUCED BY THE TYPOGRAPHIC
ETCHING PROCESS

*(The characters are etched with special tools on the wax coating of
a brass plate, from which electrotypes are taken. Adopted in
" Pitman's Shorthand Weekly " in June, 1892)*

KEY.—Our living flocks of thoughts need no longer trudge it slowly and wearily down the pen and along the paper, hindering each other as they struggle through the strait gate of the old handwriting. Our troops of feelings need no more crawl, as snails crawl, to their station on the page : regiment after regiment may now trot briskly forward, to fill paragraph after paragraph : and writing, once a trouble, is now at breathing-ease. Our kind and loving thoughts, warm and transparent, liquid as melted from the hot heart, shall no longer grow opaque, and freeze with a tedious dribbling from the pen : but the whole soul may now pour itself forth in a sweet shower of words. Phonotypy and Phonography will be of a use in the world not dreamed of, but by a few. Aye, and shake your heads as ye will, they will uproot the old spelling ; they will yet triumph over the absurdities of the dead age.— Henry Sutton's " Evangel of Love."

XXI

A NEW EPOCH IN SHORTHAND TEACHING—THE
NATIONAL PHONOGRAPHIC SOCIETY—AN EDITORIAL
JUBILEE

1890-1893

ONE of the first fruits of the Jubilee of Phonography was the State recognition of shorthand as a subject of instruction in schools aided by Government grant. " In educational circles," Isaac Pitman exclaimed, " shorthand is now the topic of the day." The Technical Instruction Act of 1889 included shorthand among a number of useful subjects for evening schools, and the Sheffield Town Council was the first municipal body in the country to arrange for instruction in Isaac Pitman's system under the new Act. For some time previous to this legislative sanction, the London School Board had taught shorthand in its schools, and this course was now rendered possible throughout the country by the inclusion of shorthand in the Education Code of 1890, among numerous optional " specific " subjects, and for the next eleven years, until " specifics " were abolished, Phonography was extensively taught in elementary day schools. Isaac Pitman had, therefore, the happiness during the remaining years of his life of seeing his ideal with regard to the mission of Phonography completely realized.

" The immediate cause of the extended practice
of shorthand," he had written years before, " was
the diffusion of knowledge among the middle
classes of society.   It has yet to be extended to
the lowest classes, and this will be the mission of
Phonography combined with Phonetic Printing."
Shorthand instruction was now made part of the
elementary educational system of the country,
but its importance was not overlooked by the high
schools of the land.   It was introduced at Rugby
School, its value being appreciated by the then
Head Master, Dr. Percival (afterwards Bishop of
Hereford), and in many other schools and colleges
throughout the country.   At this period, indeed,
Isaac Pitman was able to announce that every
year one hundred thousand persons learned
Phonography.

The considerable extension in the teaching and
practice of shorthand at this time had impressed
on the minds of many leaders in the phonographic
world the necessity of an organization framed
and conducted on national lines for the cultivation and advancement of Phonography, and for
the regulation of the teaching of the art, by the
examination of those who proposed to teach and
the granting of a teacher's diploma, which would
be recognized by educational authorities.   These
objects were promoted by the establishment of
a body conducted on national lines, entitled the
National Phonographic Society.   This Society was
successfully inaugurated at a meeting held at the

Memorial Hall, London, on 31st October, 1890, and eight years later it became the Incorporated Phonographic Society. There was a crowded gathering of phonographers at the inaugural meeting, and for an hour before the proceedings began Isaac Pitman held a kind of informal reception in the Hall. The greatest enthusiasm and cordiality prevailed, and it is recorded of him in a descriptive account of the proceedings that " white-haired, active as a stripling, and almost as erect, his happy face beamed with content as he wheeled about from one knot to another."

Lord Bury presided, and wished the new Society God-speed. He represented, he said, the outside world, which looked with admiration at the perseverance which had initiated and carried to its full extent the great art of stenography. " We have here," his lordship went on to observe, "the doyen, the head and front of the phonographic world, the man who has had the genius to succeed in establishing a system of shorthand invented by himself, not upon the ruins of other systems, but alongside them, carrying out to a still greater extent the benefits which they before him conferred upon mankind ; and he has now developed a system which I am persuaded, and the outside public are persuaded, will more and more draw within its own lines the stenographic world. It is applicable not only to the English but to all other languages." Lord Bury expressed his entire

approval of the objects of the Society which were
thus set forth :—

    (a) The discussion of (1) all questions theoretical and
        practical connected with the art of Phonography
        and its uses ; (2) the history and literature of
        Shorthand and cognate topics.

    (b) Efforts to raise the status and remuneration of
        phonographic practitioners.

    (c) The institution of Examinations of Teachers and
        others, and the granting of Certificates of
        Proficiency.

    (d) The promotion of mutual intercourse and *esprit de
        corps* among Phonographers.

The resolution establishing the Society was
proposed by Mr. Reed, seconded by Mr. E. J.
Nankivell, supported by Dr. (afterwards Sir
William) Gowers, and carried by acclamation. A
speech from Isaac Pitman followed, in which he
congratulated the phonographic world on the institution of the Society, and expressed his gratitude
to the officers for their labour in framing the
constitution. The general usefulness of shorthand
would, he affirmed, be destroyed by the practice
of many systems, but the formation of the National
Phonographic Society would do much to prevent
such an undesirable result. He became the first
President of the Society, and continued to hold
office until 1895.

It is an interesting coincidence that the Institute
of Journalists was incorporated by Royal Charter
in the year which witnessed the establishment
of the National Phonographic Society. Isaac

Pitman became, and remained till his death, a member of the Institute. In the summer of 1890 the third International Shorthand Congress was held at Munich, where special honours were paid to the memory of Franz Xavier Gabelsberger (1789-1849), " the founder of modern Teutonic shorthand," and a statue was unveiled. Isaac Pitman attended, and paid a tribute to the memory of the great German shorthand author.

One of the incidental effects of the Jubilee of Phonography was to bring about more cordial relations between its Inventor and American practitioners of the phonographic art. Isaac Pitman at this time established a closer touch with Transatlantic phonographers by sending his nephew, Mr. Clarence Pitman, to New York in April, 1890, where he has since had charge of the interests of Phonography in the Western Hemisphere.

The beginning of 1891 witnessed another Jubilee, that of the *Phonetic Journal*, which this year completed its fiftieth volume. During that long period, with only a brief interregnum, Isaac Pitman had been its editor. He had moved with the times, and had both reduced its price and enlarged its size. The Jubilee year was marked by a further extension in the number of its pages, and with an increasing circulation its usefulness was greatly extended. During this year the promotion of the National Phonographic Society occupied a good deal of attention, and in pursuance of this project

Isaac Pitman and Mr. Reed addressed a crowded
and enthusiastic gathering at the Christian Institute, at Glasgow, on 23rd September. Isaac
Pitman's subject was " Shorthand," and he made
an exalted claim for the art : " Shorthand," he
said, " develops mind ; expresses, amplifies, and
quickens thought ; and kindles and increases
affection, and thus promotes the best interests
of mankind." His address was enthusiastically
received, and at its conclusion he spoke to an
overflow meeting. Mr. Reed followed with a
persuasive address, in which he commended the
new Society to the support of the phonographers
of the North. A few days later, on the 29th
September, Isaac Pitman addressed another large
gathering assembled at the Y.M.C.A. Hall at
Bristol. The second inaugural meeting of the
National Phonographic Society was held in London
on the 21st October, when the first shorthand
teacher's certificates, awarded after examination
by the Society's Examining Board, were presented
by the Earl of Albemarle to exactly one hundred
successful candidates, and it was announced that
the Society had received an addition of one
thousand members. Isaac Pitman was unable
to be present but had spoken an address into
the phonograph, in which he congratulated the
Society on meeting for the first time to award
teacher's certificates to those phonographers who
had demonstrated their ability by passing its
examination.

On the 4th January, 1892, Isaac Pitman celebrated his eightieth birthday. The fact that he
had joined the ranks of the octogenarians was
not lost sight of by " troops of friends " in all
parts of the world, who showered upon him
innumerable friendly greetings, for which he made
a general acknowledgment in grateful terms.
" Their good wishes," he said, " cheered and
encouraged him, and he hoped to repay them by
not lessening the number of his days on earth
through overwork, as many men who undertook
important missions had done." In his early life
it was prophesied that his too assiduous labour
would bring him to an early grave, but this
birthday and his observations on it recall a passage
from a speech he had delivered at Nottingham
in 1849, which has considerable biographical
interest. " I am sometimes told," he then said,
" that I shall wear myself out in a few years, but
I think differently. I take everything very calmly,
and have acquired the habit of doing my work
quickly, in shorthand style. I have adopted
temperate habits of life and early hours of rising
and going to bed ; and I have the happiness of
being descended from a healthy stock, being the
third child of a family of eleven, only one of whom
died in youth, and the youngest of whom, Frederick
Pitman, is now (1849) on the verge of manhood.
I am now thirty-five years of age. My father,
an eldest son, is now sixty-one, and has scarcely
passed the prime of life, and his father, who is

eighty-one, gives promise of a few more years in this world. And I may add that when I was a boy I attended my great grandfather's funeral. I hope then, through the Divine mercy, I may reach the age of eighty." On the completion of his eightieth year, he was presented with a handsome illuminated address of congratulation and good wishes from the Scottish Phonographic Association.

A new phonographic weekly periodical began its career in 1892 under the title of *Pitman's Shorthand Weekly*. This was established by his sons, but Isaac Pitman took a keen interest in its success, and wrote the transfer of the lithographed shorthand of the first page of the first number. His " Greeting " was in the following terms :—

" Phonography has added a new joy to life, and given a new wage-earning employment to the nation. Its use saves time, and time is life ; it quickens thought and its expression, and thus cultivates the mind ; and it promotes intercourse between persons living at a distance from each other, and is thus ' knowledge in the making.'

" Shorthand was first printed by lithography in the *Phonetic Journal* for 1842. During the last fifty years, at a moderate computation, a hundred thousand pages of lithographed shorthand have been published, which have been read by perhaps a million persons. During the first sixteen years of the Writing and Spelling Reform, from 1842 to 1858, I wrote the transfers of several shorthand periodicals, sometimes three, in different styles, running together monthly. Then for fourteen years, to 1872, a lithographed ' Supplement ' was added to the *Phonetic Journal*, which was published at 3d. In 1873 engraved metal shorthand characters were introduced, the price of the *Journal* was reduced to 1d., and its circulation rose from 1,000 to the present 24,000.

" These recollections visit me in ushering into the phonographic world a new shorthand periodical, and in writing the transfer of this brief address. For half-a-century it has been to me a labour of love to edit the *Phonetic Journal*, and a source of gratification to find it from year to year meeting with ever increasing support. Though only a year has passed since the *Journal* was enlarged from sixteen pages to twenty-four pages, it is already found inadequate to contain the increasing variety of important matters pertaining to the study of Phonography, to the numerous interests of those who use it and teach it, and to the promotion of the Spelling Reform—a goal in the distance for which we strive.

" A general desire has been expressed for the presentation of Phonography in a recreative aspect. The adoption of Phonography in schools, mutual improvement societies, etc., has greatly increased the number of writers of the system, and there is a corresponding increase in the demand for entertaining reading matter. The *Journal* supplies three styles of shorthand, as lessons and models for learners, letter writers, and reporters ; and the present publication, it is hoped, will supply home reading adapted to amuse and instruct the vast number who every year become students and practitioners of phonetic shorthand."

In this year (1892) Isaac Pitman spent his summer holiday in the Channel Islands, to which he then paid his first visit. His system had gone before him, and by special request he gave a lecture on the art on 3rd of August in the Guille-Allès Library at Guernsey.

When a proposal was mooted that the Phonographic Jubilee of Mr. Reed should be celebrated in 1892, Isaac Pitman promoted the project with his whole heart, and his invitation to the phonographic community to support it was, without doubt, a considerable factor in the gratifying success of the movement. For nearly the whole of the preceding half-century Mr. Reed had been in the forefront of the phonographic world, in promoting the extension of the art and assisting its practitioners ; he had consequently hosts of friends in every rank of society, while his writings had made him almost a personal friend to innumerable phonographers who had never seen him. Among the speakers at the presentation, on the 23rd November, was Dr. Gray, of Oxford, who appropriately observed that the Reed Jubilee was an event in the history of Phonography which would always stand side by side with the Jubilee of 1887, and such indeed it was. The presentation, which took the form of a cheque, was made by Isaac Pitman, and the value of the token of esteem from the phonographic community was evidently greatly enhanced in Mr. Reed's estimation by the fact that he received it at the hands of one whose

words of encouragement fifty years before had
determined his career in life.

At this period Isaac Pitman was more frequently
on the platform than had been possible with
him in recent years, and special interest attaches
to what proved to be his last lecture on Phonography, because it was given at his birthplace,
Trowbridge.   It was delivered on 1st December,
1892, at the Town Hall.   The Chairman (Mr. W.
Walker) made graceful allusion to the fact that the
lecturer was a native of the town.   Isaac Pitman
gave the audience some reminiscences of his early
days, and observed that when he looked back on
his past career, he often thought of the words
contained in the verse of Scripture, " What hath
God wrought ! "   Before he concluded his lecture
on Phonography he discovered by a show of hands
that at least three-fourths of his audience were
acquainted with his system, a fact which afforded
him no small gratification.   The second portion
of his lecture was devoted to the advocacy of
Spelling Reform.   About this time Isaac Pitman
made other public appearances.   The season was
extremely wet, and the result was a serious
attack of congestion of the lungs, and for the first
time for a long period the venerable Inventor of
Phonography was confined to his bed.   He was
now residing at the Royal Crescent, Bath, himself
and family having taken up their residence there
at the time the new Institute was opened.   On
recovery, he removed his desk from the Institute

to the Royal Crescent, thus avoiding unnecessary
exposure to the weather.

In March, 1892, the Phonetic Society had been
established for fifty years, and the Jubilee list of
members was the largest ever issued, containing
5,098 names.   From this date annual lists were
discontinued, and with Isaac Pitman's withdrawal
from the Institute, the Society ceased to exist.
The phonographic functions which this Society
once discharged were now carried out in a different
way by other bodies, while its work as a promoter
of orthographic reform was continued by the
organization of a Speling Leeg, founded by Isaac
Pitman on the 4th January, 1893, with Professor
Max-Müller as President.   When on his summer
holiday at Southsea in this year, Isaac Pitman
gave an address on the objects of the Leeg at the
Portsmouth Town Hall to a number of teachers,
and a resolution of approval of reformed spelling
was passed.

In the Lecture Hall of the City Temple, in the
presence of a crowded gathering, Isaac Pitman,
on 27th September, 1893, distributed the prizes
gained by the students of the Metropolitan School
of Shorthand, of which his sons had a short time
before become the proprietors.   This was the last
occasion on which he spoke in public on Phonography, and in the course of his address he dwelt
on the great saving of time which its use had
effected in various directions.   He pointed to the
dissemination of his system through all English

speaking countries. " In every part of the world,"
he remarked, " where our noble tongue is spoken,
phonetic shorthand is written. It has been adapted
to the writing of fourteen foreign languages,
and eleven foreign systems have been published.
They are French, Flemish, German, Italian,
Spanish, Dutch, Welsh, Chinese, Japanese,
Bengalee, and Malagasy. The Debates in the
Japanese Houses of Parliament are reported in
Phonography." Later in the same year he became
acquainted with the fact that his system had also
been adapted and published in Marathi ; and
shortly before his speech a Tongan adaptation
had appeared.

XXII

" I FEEL a lessening of the joy of life now that in my old age I can no longer be with you daily, aiding in your labours and hearing the music of the machinery." Thus wrote Isaac Pitman in response to an address of congratulation promoted by the staff of the Phonetic Institute on the important event recorded in the present chapter. There is a certain pathos in the spectacle of the valiant champion of the Reading and Writing Reform having to retire through the weight of advancing years from the scene of his life-long labours. For half-a-century he had directed the Reform from his desk at the Phonetic Institute with all the zeal and ability, and with the full extent of unwearied industry of which he was capable. His inability to be there as of old was deeply felt, but without a trace of despondency or the iteration of unavailing regrets. At his home he could still work for the cause to which he had consecrated his life, and he was able to drive down in his carriage to the Institute, in order to give directions in matters there to which he still paid personal attention. At this time, however, the bodily ailment which was eventually to prove fatal had manifested itself, in the shape of disease of the mitral valve of the heart. But despite this there was the same buoyancy of spirit and cheerful demeanour exhibited during the remaining years, and almost the same activity as of old manifested now and for some time to come.

The interest felt in the career of the veteran " Father of Phonography " found expression at this period in the publication of various interviews and biographical sketches in the newspapers and popular periodicals of the day. A clever pen picture of the Inventor of Phonography in his home was published in *You and I* for March, 1894, from which we quote some passages which have a biographical interest :—

" The Royal Crescent, Bath, overlooking, from the proud eminence on which it stands, the picturesque grounds of the Victoria Park, is an ideal place of residence for the man who, in the closing years of a busy life, seeks not rest, but continues his work in the privacy of his own sanctum.

" I received a warm welcome at No. 12, the residence of Isaac Pitman, when I called upon him on a recent bright morning, for the purpose of hearing from his own lips a few particulars of his long and eventful career. He greeted me with charming cordiality, and I realized at once that I was in the presence of a man who would make friends and inspire confidence wherever he might go.

" Though Isaac Pitman is now in his 82nd year, he looks at least ten years younger, in spite of his snow-white hair and beard. His step is firm and elastic, his voice clear as a bell, and his spirits quick and merry. His fluency of speech tells of continual activity of mind. He is essentially a business man.

" The room in which we sat and conversed bears witness to this fact. The walls are lined with well-stocked bookcases, and the centre of the floor is occupied with two writing-tables.

" ' These,' said he, pointing to the volumes which filled the shelves on one side of the apartment, ' are books chiefly connected with shorthand and spelling reform. Here,' indicating another case, ' is general literature, and in the cabinet over the fireplace I have stacks of our own tracts, of which there are already fifty-five different kinds, which are continually being added to.'

" I noticed bound volumes of the *Phonetic Journal*, which has reached the 52nd year of its existence, in one bookcase ; and in another a complete set of the *Art Journal* from its commencement.

" At Isaac Pitman's writing-table we sat together and talked over many incidents in my venerable friend's career. He speaks with pardonable pride of the present position of Phonography, and the extent to which it is taught and practised throughout the country—I might almost say, throughout the world.

" ' Shorthand has become a recognized necessity amongst the acquirements of education,' he said to me ; ' and there is no doubt that it will ultimately come into general use for correspondence

and all ordinary matters of writing. For legal
documents it will never supersede longhand, but
there is no other clerical work for which it is not
suited.   Printers compose from shorthand nowa-
days, you know.   Look at this ; ' he handed me
a neatly written manuscript in shorthand.   ' That
article was set up at our office from that very copy.
Corrections, interlineations and all are in shorthand, you see. Economy in labour ; I should think
so, indeed.   Think what it will mean to reporters
and jaded newspaper men, when it is no longer
necessary for them to sit up all night to transcribe
the notes taken during a hard day ! '

" ' Phonography,' remarked Isaac Pitman, ' has
reached the top of the hill, and may now be left
to run alone.   Phonotypy has still the height
before it, and requires all the help, all the pushing
that I can give it during the few remaining years
of my life.'

" Although too much absorbed in his own
particular sphere of labour to take any prominent
part in public matters, he evinces a keen interest
in all movements which relate to educational
and social advancement.   Thus quietly and un-
ostentatiously Isaac Pitman works on,—not for
personal aggrandisement, not fame, but for the
benefit of mankind in general, and particularly of
the young men and young women, to whom, when
his own labour is done, he will bequeath the cause
to which he has given his thought—his time—
his life."

While engaged in the daily occupation the *You
and I* interviewer has so well described, Isaac
Pitman was the recipient of a letter from the then

Prime Minister, the Earl of Rosebery, which ran as follows :—

10 DOWNING STREET, WHITEHALL,

21st May, 1894.

MY DEAR MR. PITMAN,

It is with great pleasure that I make the intimation to you that the Queen has been pleased to confer on you the honour of Knighthood.   I have recommended this distinction on the ground of your great services to Stenography, and the immense utility of that art.   It was always a cherished hope of mine to obtain a recognition of these, which it is a sensible satisfaction to have realized.

Yours truly,

ROSEBERY.

To this communication its recipient made the following reply, writing his letter in longhand in the ordinary spelling, with an interlined shorthand version :—

12 ROYAL CRESCENT, BATH.

22nd May, 1894.

MY DEAR LORD ROSEBERY,

I am very grateful to your lordship for the honour of knighthood which the Queen has conferred on me by your lordship's recommendation for my services to the English language in giving it the briefest possible written form. That form was attained by classifying the sounds of speech scientifically, and then arranging the shorthand signs in harmony with the sounds. Abbreviating principles were then applied to the letters. The result is seen in the interlineation of this letter.

Gratefully, your lordship's most obedient servant,

ISAAC PITMAN.

The *London Gazette* of 25th May, 1894, announced that Queen Victoria had " been pleased to signify her intention of conferring the honour of knighthood upon Mr. Isaac Pitman, the originator of Pitman's system of shorthand."

The honour of knighthood for services in association with literature, science, art, and allied subjects, had hitherto been very sparingly bestowed, and with certain well-marked limitations. Lord Rosebery's departure in the case of Isaac Pitman and some others has been followed by succeeding Prime Ministers, and has resulted in this honourable distinction being more and more employed to show national appreciation of worthy effort. When the intention to confer a knighthood on Isaac Pitman became known, the Press of the United Kingdom and of the British Empire beyond the seas uttered a chorus of approval. The *Daily News* very fitly expressed the general sentiment in the remark that " Another of the new knights, whose title will be welcome to the whole public, is Isaac Pitman, the founder of the great system of shorthand which will always be associated with his name. The knighthood becomes more and more an order of merit as it takes account of the services of such men."

Admirers and relatives in far distant parts of the world (among whom were his two sons, then on a tour in America) as well as friends at home, vied with each other in sending hearty messages of felicitation. Addresses of congratulation reached him from Shorthand Writers' Associations in all parts of the British Empire. By a happy coincidence a distinguished citizen of Bath, whose name has already appeared in these pages, was knighted at the same time, and this gentleman, Sir Jerom Murch, was presented with his portrait on 23rd May at the Bath Guildhall. Isaac Pitman was present, and the congratulations of the citizens of Bath were tendered to both.

From the House of Commons came an address written in Phonography and bearing the short-hand signatures of Members of Parliament acquainted with the art, all (with the exception of Sir John Leng's) written in Pitmanic Shorthand. This ran as follows :—

HOUSE OF COMMONS,

29th May, 1894.

To SIR ISAAC PITMAN.

DEAR SIR,—The undersigned members of the House of Commons desire to offer you their hearty congratulations on the well-deserved honour you have received at the hands of the Prime Minister.   Wishing you long life and prosperity,

We are, yours very truly,

E. H. BAYLEY	S. D. WADDY
THOS. J. HEALY	ARCHIBALD GROVE
JASPER TULLY	T. P. O'CONNOR
T. H. HEALY	M. D. BODKIN
MAURICE HEALY	WM. O'BRIEN
CHAS. DIAMOND	JOHN LENG

The accolade of knighthood was bestowed by Queen Victoria at Windsor Castle on the following

18th July. Isaac Pitman was suffering from lameness at the time, for which he was receiving medical attention, but he was able to kneel before the Queen. Her Majesty had with gracious consideration, intimated that this part of the ceremony could be dispensed with in his case. Happily, however, he could fulfil the usual requirements in association with the ceremony.

Soon after the bestowal of knighthood, Sir Isaac Pitman retired from partnership with his sons, Messrs. Alfred and Ernest Pitman, and transferred to them his interests in the works of which he was the author. The transfer had been commenced in the Spring, but it was delayed by various causes, and it was not finally completed till 10th August, 1894. At the time of his retirement, Sir Isaac had been uninterruptedly engaged in the work connected with his invention of Phonography for fifty-seven years, and had edited the *Phonetic Journal* for fifty-two years, a record in both respects quite unique in our national history. In this year (1894) the sale of the " Phonographic Teacher " attained to a total of two million copies. It was in this year also that the National Society of Shorthand Teachers, (afterwards the Incorporated Society of Shorthand Teachers), was founded, and Isaac Pitman accepted a cordial invitation to become the Patron of the society.

XXIII

A CAREER of incessant occupation in the promotion of his mission in life left Isaac Pitman comparatively little time or opportunity for active participation in public work of the ordinary kind, or for the cultivation of his individual tastes. But there were matters outside his special concern to which he was particularly attracted, and attention may be fitly directed to these now that the story of his efforts as a Shorthand Inventor and Spelling Reformer is all but completed. Throughout his life the movements of the time greatly interested him, especially those which related to religion, politics, hygiene, and social life ; he cultivated at least one accomplishment, that of music ; and he had a good many fads, frankly owned as such, and from the promotion and advocacy of which he derived no small enjoyment.

Deeply interested in theological studies, Isaac Pitman followed, with close attention, the movement that extended over a considerable portion of his active life and resulted in the production of the Revised Version of the Bible. As we have seen, he made in early life a very close study of the text of the Authorised Version. When the work of the revisers was submitted to the public, he examined it with great interest, and expressed a preference for the revisions of the American

Committee to those which were sanctioned by the scholars who assembled in the Jerusalem Chamber. Since his acceptance of the doctrines of Emanuel Swedenborg, he was an assiduous student of the voluminous religious writings of the Swedish philosopher, and it was his custom to read a portion of them for half-an-hour early in the morning, before going to his desk at the Phonetic Institute to begin the duties of the day. To many enterprises of the New Church body he gave substantial monetary support down to the time of his death. If his zeal for the promotion of the doctrines of Swedenborg was at times a little inopportune, he had at any rate a profound respect for the religious convictions of others, and his relations with the clergy of all denominations, and with members of various religious communions were of the most cordial character. He took considerable interest in hymnology, but the popular compositions of modern authors did not arouse in him anything like the admiration he felt for the hymns of older writers.

In politics Isaac Pitman was a lifelong supporter and advocate of Liberal principles. His interest in political questions was early aroused by the popular demand for the franchise, which resulted in the Reform Bill of 1832. He gave active support to the Free Trade movement, led by Mr. Cobden and Mr. Bright ; he took a strong interest in the Irish legislation of Mr. Gladstone, and was in his later years a hearty supporter of the Home

Rule policy of the right hon. gentleman. A member of the Bath Liberal Association, he occasionally took his seat on the platform at their meetings ; his political utterances, when invited to speak, had the unusual merits of conciseness and brevity.   He was a Vice-President of the United Kingdom Alliance, and on a well-known occasion, when Sir Wilfrid Lawson addressed a mass meeting at the Bath Theatre Royal, Isaac Pitman, with some friends, occupied a box, and was evidently entertained by Sir Wilfrid's " gay wisdom." For some time he was President of the Bath Temperance Society (the parent organization of the city) and took an active part in the Jubilee celebrations of the Society in 1886.   He was a strong supporter of the propaganda of the Peace Society, but he does not appear to have ever practically considered the problem of national defence.   In several societies whose titles begin with " Anti " he took a considerable interest, more particularly in those which were opposed to vaccination, vivisection, and tobacco.

A very great love of books, and a conviction that the cultivation of a taste for reading was an ennobling thing, led Isaac Pitman to take an active part in a movement for providing the city of Bath with a Free Library.   With this object in view a committee was formed, of which the leading spirit was Mr. J. W. Morris, a zealous worker in many good causes for the intellectual advancement and benefit of his fellow-citizens.   Isaac Pitman joined

the committee and actively shared its labours.
A library of about nine thousand volumes, of
which two thousand were presented by Isaac
Pitman, was collected, and suitable freehold
premises were purchased by Mr. C. W. Mackillop
for a Reading and Reference Library. In this
building the library was supported for six years
by means of a small voluntary subscription, and
the experiment having successfully shown that it
could be maintained at the cost of a halfpenny
rate, the building and its contents were offered
in free gift to the city of Bath, on condition that
the Free Libraries Act should be adopted by the
burgesses, which would have involved the levying
of a rate of the amount just mentioned for the
maintenance of the institution. After much controversy, the offer was rejected in 1880, and consequently the library was closed. During the time
that it had been kept open experimentally Isaac
Pitman had collected at his Institute ten
thousand books with the intention of adding
them to the library as soon as it was taken over
by the city. When the project was abandoned,
he decided that he would distribute the volumes,
which he had intended to give to the citizens
of Bath, among the free libraries throughout
the Kingdom, which then numbered about one
hundred and ten. He accordingly sent out a
catalogue to all these libraries with an invitation to
them to make a selection, and in this way speedily
disposed of his collection, which included a large

proportion of useful standard works. But this generous distribution of books by no means completes the story of Isaac Pitman's gifts of books. From this time until the close of his life many institutions benefited by his liberality, but special notice of one only need be made here. Reading in the newspapers the speech of Mr. Gladstone at the opening of the new Hawarden Institute in 1893, Isaac Pitman made a present of three thousand volumes to the library of the Institute. The collection included " a large proportion of valuable and rare works, and books to suit all classes of readers " and, it need hardly be said, was greatly appreciated.

Towards the close of his life Mr. Samuel Carter Hall, the editor of the *Art Journal*, was a frequent visitor to Bath with Mrs. Hall, and became on very friendly terms with Isaac Pitman. Mr. Hall was at this time engaged in the promotion of a memorial to the poet Moore, who had been a personal friend of himself and his wife, and for whose genius he entertained high esteem. In this project he had the cordial support of Isaac Pitman. The poet with his family were buried in Bromham churchyard, in Wiltshire, and the memorial took the form of a window at the west end of the church to " complement " a memorial window to the poet's widow in the east end, placed there by her nephew. The new window, which had been subscribed for by two hundred friends and admirers of " The Poet of all circles and the Idol of his own,"

was unveiled by Mrs. Hall. It represents " The
Last Judgment."   Isaac Pitman and his wife were
among those who journeyed from Bath for the
ceremony, and after the unveiling he went to the
organ and gave a rendering of Sir John Stephen-
son's setting of Moore's stirring poem, " Sound the
Loud Timbrel," which had just before been recited
by Mrs. Hall. Afterwards another poem of Moore's,
" Lord, who shall bear that day," was recited.

The mention of Isaac Pitman's part in the
Moore memorial proceedings recalls his acquaintance with music.   In his early life, as he has told
us in a speech already quoted, he had loved the
divine art and played the flute and the piano.   At
that time new music was an expensive luxury,
and those who would provide themselves with it
had to make copies of printed scores.   In this
Isaac Pitman engaged with great diligence, and
there are in existence manuscript books containing
hundreds of pages of music written by him with
remarkable neatness and accuracy. When but
seventeen, he played the organ at Conigree Chapel,
Trowbridge, for a period during the absence of the
regular organist.   At Bath he received lessons on
the organ from Mr. George Field.   Loving vocal
music even more than instrumental, he joined the
Bath Sacred Harmonic Society, conducted by Mr
Bianchi Taylor, in which he sang bass.   As the
claims of the Writing and Printing Reform more
and more engrossed his time, however, he gave up
the cultivation of his musical ability, although he

frequently attended concerts, and occasionally wrote critiques of them for the Bath newspapers. He had a preference for sacred music and delighted most in the works of Handel.

In association with Isaac Pitman's musical efforts Mr. Reed has preserved a specimen of his work as a composer. " In his youth," Mr. Reed says, " Isaac Pitman indulged his love of harmony so far as to compose a hymn tune, an anthem on Isaiah xlix. 13-17, and the following tune to be sung to a hymn which appeared in the *Bath and Cheltenham Gazette* for 26th July, 1831 :—

When the bu-sy day is done, And up-on his couch the sun

.Rests, his course of glo-ry run, Sancte Spi - ri - tus, be with me,

Sanc - te Spir - it - us, be with me.

SANCTE SPIRITUS.

When the busy day is done,
And upon his couch the sun
Rests, his course of glory run,
    Sancte Spiritus be with me.

When the twilight shadow falls
O'er the humming waterfalls,
And zephyr unto zephyr calls,
    Sancte Spiritus be with me.

When the vesper murmurs come
Through the leaf, and from the tomb,
From the sunset's crimson gloom,
    Sancte Spiritus be with me.

When the moon is roaming high,
Like a seraph, through the sky,
And the one white cloud floats by,
    Sancte Spiritus be with me.

When the stars, those jewels rare,
Fill with diamond-lights the air,
And comes on the hour of prayer,
    Sancte Spiritus be with me.

Then when knees are truly bent,
And the hands are clasp'd intent,
And the voice to heaven is sent,
    Sancte Spiritus be with me.

—H. C. DEAKIN

" The anthem was arranged thus :—' *Chorus*—Sing, O heavens ; and be joyful, O earth ; break forth into singing, O mountains ; for the Lord hath comforted his people, and will have mercy upon his afflicted. *Solo, plaintive*—But Zion said, the Lord hath forsaken me, and my Lord hath forgotten me. *Duet, for two Trebles*—Can a woman forget her suckling child, that she should

not have compassion on the son of her womb ?
Yea, they may forget, yet will I not forget thee.
Chorus—Behold, I have graven thee on the palms
of my hands ; thy walls are continually before me.'
It was sung with much éclat, his brother Jacob
says, on the other side of the globe." In this
country, however, it does not appear to have been
rendered. The anthem was composed at the age
of sixteen.

When the discussion on the subject of uniform-
ity of musical pitch arose out of a report of
the Committee appointed by the Council of the
Society of Arts in June, 1859, Isaac Pitman drew
up a table showing the number of vibrations of
each note in comparison with every other note
in the octave (the lowest in whole numbers), which
he published in the *Phonetic Journal* for 29th
September, 1860, together with an account of
the proceedings at the meeting of the Society of
Arts held to receive and discuss the Committee's
report. As every student of musical acoustics
knows, the pitch of a note depends upon the number of vibrations produced in a given time. The
C produced by a 32 ft. organ pipe (said to be the
lowest possible music note) is the result of sixteen
double or thirty-two single vibrations per second ;
the octave above, or the lowest C of a grand
pianoforte, of thirty-two double vibrations ; the
lowest C of a violoncello of sixty-four ; tenor C of
128 ; middle C of the pianoforte of 256 ; and the
C on the treble stave of 512. The intermediate

notes are the results of vibrations represented by intermediate numbers, always increasing with the rise of the pitch. Isaac Pitman's table was as follows :—

	C below treble stave	D	E	F	G	A	B	C 3rd space treble stave
C 3rd space treble stave	2.1	16.9	8.5	3.2	4.3	6.5	16.15	
B	15.8	5.3	3.2	45.32	5.4	9.8		15.16
A	5.3	40.27	4.3	5.4	10.9		8.9	5.6
G	3.2	4.3	6.5	9.8		9.10	4.5	3.4
F	4.3	32.27	16.15		8.9	4.5	32.45	2.3
E	5.4	10.9		15.16	5.6	3.4	2.3	5.8
D	9.8		9.10	27.32	3.4	27.40	3.5	9.16
C below treble stave		8.9	4.5	3.4	2.3	3.5	8.15	1.2

The table, it was explained, is to be used like
a multiplication table ; thus, lower C with G above
gives the vibrations as two to three, while the next
note D, with A above, gives twenty-seven to forty,
etc.   In the chord D, F sharp, A, the vibrations
of A, to agree with the chord C, E, G, should be
forty-and-a-half instead of forty, or D should be
twenty-six and three-quarters instead of twenty-
seven.   We thus see, says Isaac Pitman, a mathe-
matical demonstration of the distinction which
every musical ear feels in the perfection, or round-
ness, of the C chord, compared with the chord
of upper D, F sharp, A ; and of the difference in
quality, as it may be called, between the various
" keys," ranging from C natural, through G with
one sharp, F with one flat, D with two sharps, B
flat with two flats, A with three sharps, A flat with
four flats, and E with four sharps, etc.

Probably few men of his generation so con-
sistently lived the simple life as Isaac Pitman.
His dietary was limited to three moderate meals
per day from the fruits of the earth ; of alcoholic
liquors he never partook, and until late in life it
was not his custom even to drink tea ; he did not
smoke, and had a pronounced antipathy to the
use of tobacco by others.   At the public luncheons
and banquets which he attended he never departed
from his simple vegetarian dietary, a fact over
which the gourmands present were apt to chortle, [1]

---

[1] When the Lord Mayor of London entertained the International Shorthand Congress to luncheon at the Mansion House,

forgetting that with Isaac Pitman " plain living " meant a wonderful measure of bodily health and high spirits, and total freedom from the ailments which attend on so-called " generous living." He was for many years a supporter and a Vice-President of the Vegetarian Society. His experience was embodied in a letter he addressed to *The Times* in 1879, which ran as follows :—

Ser,—A frend sujests tu me that I ought tu reit a leter tu *The Times*, plasing mei leif-eksperiens in kontrast with the editorial suming-up on Mr W. Gibson-Ward's vejetarian leter in *The Times* ov last Thurzday. The konkluzhon areivd at iz : " So long az no speshal kall iz tu be made on the strength, a piurli vejetabel deiet may sufeiz." Az mei leif haz been wun ov eksepshonal aktiviti, the fakt that it haz been maintaind on a vejetabel deiet ought tu be known, nou that a diskushon on deiet haz been admited intu *The Times*.

Mei deietetik eksperiens iz simpli this,—Abuv forti yearz ago dispepsia woz kariing me tu the grave. Medikal adveizerz rekomended animal food three teimz a day insted ov wuns, and a glas ov wein. On this rejimen I woz nuthing beterd but rather grew wurs. I avoided the meat and the wein, gradiuali rekuverd mei dijestiv pouer, and hav never sins nown, bei eni pain, that I hav a stumak.

Isaac Pitman's vegetarianism—he partook of a potato and a glass of water—attracted the attention of his Lordship's Chaplain, who wrote impromptu the following Latin epigram which he handed to Mr. Reed :—

Vina negat ; ventri indulget non omne legumen ;
Angulus ingenio multus ubique latet,
Ast ubi jam cœpit tabulas implere capaces
Verba fluunt : scriptis angulus omnis abest.

(He refuses wine, and eats only vegetables ; many angles are to be found in his mind, but when he writes the words flow and every angle disappears.)

Theze forti yearz hav been spent in kontiniuus labor in konekshon with the invenshon and propagashon ov mei sistem ov fonetik shorthand and fonetik speling, korespondens, and the editorial diutiz ov mei weekli Jurnal. Though siksti-feiv [66] yearz ov aje, I kontiniu the kustom I hav folowd all through this period, ov beïng at mei ofis at siks in the morning, sumer and winter. Til I woz fifti yearz ov aje I never tuk a holiday, or felt that I wonted wun ; and for about twenti yearz in the ferst part ov this period I woz at mei desk fourteen ourz a day, from siks in the morning til ten at neit, with two ourz out for mealz. Twenti yearz ago I began tu leav of at siks in the evening.

I attribiut mei helth and pouer ov endiurans tu abstinens from flesh meat and alkoholik drinks. I kan kum tu no uther konkluzhon when I see the efekt ov such ekstended ourz ov labor on uther men who eat meat and drink wein or beer.

I hav riten mei leter fonetikali, az iz mei kustom, and shal feel obleijd if it be aloud thus tu apear in *The Times.*

EIZAK PITMAN.

Fonetik Institiut, Bath, 27 Janiueri, 1879.

He bore somewhat similar testimony in a contribution to a work entitled " Study and Stimulants," edited by Mr. A. Arthur Reade, containing the personal experiences of many eminent men, which was published in 1883. " From my own experience," he wrote, " of the benefits of abstaining from the sedative alcohol, and the stimulants tobacco and snuff ; and my observations of the effects of these things on persons who indulge in them, I have a firm conviction that they exercise a deadly influence on the human race." Isaac Pitman's repugnance to tobacco led him at times to a very active campaign against the offending

weed. In 1895 he addressed a circular to the
members of the Bath Town Council on the subject,
which may be quoted here as typical of his attitude
towards tobacco. " The bright days," he wrote,
" when the breezes from our hills will not be
polluted by tobacco smoke as they descend into
the streets of our beautiful city may be very distant ; but that the change will come I have no
doubt. Such a change of public opinion and practise as would permit the Council to enact a by-law
against smoking in the streets *may* begin by a
perusal, by the Council, of the Anti-Tobacco
literature which I have the pleasure of sending."

For the autograph hunter Isaac Pitman had
the keenest aversion. No man probably ever
wrote so many letters to unknown correspondents
as he did in shorthand on matters relating to his
system, or in reformed spelling on questions
concerning that branch of his work. But he had
a great contempt for the trifler who wrote " to
know if you would give me one of your autographs,
as I am collecting them, and should like to have
one of yours in my collection." For all such he
had prepared a printed tract which dealt in somewhat trenchant fashion with " the power of being
a nuisance." A copy of this was addressed by a
junior clerk to the autograph hunter, who, if he
was disappointed in his quest, at least received
wholesome advice on the error of his ways.

There was at different times a certain *rapproche-
ment* of Phonography and Phrenology, which

probably arose from the fact that in the early part of Isaac Pitman's career a good many people were enthusiastic students and advocates of the two subjects. At any rate, both were associated in the denunciation of the Rev. E. Bickersteth, to which reference has already been made. Isaac Pitman's interest in Phrenology no doubt arose in the first place from his contact with Mr. L. N. Fowler, of the firm of Messrs. Fowler and Wells, of New York, who was a well-known exponent of it in the early days of Phonography. In later years he submitted his head for examination several times, and lastly, towards the close of his life, he was " phrenologically examined," by Mr. James Webb, a past President of the British Phrenological Association, whose report was "privately printed" in the form of a pamphlet. Mr. Webb's examination, with the aid of measuring tape and calipers, was also a semi-interview, in which Isaac Pitman mentioned some of the facts of his life and gave expression to a few opinions. Mr. Webb himself notes certain data which are worthy of reproduction. He found that Isaac Pitman's head was large, which was due not only to the circumference of nearly 23 in., but to the large coronal development from the root of the nose to the occiput of $12\frac{1}{4}$ in. Mr. Webb also noted the transparency of his skin, the exceeding fineness of his hair, and the clearness and purity of his eyes. At the time of this examination Isaac Pitman was in his eighty-third year.

The investigation does not appear to have disclosed any appreciation for art. His brother Benn says that " Isaac was somewhat deficient in æsthetic taste. He was precise, orderly, methodical, and clean in body and mind ; and with a simplicity and directness of soul that we look for only in the innocency of childhood. But he had little appreciation of, or care for, things of beauty, or of the fine art works." Against this criticism it is only just to Isaac Pitman to mention his great interest in the *Art Journal*, and his anticipation of a time when he should enjoy the perusal of a set of the volumes of this magazine, which he took much pleasure in completing and in binding in a style befitting the artistic treasures the volumes contained. And the testimony of his brother Henry deserves to be quoted : " Isaac had intense love for all things beautiful. Why did he visit the Art Treasures Exhibition at Manchester ? He spent many hours there examining the pictures."

A point in Mr. Webb's delineation indicated an amiable weakness. His " Caution " was large but somewhat eccentric in action, so that there was some likelihood of his being deceived by the plausible, etc. Isaac Pitman was, in fact, inclined to trust a little too readily to the truthfulness of those who aroused his sympathy. A single instance may be mentioned. At the time when the feelings of the nation were excited by the sufferings of the Poles, there came to Bath a certain individual who described himself as a Polish refugee. Isaac Pitman went to the trouble and expense of printing the man's story for circulation among the benevolent, but it was afterwards found that the interesting stranger was not what he represented himself to be.

One day, when the subject of this "Life" was absent from home, an American gentleman presented himself at his private residence and informed the astonished maid that he was Isaac Pitman! Later on the two Isaac Pitmans had an opportunity of fraternizing. Although they were not doubles in the sense of having a personal resemblance, they yet possessed many striking similarities. This will be best indicated by the reproduction of a letter which Dr. Thomas Hill, a former President of Harvard University, wrote to Mr. Benn Pitman, as follows :—

WALTHAM, MASS.,

22nd June, 1891.

I have wanted to tell you, if I have not done so, of a curious coincidence. Professor Barber, at Meadville, told me that when he was in Somerville, Mass., he had a parishioner named Isaac Pitman, a very enthusiastic phonographer. This American Pitman went to England, and while there called on your brother Isaac Pitman. The two men had been born and brought up on opposite sides of the Atlantic, but were of no known relationship. But they were of the same age, of the same name, with the same zeal for Shorthand, with the same devotion to Swedenborg, and with the same adherence to two or three other isms ; Professor Barber thinks that homeopathy and vegetarianism were among them. This is, it seems to me, a very curious set of coincidences, and would seem to indicate the probability of mental peculiarity inherited from a common ancestor several generations back.

It was in the early seventies that the American Isaac Pitman visited the Inventor of Phonography. The American namesake's death occurred on the 3rd April, 1895, and the notice of it in the American papers led some people to suppose that the English holder of the famous name had at that time departed this life, an idea which was promptly contradicted by the newspaper correspondents.

XXIV

1895-1897

ON a wintry day at the beginning of 1895, when Bath was covered with a mantle of snow, Mrs. Sarah A. Tooley paid a visit to the city, and had an interview with the Inventor of Phonography at the Royal Crescent, an account of which was soon afterwards published in *The Young Man* under the title of " Sir Isaac Pitman at Home."

" Now I knew," Mrs. Tooley wrote, " that the morrow (4th January) was the eighty-second (third) birthday of the Grand Old Man of Phonography, and had he received me in an easy chair by the fireside it would have seemed the most natural thing possible on a cold afternoon in midwinter. Instead, I found him in his study, seated at his writing-table immersed in correspondence, and with no apparent thought about fire. He rose quickly to greet me in his simple, kindly way, and I saw that though his back was slightly bent, and his hair and beard were white as the snow outside, his eye was bright and keen, and his face ruddy as a winter's apple. His speech is rapid and clear, but he is so full of action, and has so many things crowding in upon his mind, that it is with difficulty he talks upon one subject for any length of time. Small wonder that, with his active temperament, he early discovered longhand

318

AUSTRALIAN ADDRESS PRESENTED IN 1894

NO. 17 ROYAL CRESCENT, BATH

to be an unmitigated nuisance, and the ordinary method of spelling an unendurable bore. After being in Sir Isaac Pitman's company for five minutes, I was amazed, not that he had taught people to write at more than two hundred words a minute, but that he had not also invented a 'shorthand' form of speech."

A graphic sketch of Sir Isaac's career followed, and then the interviewer proceeded :—

"I had been talking with Sir Isaac in his handsome dining-room, but I wished to see him in his own special sanctum, and he kindly led the way to what I should call a 'study,' but he prefers the designation of 'office'; 'I do not study,' he said, 'I only work.' The office is a long room, with writing and other tables running down the centre. At the window sits Sir Isaac at his desk ; rows of neatly kept pigeon holes surmount his table, and above them is a handsome testimonial in an oak frame, presented to him by the shorthand writers of Australia, as a mark of their appreciation of his lifelong services to Phonography, and also as a congratulatory tribute to him upon his recent knighthood. Sir Isaac jumped nimbly on to the table and brought down the testimonial for my inspection. Well-filled book-cases cover every available inch of the room. Above the book-cases are the seven cartoons of Raphael, and over the largest book-case is a bust of Milton. Phonetic literature lies in piles on the tables and floor, but there is no disorder. . . . Directly Sir Isaac enters his office it seems that he must sit down to his table to write, and it is deeply interesting to note the truly wingèd swiftness with which he makes the signs of Phonography.   He showed me with pride a letter in shorthand from Archbishop Walsh, of Dublin, a disciple of whom he is very proud."*

Few indeed are the number of reformers who, having passed their eightieth year, have still the inclination and the strength to work for their cause as they did in earlier years.   Isaac Pitman has this unique distinction, for it may be said with truth that from the time he set his hand to the Spelling Reform in the early forties until the closing days of his life he never relaxed his efforts. After the date of his retirement from partnership with his sons, until the final phase of his last illness —a period of nearly two years and a half—he worked for the Spelling Reform with unabated persistency, and expended more than one thousand pounds a year in the promotion of the cause. For the accommodation of a publishing staff his " office " at the Royal Crescent was unsuited ; the Phonetic Institute was too distant from his home to permit of his personal attendance there to supervise whatever work he had in hand. Accordingly in March, 1895, he engaged two spacious rooms on the first floor at No. 43 Milsom Street, the leading business thoroughfare in Bath, and there opened The Institute of Spelling Reform.

---

* The Archbishop when on a visit to Bath some time previously had called on Isaac Pitman at the Phonetic Institute.

The new office was an easy distance from the Royal Crescent, but as his power of walking had greatly diminished, he availed himself of wheel-chair conveyance when he felt that he needed this assistance. " I have now recovered my wonted health," he wrote in July, " and am at my desk as of old at six o'clock in the morning."

In the autumn of this year Isaac Pitman was visited for the last time by his old disciple, Mr. Reed. Fifty-two years had passed over the heads of both of them since the latter, then a stripling of sixteen, made his earliest visit to the first Institute established in the city of Bath. As on that occasion, he found Isaac Pitman at his desk promoting the Reform with his ever-ready pen, and around him as of old was a staff engaged in the distribution of its literature. Mr. Reed enters into details, and some of these may be quoted as typical of the work which was carried on from day to day to the end. He found Isaac Pitman in Milsom Street superintending the distribution of a letter and literature on Spelling Reform which was being sent to the 28,000 members and 5,000 officers of the National Union of Teachers at a cost of over £200. " Nothing," he exclaims, " could be more characteristic of his marvellous energy and patient toil. For this outlay of time, labour, and money he will not receive a penny return ; the only recompense he seeks being the satisfaction of contributing to the removal of the ' Spelling Difficulty ' which—to use his own words—' broods like a nightmare over all branches of education.' It was in this persistent, determined way that more than half a century ago he sent forth Phonography into the world, and laid the foundation for its becoming co-extensive with the English language. His phonographic enterprise brought him fame and material means, both well deserved. The latter he has, for years past, liberally dispensed, and is still dispensing, in furtherance of his darling project of lessening the toils of infancy, and removing a standing reproach from the noble English tongue. I confess that, familiar as I am with his indomitable perseverance, I am amazed at the energy he still displays."

In addition to his efforts on behalf of Spelling Reform, Isaac Pitman manifested during these years considerable activity in another direction. He desired to make certain changes in Phonography, which would have had the effect of turning the system as it exists in the present day into the Tenth Edition of 1857, while at least one of the proposals showed a reversion to a much earlier edition. A protracted and strenuous controversy arose over the project which—whatever its merits or demerits—would without question have disastrously affected the progress of the art. Its inventor did not realize that the day for making fundamental changes in his system had passed now that Phonography had taken its place among educational subjects which are universally taught. The proposals were finally submitted to a

committee of phonographic experts, and as their
verdict was unfavourable to the alterations, it
was not considered advisable to change the presentation of the system—a decision, however, in
which the originator of Phonography did not
acquiesce.

For the promotion of the projects enumerated
above Isaac Pitman in January, 1895, began the
publication of a new monthly periodical which
he named *The Speler*. This was designed for the
promotion of six objects, which were set forth
under the title. The first three related to the
inculcation of Swedenborgian belief and practice,
and in this association he published, under the
heading of " Reminiscences," a full account of
his reception of the New Church doctrines nearly
sixty years before. The fourth object was Spelling
Reform, *The Speler* being printed throughout in
the " First Stage " style, with articles explaining or
advocating the method. The fifth object was Shorthand, and was devoted chiefly to advocacy of the
changes he was now proposing. The sixth object
was Peace, and included matter relating to the
objects and aims of the Peace Society. The
" Reminiscences " and some other contributions
in *The Speler*, were reproduced in book form.

Isaac Pitman's last appearance on a public
platform in advocacy of the Spelling Reform was
at a meeting of the Bath branch of the National
Union of Teachers on 20th June, 1896, when " the
oldest British schoolmaster alive " delivered to an

interested audience a lucid address on the need
and practicability of orthographic reform.

On the 8th September, 1896, a statement
appeared in the newspapers which was received
with widespread expressions of regret wherever the
English language is spoken. It announced that
the state of health of the venerable Inventor of
Phonography was occasioning considerable anxiety
to his family. He was again suffering from
congestion of the lungs, and although in about a
month's time he was able to leave his bed, there
was no recovery of strength, and during the
autumn he gradually grew weaker. At Michael-
mas the family removed from No. 12 to No. 17
Royal Crescent, and the move was effected without
occasioning the smallest discomfort to the invalid,
who was indeed greatly interested in it.   "It is
often said," it was observed in the *Bath Herald* at
the beginning of December, " that hope on the
part of the patient has an excellent effect, and,
if that is so, Sir Isaac possesses a very valuable
quality, for he would be the last to give way. . . .
He is, however, quite confined to his bed and
sitting rooms, which open one into the other,
and finds his daily self-imposed task of inditing a
few letters and dictating others to a clerk, all
that his strength can accomplish, and even this
sometimes occasions great exhaustion."

Throughout his last illness the serenity and
cheerfulness of mind displayed by Isaac Pitman
made a striking impression on his many friends.

His increasing bodily weakness was felt by the veteran worker, but it was not a theme of complaint, or of despondency. Writing to his brother Henry at this time he said, " I must expect a continual decrease of strength until the heart gives its last pulsation, and the angelic messengers who wait on the dying draw out the spiritual body from this one. Then I shall have a sound heart, and get to work in my new sphere of life."   On his 85th birthday, on the 4th January, 1897, he was in excellent spirits, but being very feeble, he was wheeled in an armchair into the sitting room adjoining his bedroom, where many friends visited him to offer sympathetic congratulations. The day was wintry, and on grasping the hand of one of his visitors the veteran observed that the weather must be cold : " They take so much care of me," he added, alluding to the warmth of the room, " that I am not aware of the cold out of doors."   After his birthday increasing weakness gave to Isaac Pitman unmistakable warning that his earthly career had almost run its course. He arranged for the January issue of his periodical, and he then performed the last public act of his life, by presenting through Mr. J. W. Morris, a valuable collection of works of reference to the Bath Corporation, which had at that time realized one portion at least of the scheme for which he had worked with Mr. Morris in earlier years, by establishing a Free Reference Library in the Municipal Buildings.

His death occurred at ten minutes to eight o'clock on the morning of Friday, 22nd January, 1897 ; he was free from pain, and conscious almost to the last. On the eve of the final summons he had simply and touchingly described his end in a message he entrusted to the Rev. Gordon Drummond, at that time the Minister of the New Church at Bath, which was in these words :—

" To those who ask how Isaac Pitman passed away, say, Peacefully, and with no more concern than in passing from one room into another to take up some further employment."

XXV

His long illness had prepared Isaac Pitman's many friends and disciples for the inevitable end, but to numbers of those who had been in frequent communication with him till within a day or two of his death, there seemed a sense of unreality in the announcement. Could it be true that the hand of the unwearied worker in the cause of brief writing and spelling reform, and of many movements designed for spiritual or social amelioration, was for ever still ? The Press of the country which told the story of his life and gave its estimate of his work left no room for doubt. Most of those who dealt with his career in the newspapers were writers of Phonography, and there were here and there indications that they felt the loss of one whose art had aided them so much as though it were that of a personal friend. From all parts of the world, from individuals and from societies, expressions of sympathy reached Lady Pitman and her sons.

The funeral service was held at the New Church, Henry Street, Bath, on Wednesday morning, 27th January, and was attended by the Mayor of Bath (Mr. G. Woodiwiss) and a large and representative company of the citizens of Bath. After the service the body was conveyed to Woking for

cremation, in compliance with the following
direction left by Isaac Pitman : " I desire that on
my departure to the spiritual world my body may
be cremated, as a more wholesome and more
pleasant manner of disposal than burial in the
earth." There was on the following day (Thursday) a service in the hall attached to the Woking
Crematorium, which was conducted by the Rev.
J. Ashby (President of the New Church Conference) and the Rev. Gordon Drummond. After
cremation, the ashes of the departed were preserved in a casket of bronze, which is in the keeping
of his family.

Simultaneously with the proceedings at Woking
a large congregation assembled at a Memorial
Service at the New Church, Argyle Square,
London, which was conducted by the Rev. A.
Faraday. A similar Memorial Service was held
at the Bath Abbey Church, and was attended by
the Mayor and a number of leading citizens.
From the pulpit of the venerable Abbey Church,
the then Rector of Bath, afterwards Bishop of
Sheffield (Dr. Quirk), had on the previous Sunday
morning paid an eloquent tribute to the departed,
and had spoken of his career as an illustration of
self-sacrifice.

Isaac Pitman's system is his best memorial, but
record must here be made of honours paid to his
memory. The Corporation of the City of Bath
marks with suitable mural tablets the dwellings of
celebrities of the historic past, but on 15th July,

1901, it placed on the house where Isaac Pitman died the first tablet erected to a worthy well known to the majority of those who assembled at the

MEMORIAL TABLET PLACED BY THE BATH CORPORATION ON NO. 17 ROYAL CRESCENT, BATH

unveiling ceremony, which was performed by Mr. Arthur W. à Beckett (President of the Institute of Journalists).

Directly after the death of the Inventor of Phonography a movement was initiated with a view to the provision of a permanent national memorial. Twelve hundred friends and admirers in all parts of the world contributed, and it was decided that the memorial should take the form of a portrait in oils. The work was undertaken by Mr. Arthur S. Cope, R.A., who produced a portrait universally acknowledged to be an admirable likeness. A photogravure from this portrait forms the frontispiece of the present volume. In July, 1908, the Memorial Committee offered the portrait to the Trustees of the National Portrait Gallery, London, by whom it was accepted. It is hung in Room XVIII, the central corridor on the first floor.

A memorial window subscribed for by Isaac Pitman's co-religionists was unveiled in the New Church, Henry Street, Bath, in 1909, the service being largely attended by those taking part in a Joint Conference of the national phonographic societies then in session at Bath. The subject of the window, which is at the left side of the altar, is a symbolical figure guarding the Open Word from profanation. Below the window is a brass plate bearing the following inscription :—

" Now it is permitted to enter intellectually into the mysteries of faith." Swedenborg, T.C.R., 508.

The above window was dedicated to the glory of God and in memory of the late Sir Isaac Pitman, the Inventor of Phonography, one of the original trustees of this Church, and for ten years its honoured President (1887–1897).

5th September, 1909.

In the many estimates of the life work of Isaac Pitman which appeared in the Press of the world at the time of his death, there was no truer observation than that of the *Cologne Gazette*—representative of German opinion—that in the two directions of stenography and phonetic spelling " he must be reckoned among those who have exercised an unusually great and happy influence upon their race." An American estimate was expressed at a somewhat earlier period by the Rev. Edward Everett Hale, who in remarking on the gratitude due to Isaac Pitman from the English speaking race, pointed out that " the step forward in written language, which was due to his ingenuity, his science, his steadfast perseverance, is a step which marks, not only the literature of our time, but its commercial transactions, its mechanical work, and quite as directly its scientific activity."

A moment's reflection will show that Isaac Pitman's achievement is unique, and that its success has been phenomenal. The majority of the systems of English shorthand have passed into oblivion, or are practised only by a few, while the method of writing for which the world is indebted to his genius has come into universal use. In the United Kingdom, except in the most thinly populated parts, it is everywhere taught ; it is practised in Africa, wherever the English language has penetrated ; in India votaries of the art are found from Colombo to the Himalayas; in Australia Phonography has been taught and practised as long as in the old country. Across the Atlantic we find the method held in high esteem both in Canada and in the United States, and universally employed ; in South America it is in general use in Spanish adaptations. What is said of the British Empire may be said of Pitman's Phonography—the sun never sets upon it.

To an age which appreciates time and labour saving inventions Isaac Pitman's shorthand appeals with especial force. But to his strenuous advocacy of the much needed reform in our spelling it has been comparatively indifferent. Some day, and possibly sooner than anticipated, the reform of our orthography will become a practical question. When that time arrives the lifelong labours of Isaac Pitman in this direction will not have been in vain.

(From *The Literary World.*)

IN MEMORIAM.

SIR ISAAC PITMAN.

Say, Mercury is dead! He whom the gods
Deputed to the task of teaching men
The way to quicken thought, to give it wings,
And bind the broken fragments of discourse.
Not in this age shall honour due be paid
To him who more than most helped to advance
The human race along the paths of peace.
Succeeding generations will proclaim
With clearer voice the victory he won—
Will rank him higher than the men who slew
Their fellow-men in thousands on the field,
Or grabb'd at honours in a Party's cause,
With self the sole objective unconfessed.

F.

APPENDIX I

A REPRINT OF " STENOGRAPHIC SOUND-HAND."
By Isaac Pitman.
(1837).

SHORT-HAND,*

FOUNDED ON

" WALKER'S PRINCIPLES OF ENGLISH
PRONUNCIATION."

INTRODUCTION.

1. THAT Short-hand is an invaluable acquirement, every one
practically possessed of it is convinced ; and without making one's
self liable to the charge of arrogancy, it may be asserted, that
the person who makes a regular use of it, is raised almost as
high above the individual who knows only long-hand, as the
man of science with the powers of steam at his beck, is above the
common labourer. In this " Introduction " we shall speak of
the art apart from any particular system ; we shall show in its
proper place the excellency of *this* system with regard to *writing
by sound,* and how former Stenographers have failed here ; also,
that though it is capable of expressing by a single mark every
sound in the language, pure or mixed, it is at the same time
*the plainest practical plan of putting pen to paper for the production
of peerless poems or profound and powerful prose for the press or
for private pursuits, ever published.* As some of our readers will
not go beyond the " Introduction," we are anxious to set before
them at once the beauty and simplicity of the system here
recommended to their notice. In plate 2, at the right hand
corner, are some Short-hand " Examples ; " they will find the
above alliterative sentence written in the first three lines, from
1 a to 3 g.

2. The thousand advantages accompanying the practice of this
art, and the power of usefulness which it gives, it is impossible
to enumerate here. Two or three only shall be specified. FIRST.
In literature you may make extracts at little expense of time and
paper, from books which cannot be obtained, either because of

---

* Facsimiles of the plates which accompanied this work are given between
pp. 34 and 35 *ante,* and a facsimile of the cover faces p. 40.

their high price or scarcity. SECOND. Every composer finds that frequently his thoughts outstrip his pen, and many embryo ideas perish as soon as they are conceived, there being no means for their delivery according to our present circuitous mode of writing. Here Short-hand steps in, and adds a sevenfold celerity to writing, enabling it to keep pace with invention, and by its reflex power quickens the conception and delivery of future thoughts. THIRD. It is a short way of keeping copies of letters and memoranda of all important events. You want to write to your friend—and you have enough on the tip of your tongue just now to fill a sheet. Get your letter-book, and make your thoughts appear in dots and strokes ; while doing it you will be thankful that you can save all that which, without the assistance of Short-hand, would evaporate ; and you will need no other proof of the last-named advantage. At your leisure transcribe it in long-hand, and post it. This is the writer's constant practice. To the clergy, to barristers, and all who attend courts of law, to journalists and travellers, the science is invaluable ; and when fairly written, it is more easily read than long-hand. The FOURTH advantage is so well known and appreciated, that it shall be merely named—taking down lectures, speeches, and sermons, either in full, or according to their heads and divisions. Speaking in a general way, without Stenography, there would be no reporters—without reporters, no newspapers—without news-papers, no readers—and without readers, England would be thrown back two or three centuries in the march of civilisation. FIFTH. By the practice of Short-hand there is a great saving of time. A Stenographer can accomplish in eight or ten minutes, (according to his proficiency,) what would occupy him an hour if he were ignorant of it. The amazing increase of power, and the additional means of doing good, which may be calculated upon, under this head, are incredible. Take a very common case. Suppose a man, who, in addition to his daily avocation, employs an hour a day in composing books for the instruction and benefit of mankind ; with Short-hand he is able to write six times as much as by common hand ; and there is no doubt that his inventive powers will keep pace with his pen. He need not transcribe it himself, this may be done by a school-boy. Esti-mating then that he spends fifty years of his " threescore years and ten " in this work (which it is very likely will be productive of more good to the community than his manual labour during the remaining part of the day) he accomplishes in his life the work of 300 years !   Reader, " Persevere."

STENOGRAPHY.

3. The name of this science is derived from two Greek words, STENOS, *short* ; and GRAPHE, *a writing*. Common writing enables

us to make our thoughts appear on paper ; Stenography or Short-hand does the same, with one seventh of the time and trouble ; and, according to this system, with seventy times seven as much consistency.

The strange title prefixed to this system, " Stenographic Sound-hand," may perhaps require a little explanation. It is a *system of Short-hand, shorter than any practical system yet published ; and the words are written exactly as they are pronounced.* Systems of short-hand that depend for their existence upon *staves* like music, or even on a *single line*, by which the letters have a three-fold power of expressing different words *above*, *on*, or *below* the line, seeing that short-hand is generally written without lines, and without the possibility of getting any, such systems are certainly *practicable*, but they are not *practical ;* and this is the highest censure that can be passed upon them. Systems containing letters of different sizes, or the same size more or less curved, are equally objectionable.

4. Every language is composed of two kinds of sounds. The first class is formed simply by opening the mouth to a greater or less degree, and making the voice to issue. These are called *vowels*, or *vocal sounds*, as *e*, *o*. Sometimes two of them coalesce, as *e*, *oo*, forming *u*, or *au*, *e*, in *boy*. These are called *diphthongs*, or *two sounds*. Those of the second class cannot be formed unless a vowel be joined to them. Their pronunciation consists in pressing together different parts of the mouth, such as the lips, the teeth, the tongue, the palate, etc., and making a vowel sound either before or after the concussion of the organs, as *b*, which is made by a pressure of the lips, and impelling the breath against them ; still there is no sound till the vowel *e* is heard. *P* is produced in the same way, by a brisker appulse of the organs. In sounding *m* the vowel is heard *first*, then the lips close as for *b*, and the sound is continued through the nose. These letters are called *consonants*, that is, letters *sounding with* others.

It is neither necessary nor possible here to enter into an examination of *all* the letters, as to their names and manner of formation ; this is already well done in the work mentioned at the head of these remarks ; our object is merely to put them down on paper, in the simplest and most expeditious form possible.

5. Two of the consonants, called *liquids* or *melting letters*, namely, *l* and *r*, possess the peculiar privilege of coalescing with the others without the intervention of a vowel : so that the two are pronounced as one. Example : the word *bless* is pronounced by closing the lips and forcing the breath against them for *b* ; then placing the tip of the tongue to the gums of the upper teeth for *l ;* and causing both to be enunciated in the following vowel, *e*, sounded as *a*. All this is done as quickly, and with as little effort as if it were only a single letter ; *s* closes the sound, and completes the word. *L* unites with five letters in this manner, and *r* with

nine, and there are thousands of words in which these combinations occur. There are also a few others which may be seen in Plate 1.

6. To every utterance of the voice forming a vowel or diphthong, and every consonant, single or double, we have here given a simple mark. The vowel and diphthongal sounds are written according to the order of nature, beginning with the simplest, requiring the least opening of the mouth, *e* (heard in *see*). A wider opening makes *a* (*say*). The next sound in order is *a* (*mar*) [Note a.] By expanding the organs a little more the broad German *a* (*all*) is produced. This sound is expressed by *au*. Contracting the sides of the mouth a little, *o* (*no*) is formed, and by bringing the organs into a round shape, we have *oo* (*do, too*). These six vocal sounds have corresponding short ones. The diphthongs are *i, u, oi*, and *ou*, which being mixed sounds cannot be shortened. That the short sounds of *i* and *u* are miscalled so will appear by and by. *I* is composed of *a e, u* is *e oo, oi* is *au e*, and *ou* is *au oo*, pronounced as quickly as possible. What are commonly called diphthongs and triphthongs, as *oa* in *boat, eau* in *beauty*, are so only to the eye.

7. The Short-hand marks for these letters, are as simple and as orderly placed as their sounds. The first three are made by a *dot*, placed at the beginning, the middle, and the end of the consonant with which it is associated. The next three, which are of a broader sound, have the dot made broad, that is, *a short stroke*. Three of the diphthongs have a *curve*, or half of a small circle, and the other a *small angle*. The " wheel-about " shape of these four corresponds very well to their " turn-about " sound ; and if the language should ever become receptive of two more such, we have angular situations for them. These marks must point in that direction which renders them most conspicuous. A *long* vowel is made with a *heavy* dot or stroke, and a *short* vowel by a *light* one. With respect to situation, the places are counted downwards with perpendicular and leaning down strokes ; from left to right with horizontal letters ; and upwards with *h, l, r,* and *y.* Though *s* may be made up or down, as expedition or beauty of conjunction may dictate, let the vowels' places be always counted downwards when it stands without another consonant in a word. In other situations it must follow the general rule.

8. The correct sound of these six long vowels, six short ones, and four diphthongs, which are all that are to be found in the language, will be understood from these words, which are written in the examples, plate 2, (3h..4 i). *Tea tin, pay pet, father fat, daw dot, show shut, coo could, fine, duke, boy, vow.* All these sounds may be discovered in the following sentence : " Fear thou the Lord in thy youth, hate and avoid evil, love and pursue good, and so walk in the paths of life." This is pronounced, and according to our system would be written in full, thus : Fēr ᴛʜou ᴛʜă Lăŭrd ĕn ᴛʜi yōōth, hāt ănd ăvoid ēvl lŏv ănd pŏrsu

gŏŏd ǎnd sō wāūk ĕn thǎ pǎтнz ǎüv lif (5 a..7 c.). [b]. There
are very few words in our language whose sound is composed
of the sound of the letters ; and to surmount the difficulty of
acquiring a proper pronunciation is the most arduous task in
ascending the hill of knowledge, especially when we remember
that it must be done in youth. Stenographers have endeavoured
to remedy this evil, and have directed their pupils to *spell as
they pronounce.* This has been attended to generally, with
respect to the consonants, but they have made no distinction
between the vowel in *pate & pat, hall & hat, seat & set, pine & pin,
bony & bonny, tune & tun* [c]. In these pairs, besides the difference in the length of the vowels, the sound of the long one is in
no case the sound of the short one. By SOUND HAND, then,
we mean *where every vocal utterance in the language has its mark,
which mark is never used to express any other sound.* It is hoped
that now the reader will understand our meaning in saying, that
in this Stenographic Card the *English language* is WRITTEN AS
SPOKEN, a custom professed, as we have observed, by all short-
hand-writers, but practised hitherto by none. To produce only
one instance of their inconsistency, they dispense with *w & y* as
vowels, and yet write them for *au* in *saw, oi* in *boy,* &c. In this
system these two letters must never be used except when they
begin a syllable. Some words, former stenographers have been
utterly unable to write Ex. : *anguish* would be transformed into
an-gish, and it might be read *an-jish* in those authors who do not
thicken *g* for *j ;* to say nothing at present of the impropriety of
considering these letters relatives. The word is written in this
system by three simple marks, *ang-gwish,* as it is pronounced, (7 f).
This observation, however, does not properly belong to this
paragraph.

9. We come now to consider the *consonants.* It will be seen
in our alphabet that the sharp and flat letters *f v, k ga, p b, s z,
t d, ch j, sh zh, & th* TH, are made with one mark for each pair,
the only difference between them is, that in pronouncing the last
of each pair there is a greater pressure of the enunciative organs
than in sounding the first. This is very properly denoted on
paper by a *pressure of the pen.* That the same organs, and in
the same position, are required for their utterance, needs no
other proof than the pronunciation of the following words :

fowl vowel	ba*th* baTHe
cap (kap) gap	wafer waver
pear bear	class glass
dose doze	plush blush
tear dear	muscle muzzle
cheer jeer	try dry
rash rasure (pronounced razhur)	chump jump
mesh measure (pronounced mezhur)	e*th*er eiTHer

It has been objected that it is difficult to make the heavy strokes for the flat letters. This is admitted when they are written with a black-lead pencil ; and as to *b* and *ga*, with their compounds, when written with a pen. (The pupil must use the latter.) [Messrs. Mordan & Co. will confer a favour on the public by producing an *ever-flowing pen*, similar to their *ever-pointed pencils*.] But even if every flat letter were made with a light stroke, the inconvenience in reading would be very trifling. Ex. including them all, " Get wisdom, knowledge, and virtue ; and prize them as the greatest treasure." If this sentence were written under circumstances which prevented the making of heavy strokes, (as black lead pencil on ivory,) we should read it thus, " Puy wistom, knowlech ant firtue, and price *t*hem as *t*he kreatest treshur." No one could mistake the meaning of one word here. Stenographers have always classed two of these flat letters, *v* and *z*, under the same marks as their respective sharps. They have taken no notice of two others, flat, *sh*, (*zha*) and *th* (*dha* pronounced like *they*), writing the last syllable of *mission* (*mishun*), and *vision* (*vizhun*), alike ; and also using the same marks for *breath* and *brea*THe *;* and they have misclassed the letters of two other pairs, namely, *ga* (get) with *j* (jet), and *k* (keen), with *q* (queen). Certainly it is better to have a choice band of eight men, with regular pairs of arms, &c. right and left, than only six, two of whom have only one arm, one leg, &c., and two more are monsters with a leg sticking out at the shoulder, and an arm protruding from the thigh !

10. No apology can be necessary for the use of *double letters*, (see the latter part of Plate 1). In words which require more than one motion of the pen, they are used more frequently than the single letters of which they are composed. We have taken all that occur without a vowel between them, and which are consequently pronounced with one effort of the organs. Such combinable consonants have as good a claim to a place in the alphabet as *q & x*. The small vowels (*i & e*) placed among them, (*a & e*) with the single aspirated dentals, are to assist in pronouncing each as one syllable. In placing *q* (*kw*) and *x* (*ks*) in this class, which is their proper place, it was necessary to alter the sound of the former a little, because of its flat *gwe*. It has now the same sound as when pronounced in a word ; this should be the case with every letter. Whenever the short-hand letter *g* is mentioned, call it *ga* that it may answer to *k*. Whenever *h* is pronounced, call it *he*, like the personal pronoun. Perhaps some of our readers who are not accustomed to aspirate this letter in their reading and conversation, will pronounce it like the vowel *e*. Such persons must seek oral instruction on this point. The name *aitch* for a forcible aspiration is only one of many misnomers in the English alphabet. The rectification of the others, however, is left for another time. Without this alteration we should call

the first consonant in *cheer* by the same name as the first in *hear* !

11. DIRECTIONS.   Write every word according to its true pronunciation, and follow " Walker " till you have a *better* guide [d].   Be exact in the shape of the letters ; *f* or *p* not leaning sufficiently would be *t*.   To assist in acquiring their formation, construct a diagram like the one in Plate 2, several times, till you have a tolerably good circle, by making the *box* of the wheel first, then the *spokes*, next the *circles*, inner and outer.   Make it without ruler or compasses.   With the exception of *q* and *x*, all the letters which succeed each other in the language, can be joined by their respective shorthand marks, without taking off the pen.   Conjoin the whole thus : *bb, bd, bf,* &c. to *bzhr* (7 g..i.).   Then *db, dd, df,* &c. (8 a..c.).   The loop *s* is joined in this manner, *sp, st, sf, sk, sr, sm,* (8 d..i.).   The pupil may also run through the changes with the *stroke s*, making it up or down, according to convenience, *sb, sd, sf, sg,* (9 a..d.).   Further directions concerning this letter will be given n. 12.   The hooks of a few of the double letters must, in joining, be made less bent ; the worst examples are *rbl, pkr,* (9 e. f.).   Repeat a letter thus : *ff, mm, prpr.* (9 g..i.).   Many of the combinations thus obtained cannot be pronounced, but it will be well to do the whole for the sake of exercise, and to imprint the forms of the letters upon the pupil's mind.   When the conjunction of all the consonants is thus accomplished, begin to write sentences ; and here particular care must be taken in ascertaining the exact sound of every word.   The greatest difficulty will be to discover the vowel sounds, so as to write them according to the natural order in which they are placed in this system.   The difficulty will arise from this circumstance.   By education and custom we are taught to call the short sound of *a* short *e* or short *a ;* thus : *mate met, hate hat,* and so with every other vowel, *the short sound of it is found under another letter,* Ex. *seen sin, boat but, raw rot, pool pull.*   The reader will be assisted here if he remember to write the second vowel in this list for the first ; it is Walker's notation :

$\overset{1}{\text{Fate}}$	ā	$\overset{1}{\text{pine}}$	i	$\overset{1}{\text{tube}}$	u
$\overset{2}{\text{far}}$	ā	$\overset{2}{\text{pin}}$	ĕ	$\overset{-2}{\text{tub}}$	ŏ
$\overset{3}{\text{fall}}$	āū	$\overset{1}{\text{no}}$	ō	$\overset{3}{\text{bull}}$	ŏŏ
$\overset{4}{\text{fat}}$	ă	$\overset{2}{\text{move}}$	ōō	$\overset{3\,2}{\text{oil}}$	oi
$\overset{1}{\text{me}}$	ē	$\overset{3}{\text{nor}}$	ăŭ[e]	$\overset{3\,3}{\text{pound}}$	ou
$\overset{2}{\text{met}}$	ă	$\overset{4}{\text{not}}$	ăŭ		

After a time it will be found that it is much easier to *write by sound* in *every* case, than according to what is called by some misnomer, *orthography.*   Persons who have never learned any system of short hand, and are inclined to make an attempt at this, which is strongly recommended to them, should at first write every word in full, that is, as it is pronounced in good society. An example both of spelling and writing is given in n. 8. To adduce another instance, the Great Precept might be written by a beginner thus : " Thou shălt lŏv thǝ Lǎürd thi Gǎüd wēth āül thi hǎrt ǎnd thi nābŏr ǎz thisǎlf." After a little practice, many of the vowels may be omitted ; and every letter may represent two or three of the commonest words, and sometimes a prefix, or an affix. To the double letters only *one* word is appropriated, (see Plate 1.). The same example written by this rule would be reduced from 49 marks to 22.

12. SHORT-HAND RULES. When a letter has two forms, which is the case with *l, r, s, & ng,* the first is for joining, and the other is to be used when such a letter stands alone for an alphabetical word, or without another consonant in the word ; Ex. of their use in the three cases ; *least, all, oil ; right, our, raw ; case, us, see ; among,* (*ng* is not used for an alphabetical word, but as a representative for *into* and *unto*) *owing.* (10 a..11 b.) In these circumstances the second mark must be used. Whenever *l* occurs with no other consonant following but *l, r,* and *s.* Ex. *loll, liar, lose, also, loller, lolls, laurel, liars, loser. R* with only *l, r, s,* and *ng.* Ex. *real, error, rose, ring, roller, rails, roaring. S* when repeated, when it is the only consonant in a syllable, and when followed by *l* or *ng* only. Ex. *assize, mercy, ascend, soul, sing.* Also use the stroke *s* whenever the other would cause ambiguity [f] or hinder the freedom of the writing ; in all other cases the *loop s* will be found exceedingly convenient. *Ng* must be made with the second mark when preceded by *p, sp,* and *y* only ; and when it does not end a word. Ex. *paying, sapping, young, anguish, ringlet, beings, flinging.* The pupil is requested to write all these words according to the rule. The small *ng* may be turned in any direction, it is merely a hook at the end of the preceding letter. The large *ng* is a thick *n,* but as this letter is never made heavy in a word for any other purpose, there can be no mistake here. *Spr, str,* and *skr,* may be made with one stroke, thus : *sprain, strong, screw* (11 c..e.). This will not interfere with *sp, st,* and *sk,* because when these letters begin a word, the loop is placed on the other side. (See n. 11.). *S* before and *w,* with which it will combine, may be made with the *oop* or *stroke.* The former plan is the best. Ex. *splinter, swing,* 11 f..12 a.). It may also be written with the *loop s,* and separate letters for *p* and *l.* When *s* comes before a double letter *in the middle of a word,* the double letter must generally be divided, or the *long s* made. The first is the preferable plan. Ex. *principle, nstruct,* (12 b..f.). *Possible, toaster, whisper,* &c. may be written with both the loop and double letter, (12 g..i.) *X* is nothing more than a stroke *across* the letter preceding or following. Ex.

maxim, sticks, (13a. b.) *Q* is a stroke *adjoined* to the letter preceding or following. Ex. QUEEN, *request.* (13 c. d.) Both letters should be made with a heavy mark when they have the flat sound. Ex. *exist* (egzist), *languish,* (13 e. f.) Let not *l* run into *m.* Ex. *lame,* (13 g..i.) Nor *m* into *shr, ch* into *n, th* into *ch.* Write *beyond* thus : (14 a.) *Y,* which is of difficult conjunction, seldom occurs except ·vhen beginning a word. When several down-stroke characters succeed each other, as in *statistics,* (14 b.) take off the pen and begin again. The beauty and lineality of the writing is thus preserved. This trifling inconvenience of stopping, in about one word in a hundred, which besets every system that has been, or can be invented, as it cannot be cured must be endured. Incipient vowels must commonly be written. Ex. *open, alter, altitude,* (14 c..e.) Without the first vowel these words might be read, *pen, letter, latitude.* A vowel between two consonants may be made either *after the first* or *before the last.* Ex. *mood, tune,* (14 f..i.) The rule is this : for *α, oo,* and *oi,* place the mark *before the last,* and put the other vowels generally *after the first mark.* When a long vowel comes between the double letters, as *o* between *b* and *l* in *bolster,* between *p* and *r* in *pardon,* always write the single letters. When double letters occur, with a short vowel between them similar in sound to the names of the letters in the alphabet, they may be used without scruple, as *per* in *permit, pur* in *pursuit, ter* in *clatter, cal* in *methodical.* Prefixes and affixes must not be joined to the other part of the word. Ex. *transact, wisdom,* (15 a. b.) Any alphabetical word or representative may be used for this purpose. Ex. *childhood, without, forward,* (15 c..e.) Prefixes and affixes need never be used except there is an advantage gained by it, either as to beauty or brevity. Ex. the words *distemper, comprehend, satisfaction,* and *indecision,* should be written WITH them ; and *discover, common, motion, decision,* WITHOUT them. Make a plural affix by adding the loop *s.* Ex. *professions, contents,* (15 f. g.) A prefix or an affix may be made in the middle of a word. Ex. *incomplete, missionaries,* (15 h. i.) Alphabetical words, when *nouns,* may express the plural number, and when *verbs,* the third person singular by adding the loop *s* only. Ex. *thoughts, comes,* (16 a. b.) The *second person singular* of the verb may be written as the *first,* without any danger of mistake. Ex. *Thou mayest,* (16 c.)

Write figures as usual ; high numbers may be abbreviated thus : 300—60,000—300,000, (16 d..f.) Ordinal numbers, with a dot above the figure, Ex. *second, third,* (16 g. h.) Adverbial numbers, with a dot under, Ex. *fourthly,* (16 i.) Numerals may occasionally be written as *words,* because they have a plural number, and the word *one* has a possessive case ; it should be written *won.* Put proper names in long-hand. Underline important words with a zig-zag line. Important sentences may

have a straight line.   See examples in the first " Rule of Life,"
n. 13.   Stops as usual, except the *period*.   Ex. comma, semicolon,
colon, period, exclamation. interrogation, irony [g] parentheses,
brackets, hyphen. quotation marks, (17 a..h.)   Contractions of
long words may be made by adjoining one letter to another, or
by making a comma under.   Ex. *notwithstanding, nevertheless,
indispensable, incomprehensible, satisfactorily*, (17 i..18 d.)
According to one of our rules, this first plan would frequently
make *q*, but as this letter never ends a word, there is no danger
of ambiguity here.   Another method of saving time is to join little
words together.   Ex. *as it is said, there are*, (18 e. f.)   Theological,
parliamentary, and law phrases, may be written by the initial
letters of the words joined to each other.   Ex. *kingdom of heaven,
His Majesty's ministers, practice of the court*, (18 g..i.)   These aids
will enable a writer to follow the swiftest speaker in the world
that is worth following.   Should other methods of abbreviation
be required by a slow writer, they may be found in short-hand
treatises.   It must be remembered that contractions are a license
granted to reporters only.   To conclude these rules (which cannot
be lengthened without producing *tedium*, nor abbreviated without
causing *obscurity*), give the letters their full shape, and in commencing, make them a quarter or even half an inch in length ;
the size may be reduced gradually to one-eighth or less, and if
they be properly formed, and sufficient vowels inserted to give the
sound, it is impossible that mistakes can arise.   Let the reader
practise the system, and he will find all difficulties vanish as he
proceeds ;   and with reference to one of the " babbling speeches
of this babbling earth "—the English, which is not the most
harmonious or consistent—he will be able to sing as he proceeds,

> " For every evil under the sun
> There is a remedy, or there's none ;
> If there *is* one, try to find it,
> If there's *not* one, never mind it."

13. THE LORD'S PRAYER. Our Father which art in heaven,
hallowed be thy name : thy kingdom come : thy will be done
in earth, as it is in heaven : give us this day our daily bread :
and forgive us our debts, as we forgive our debtors : and lead
us ; [h] not into temptation, but deliver us from evil : for thine
is the kingdom, and the power, and the glory, for ever.   Amen.
Mat. vi. 9-13.

PSALM 100. 1. Make a joyful noise unto the Lord, all ye
lands.   2. Serve the Lord with gladness ; come before his
presence with singing.   3. Know ye that the Lord he is God :
it is he that hath made us, and not we ourselves : we are his
people, and the sheep of his pasture.   4. Enter into his gates
with thanksgiving, and into his courts with praise ; be thankful
unto him, and bless his name.   5. For the Lord is good, his
mercy is everlasting ; and his truth endureth to all generations.

RULES OF LIFE. FIRST. To read *often*, and to meditate *well* on the WORD OF GOD. SECOND. To be always content and resigned under the dispensations of Providence. THIRD. Always to observe a propriety of behaviour, and to preserve the conscience clear and void of offence. FOURTH. To obey that which is ordained ; to be faithful in the discharge of the duties of our employment ; and to do everything in our power to make ourselves as universally useful as possible. Always to remember "The Lord will provide."

14. These three examples are written according to this system in the second plate. Compare them word by word with the shorthand copy. This will explain much more than several pages of letter-press. It proves the superiority of this system, that these specimens are written with 377 motions of the pen ; while Byrom's takes 555, Taylor's 458, and Lewis's 508 [i.] Add to this, that by neither of these authors, nor by any other, can the proper sound of the words be written ; and that here there are no arbitrary marks either used or needed ; but every word is written exactly as it is pronounced, with the common allowance of leaving out some vowels, and making every letter represent one, two, or three words. The average of the whole alphabet is less than two to a letter. Stenographers have hitherto split their science between a correct pronunciation of the language, indicated by simple and infallible marks ; and the anomalies of long-hand, in which "a *perfect knowledge of the letters* affords no *clue* to the sound of the word." To attain proficiency in writing this, or any other system, the pupil must practise half an hour, and, if possible, an hour a day ; and read over twice everything he writes. His constant motto must be, "PERSEVERE." He should keep out the elbow, and for short-hand, use short lines. In this system, when written by a reporter, there will be about as many *strokes* as *syllables ;* consequently the pen can easily keep pace with the tongue ; and if our language were written and printed by it, the labour and expense of education would be reduced 50 or 80 per cent. We should then teach a child to call *medicine f i z i k* (or more properly *f ĕ z ĕ k*), *fizik*, instead of *pe* p, *aitch* h, *wi* y, *es* s, *i* for i, *see* c, *physic* !

15. The writer is preparing a "Manual of Stenography," including an analytical sketch of the English language, and the application of it to short-hand characters ; also a scheme of an alphabet according to nature ; which shall be published another day if it is worthy of publication ; to ascertain which, this card, containing the *principles*, is thrown out as a *feeler*. The system required many schemes, and many experiments with the language, before it was brought to its present state. Forcible reasons could be given for the selection of every mark to express the sound to which it is appropriated ; some of them have appeared to former stenographers, consequently it will be found that the letters *f,*

m, *n*, *r* and *t*, are the same here as in some other systems. Let the attentive reader examine every letter, remembering that the commonest sounds must have the simplest marks ; and that those letters which frequently succeed each other, should have characters that run into each other without an angle ; and we presume he will discover that not one of them could be altered to advantage. With reverence be it spoken, that the characters *appear* to be adapted to the sounds, as though the circle, mathematically dissected, were contrived by the Great, the Wise, and the Benevolent Author of Nature to suit the English language ; a dot or a stroke to a sound. The coincidence appears in its most striking light, when we consider that there is not one sound unexpressed ; that not another character could be introduced without causing confusion ; and that every two or three consonants that will coalesce in the beginning of a syllable, as *pl*, *sm*, *str*, &c. are made with *one stroke*.

16. The short-hand placed above the Diagram, plate 2, is, " This alphabet contains sixteen vowel sounds, twenty-five single consonants, and twenty-four double ones ; total sixty-five letters, including every vowel sound in the language, and every combination of consonants that will commence a syllable, all drawn from this Diagram." The system must stand upon its own legs if it stand at all ; or, to change the figure, *it must roll upon its own wheel*, and if it sink into oblivion after a reasonable trial of its capabilities, it will be because it deserves no better fate. By the author it is practised and taught daily, without any inconvenience arising from heavy letters ; and after eight years' extensive use of the best system hitherto published, Mr. Taylor's (sometimes miscalled Harding's, and lately sent forth without any reference to Mr. Taylor's name) and an examination of many others, he hesitates not to say, it is as good again as *that*. This observation might certainly be spared for the sake of modesty, and also with regard to those readers who have learned Mr. Taylor's and will now give this a fair trial ; but we know well that, with many persons, stenographic perseverance is a rare virtue ; and the experiment, with its result, is here mentioned for their sakes. Among the author's pupils are more than twenty boys (in his school,) about the age of ten years ; and it may confidently be asserted that they could not have learned so easily any other system extant.

17. Never before were forty-nine consonants expressed by twenty-five marks, and sixteen vowels by four marks ; all as simple in shape as a *coach-wheel ;* and at the same time as expressive of the thoughts and affections as long-hand, with a saving of at least five hours out of six. And what is of more importance, *the marks are suited to the sounds, so that* WHEREVER A LETTER IS RELATED TO ANOTHER, EITHER BY ORGANIC FORMATION, OR BY BEING COMBINED WITH OTHER LETTERS, IT IS SIGNIFIED

BY ITS SHAPE. Still it is not sent forth as a *perfect* system. It strikes out a new path, especially as to the manner of writing the vowels. It is a wonder to the author that it *is* new, being so very simple and natural. The truth is, we are come upon the most *unnatural* period of the world's existence ; scarcely anything is in the order of nature, still less in the order of heaven ; and our language, as though partaking of the common declension (most appropriately termed *" the fall,"*) exhibits the sad spectacle of having almost every word pronounced contrary to the sound of its letters. As any change at the worst point must necessarily be for the better ; and as the world is now beginning to experience a *wondrous* change, we have the assurance that a bright period is opening up upon us ; order will be restored ; and according to the sure declaration of HIM who maketh " all things new," heaven will yet descend upon earth, and " wisdom and knowledge will be the stability of the times." The road here struck out, to assist in conducting to this delightful state, being *new*, will require travelling and repairing to constitute it a good one ; then, we doubt not, it will bear a comparison with any of the numerous paths leading to the temple of wisdom. Should it be denied that we have produced the *best* system of short-hand, it must be conceded that we have produced the *cheapest*.

18. In conclusion. Convinced as the writer is of the unspeakable importance of the art of writing, and more especially of shorthand, to man, while an inhabitant of this material world ; convinced also of the superior excellency of a language *written as pronounced*, above one, like the English, where the sound of the letters is continually at war with the sound of the words ; keeping in mind too the discoveries, the improvements, and the facilities of every description that characterise this new age ; he thinks he is not too sanguine in expecting, that, ere long, short-hand will be the common hand, in which the imperishable Word of God will exist no larger than a *watch* [j], and be as constantly used for the discovery and regulation of man's *spiritual state*, with reference to *eternity*, as the pocket chronometer is for the discovery and regulation of *time* with reference to *the present life*.

POSTSCRIPT.

WE did not intend to give the translation of the two brief shorthand sentences in Plate 1, but to leave them as an exercise of the reader's sagacity ; but as there is a superfluous dot in one of the words, which might cause a difficulty in reading it, it is thought necessary to give the long-hand here. " N.B. Each letter may represent the words, &c., placed to it." " Pronounce each as one syllable."

In Plate 2, fourth line, third word, the short-hand letter *l* should be *w* (will).

In " The Lord's Prayer," haloud should be halōd. This last error exists only in some impressions.

NOTES.

[a] To express this sound of *a*, called the middle or Italian *a*, we adopt the Greek alpha (α). The reader is to pronounce this letter, then, wherever it occurs, as in *far*, *father*, which is similar to the cry of a sheep, *baa*.

[b] Be careful to sound the vowels as in the preceding classification, n. 6. According to the usual practice, a *long* vowel has a *stroke* over it, and a *short* one a *curve*. *Th* (in italics), signifies the sharp sound, and ᴛʜ (in capitals), the flat sound. See the reason, for pronouncing the article *the thă*, in Walker's dictionary, under the word.

[c] There is one exception to this remark. Mr. Towndrow, who, it appears, is a transatlantic stenographer, has separate marks for the long and short vowels, but in his classification of them, he has followed custom, as in the above pairs, instead of following *nature*, as is done in this system. Mr. T.'s theory of short-hand appears to be little known in England. After a careful examination of it, we are led to say, that, on the whole, it is clogged with difficulties which appear to us insuperable.

[d] The reader is earnestly requested to peruse and reperuse this gentleman's " Principles of English Pronunciation," prefixed as an *Introduction* to his admirable " Pronouncing Dictionary." Should he be unacquainted, we mean *practically* unacquainted with this standard of orthoepy, this able exposition of the English language, he will read the present attempt to express it in short-hand without interest, and condemn it without scruple. From such critics may Heaven preserve us !

[e] This third sound of *o* (*nor*), is the same as the fourth (*not*), except that the hollow sound of *r*, necessarily lengthens the vowel a little.

[f] To give a case of ambiguity by using the round *s*, *ask* is written like *sack*, and *east* like *seat*. This is near enough for a reporter or even for private writing ; but if ever the system should be printed (the probabilities of which are greater than the probabilities of long-hand, 500 years ago), one of these rules must be added : make *s* with a stroke when it begins a word followed by a vowel ; or, make *s* with a stroke when a word begins with a vowel, followed by *s* and another consonant.

[g] Many have said that as there are notes of interrogation and exclamation, there should be one for *irony*. But no writer that the author is aware of, has given any. If this attempt to make a smile appear on paper, conveying at the same time an intimation that the words are to be taken in a contrary sense, be approved of, it may be adopted by the reader. The shape of the

note is something like that of a conceited puppet, with an empty noddle.

[h] The punctuation of this petition was suggested to the author by a friend. It appears preferable to the common mode for many reasons, for which, however, we have not room here.

[i] The following are the particulars :—

	Straight or curved strokes.	Loops	Strokes with hooks or dots.	Separate dots and marks.	Pen off for prefixes and affixes.	Two letters in one stroke.
Byrom ..	458	86		120	17	23
Taylor ..	395	97	24	71	32	8
Lewis ..	368	38	33	158		18
Pitman ..	326	37	84	68	18	17

In this calculation every author is allowed the full privilege of his alphabetical words, arbitraries, &c., and when a word is neither the one nor the other, all the consonants that are sounded are written, and when there is but one, and a vowel, *that* is put. The number of *other* vowels that have been counted may be seen in the specimens, plate 2. The fairest way of judging between the systems appears to be this :—Take the number of straight or curved strokes, and reckon every *loop, hook, dot*, or *taking off the pen* as equal to *half* a stroke. Deduct all the letters that follow as a continuation of the preceding letter. The result is, B. 546, T. 499, L. 464, P. 412. In n. 14 we have added the strokes to the separate dots, &c., deducting every two strokes made as one.

In the above table Mr. Lewis's separate loops for *s* are counted in the *first* column, because they require as much time as plain strokes. The loops in the *second* column are those that occur in conjunction.

The last column includes all double letters made by straight strokes, as *ff, tt*, and such strokes as *fn, nr*.

[j] This is no airy imagination, but a conclusion from these premises.

The Bible contains in round numbers 770,000 words. One of the best editions of the Holy Word, either for the pocket or the study is, without controversy, Mr. Bagster's " English Version of the Polyglott Bible." The type is sufficiently large (*nonpareil*, the same as is used in this card), and the paper excellent. If the worthy publisher will accept our judgment (the work is above our praise) we should say it is the best small bible in the world. Now, by *nonpareil short-hand* (if the printers will excuse the term,) fourteen lines of eighteen words each can be written in a square inch, = 252, or in a page of two inches square, 1008 words.

770 pages, therefore, would contain the Bible, and judging by the same work as a standard, these pages would occupy three-fourths of an inch in thickness ! Allow one-eighth of an inch all round for margin. Here then we have the WORD OF GOD quite large enough for reading, two and a quarter inches square, and three-quarters of an inch thick ! As it would be advisable to have all the proper names in long-hand, this would make the thickness seven-eighths of an inch. Success to the publisher who may undertake it !

APPENDIX II

THE EVOLUTION OF PHONOGRAPHY

IN the narrative of the Life of Sir Isaac Pitman given in the preceding pages, reference is made to the main features in the development of his system of Phonography. But to students of the art, to teachers, and to those interested in shorthand bibliography, a more minute description of the evolution of the system will, we believe, prove acceptable, and it is consequently here presented. It should be explained that the changes noted are those only which were actually made in the text-books issued in the successive editions, no account being taken of innumerable suggestions and experiments for the improvement of Phonography which were discussed from time to time in the shorthand periodicals, but were never incorporated in the system.

FIRST EDITION (1837).—The complete text of " Stenographic Sound-hand " is given in the immediately preceding pages ; the two illustrative plates appear between pp. 34-5. In this book the consonants were given in the order of the common alphabet in Plate 1, but they were grouped in pairs in the text of the work. The instances in which the signs were changed in the subsequent editions are indicated by small capital letters in the following list—

/ B, | d, \ F, ___ g, ✓ H, ⌐ J, — k, ⌠ l, ⌢ m, ⌣ n, / P, ⫽ r (up), °⌡ s, | t, \ v, ⌠ w, ✓ Y, °⌡ z.

To these were added—

⌠ WH, ⌐ CH, ⌠ SH. (th, (thee, ⌠ ZH, ⌣ ng.

Straight letters were hooked initially for l and r, thus ⌐ kl, ⌐ kr, and there were large initial hooks for ⌠ dw and ⌠ tw, and forms for ⟍ shr,) thr,) theer, and ⟍ zhr.

The vowel scale and diphthongs were as under—

˙	ee	‾	aw	ᶜ	ĭ	ᵛ	ou
˙	a	‾	o	ᶜ	u		
˙	ah	‾	oo	ᶜ	oi		

349

The short vowels were not shown in the plate, but instruction on their representation was given in the text, and was thus epitomized : " A *long* vowel is made with a *heavy* dot or stroke, and a *short* vowel by a *light* one."

The following arbitrary characters appear in Plate 1—

⊤ *kw,* ⊤ *gw,* ＋ *ks,* ＋ *gz,* used to represent *question (kw) ; language (gw) ; except (ks) ;* and *example (gz)* respectively.

Writers were recommended to " join little words together " (phraseography).

SECOND EDITION (January, 1840).—In Phonography (the " Penny Plate ") the consonants were arranged in phonetic order and paired (in accordance with a promise made by the author in the First Edition that he would subsequently publish an " alphabet according to nature "), while the significance attached to some of the signs was changed, as will be seen from the following list of consonants—

＼ *p,* ＼ *b,* | *t,* | *d,* / *ch,* / *j,* — *k,* — *g,* ＼ *f,* ＼ *v,* (*th,* (*thee,* ○) *s,* ○) *z,* ⌡ *sh,* ⌡ *zh,* (*l,* ∕ *r,* ⌢ *m,* ⌣ *n,* ⌣ *ng,* ＼ *h.*

The consonant signs for *w* and *y* were discontinued, also the hooked forms for *tw, dw,* and *wh,* and the four arbitrary characters for *kw, gw, ks,* and *gz.*

Small initial hooks for *l* and *r* were added to curved consonants thus : ＼ *fl,* ＼ *fr,* and the thickened sign (was allotted to *lr,* the heavy sign ＼ to *hr* and *m* was thickened thus, ⌢ for *mp,* while ⌢ represented *mr* and ⌣ *nr.*

Final hooks which add *l* or *r* were introduced read *before* the stem letter, thus,

＼ *pl.* ＼ *lp ;* ＼ *pr,* ＼ *rp ;* ＼ *fl,* ＼ *lf ;* ＼ *fr,* ＼ *rf.*

The halving principle was introduced, thus, ＼ *p,* ＼ *pt ;* ＼ *b,* ＼ *bd,* but with the following and some other irregular applications :

) *tn,*) *dn,* ⌡ *chn,* ⌡ *jn,* ＼ *fn,* ＼ *vn,* ⌢ *kn,* ⌢ *gn,* (*nt,* (*nd.* Under this principle *Phonography* was written ⌣ the first

sign ⟍ represented *phono*, and the second the suffix for
-graphy.

The short vowel scale was illustrated thus : ⌐ i   ⌐ ŏ
⸱ e   -̣ ŭ
⸠ a   ⸜ ŏŏ

though different letters from those here shown were used to
indicate their significance. The following four angular double
vowels were introduced, namely, ᵛ⁞ *i*, ᵥ⁞ *ăō*, ^⁞ *oi*, ᴧ⁞ *ou*, and
four angular treble vowels, ᴸ⁞ *wi*, ∟⁞ *wăō*, ⁊⁞ *woi*, ¬⁞ *wou*. Some
of these characters were intended, the " Penny Plate " states,
to represent foreign or provincial sounds. The *w* and *y* series was

introduction : ᶜ⁞ *we*   ᵛ⁞ *ye*
ᶜ⁞ *way* etc.,   ᴶ⁞ *yay* etc., both long and short.
ᶜ⁞ *wah*   ᴶ⁞ *yah*

THIRD EDITION (September, 1840).—The consonant representation remained the same. The vowel signs were exhibited in
tabular form with the " Single or pure vowels " at the head, thus :
Long—*e, a, ah ; au, o, oo*. Short—*i, e, a ; o, u, oo*. Under
" Double Vowels " were shown the *y* and *w* series, and another
ᴸ⁞ series of angular signs, with some additions for foreign sounds.
There was a table of " Treble Vowels," including ᴸ⁞ *wi*, and a
series of fourteen signs for representing foreign and provincial
sounds.   These were indicated by the sign just shown, in different
positions, and by ᶜ⁞ *yae*, etc.

FOURTH EDITION (1841).—The termination *-shon* or *-tion* was
represented by a tick or a curve as ∟ ⌣ The angular
double vowels were reduced to three by the omission of *ao*, the
angular treble vowels to two by the omission of *wao* and *woi*,
and the *yae* series of signs omitted altogether from the body of
the work, and placed at the end, in an Appendix devoted to
" Foreign Sounds and Provincialisms."

FIFTH EDITION (1842).—The sign ⟍ was allotted to *r*, with
⟋ *r* as a duplicate sign (it was hooked ⌒ for *rch*), and the
signification of ⟍ was changed to *rl*. The aspirate was repre-

sented by a reversed comma, thus : ᶜ⁞ *he*   ⁾⁞ *haw*   When
ᶜ⁞ *ha*   �⁞ *ho*
ᶜ⁞ *hah* ⸲⁞ *hoo*

needful the aspirate mark was enlarged to the size of a consonant,
thus, ⸜ₒ *hew*.

Intersected and Contracted Words introduced; list of Phraseograms given.

SIXTH EDITION (1844).—This edition, in the form of a " Penny Plate," anticipated some of the improvements which were in preparation for the next (Seventh) Edition. The sign ⌐ was allotted to *rl*. The aspirate was now expressed by adding a dot to the following vowel, thus, `"|` *heat.*

The final hook was given the signification of *n* when on the left side of a straight consonant, thus, `↘` , and *shn* on the right side, thus, `↘` . A hook at the end of any curved consonant represented *n*. All consonants except *ng*, expressed the addition of *t* or *d* when half length.

The number of simple long vowels was increased by one and now ran as follows :

     `"|` *e,*   `·|` *a,*   `.|` *ah,*   `¯|` *au,*   `-|` *uh,*   `•|` *oh,*   `_|` *oo.*

The new vowel sign *uh* necessitated a similar change in the short vowels, and the addition of the following new signs in the *w* and *y* series, namely, `⌐|` *yo* and `ǃ|` *wo.*

Grammalogues were introduced, the first list consisting of *the, and, of, to, in, that, it, is, as, for, which, have, their, from, more, them, shall, upon, Lord, been.*

SEVENTH EDITION (1845).—The double consonant *lr* was represented by `ƒ` and `ƒ` and *rl* by `⌐` . The sign `⌐` was adopted as unhooked *vr*. The method of vocalizing consonants of the *pl* series was introduced.

The termination -*tion* following a curved consonant was represented by a large hook, thus, `⌣⌐` *nation.* Loops for *st* and *str*, and the *s-shon* termination were introduced, thus `↖` *stp*, `↘` *pstr*, `↖` *ps-shon.*

From this edition the list of Arbitrary Words given in the preceding six editions disappeared, an extended list of Grammalogues taking their place. Under the discontinued arrangement each single or hooked character had, in addition to its alphabetic name, assigned to it the representation of one or several words. The list had been greatly reduced in 1841.

EIGHTH EDITION (1847).—The use of *n* before the treble consonants introduced, thus, `↘` *inspiration.* From the vowel scale `-|` *uh* disappeared, and the sign henceforth represented *ō*.

From 1837 the second-place vowels, both long and short, had been written after the first when between two consonants ; in 1841 there was a rule that a second-place vowel could be written either after the first or before the last consonant. Now (1847) the rule was introduced that second-place vowels are written after the first consonant when long, as ˙⌐ *gate*, and before the second when short, as ⌐ *get*. " The length of a second-place vowel will thus be determined by its position, if it should not be indicated by its size."

NINTH EDITION (1852).—Consonant forms provided for *w* and *y*, namely, ⟍ *w*, ⌐ *y* ; also ⌐ for *h*, in place of ⟨ ; ⌐ *wl*, ⌐ *wr*, ⌐ *wm*, ⌐ *wn*. The writing of a curved consonant twice its usual size to express the addition of the heavy *thr* introduced.

Among the diphthongs ⌄| is re-introduced to represent *ai*.

TENTH EDITION (1857).—In this edition the order of the consonants was altered as follows : *k, g, t, d, ch, j, p, b, sh, zh, s, z, th, thee, f, v, l, r, ng, n, m.* The additional form ⟋ (down) was introduced for the consonantal representation of the aspirate, in addition to the character employed in the preceding edition.

The small final hook on the right side of a straight consonant, or above it, as in ⎩ and ⌐ was assigned to the representation of *f* and *v*, and *-tion* was indicated by a large final hook attached to a straight consonant, as ⎩ and ⌐ . The aspirated *w* was indicated thus, ⟍

The vowel scale was changed from ⋮| ēē / ā / ah to ⋮| ah / ā / ēē with the following explanation : " Experience has shown that the present arrangement is more in accordance with the laws of phonetic writing, and more convenient for the writer." Similar changes were made in the short vowels, and the *w* and *y* series.

The diphthong *ai* was altered to the following form ⌐|

ELEVENTH EDITION (1863).—The following additional consonant signs introduced : ⌐ for *w*, in addition to ⟍ ; ⌐ for *y*, in addition to ⌐ ; and for *h* ⌐ and ⟋ ; the tick *h* was also used as in ⌐ *hm*.

Large initial hooks were introduced to indicate the addition of *l* to curved letters and duplicate forms assigned as follows : ⟋ (down) ⌣ (up) *shr*, ⟋ (down) ⌣ (up) *shl ;* ⟨ ⟩ *thr ;*

⟨ fr, ⟨ fl ; ⌣ nr, ⌢ nl ; ⌒ represented mpr. The aspirated w indicated by a thickened hook, thus, ⌄ wh, in addition to the Tenth Edition form. The back hook for adding the prefix in- employed in ⟍ inscribe, ⟋ inhabit, etc.

The following changes were made in the diphthongs : ⌐ai, ⌐oi. The ⌐ ah-e series of disyllabic diphthongs introduced.

TWELFTH EDITION (1868).—The order of the phonographic consonants was altered as follows : p, b ; t, d ; ch, j ; k, g ; f, v ; th, thee ; s, z ; sh, zh ; m, n, ng. Only one consonant form was now assigned to y, namely, ⌐ , and ⌐ represented lr instead of ⌐ , which was assigned to wl.

After this issue " Editions " were discontinued.

1870.—The triphthong ⌐ wi discontinued. The signs ⌐ thl, ⌐ thl introduced.

1871.—The character ⌐ was assigned to wh ; ⌐ to wl, and ⌐ to whl. The sign ⌐ was given the significance of rch, rj.

1873.—In the list of Grammalogues ⌐ was substituted for ı to represent he.

1881.—The double-length principle was applied to a straight consonant when following another, as ⌐ conductor. (There was a preliminary introduction of the principle in 1879 at the end of " Key to the Reporting Exercises.")

1884.—The double-length principle was extended to straight consonants ending with hook, or circle ns, as, ⟍ printer, ⌐ counters.

1885.—In the list of Grammalogues ı replaces ⌐ for he.

1886.—It was announced that the perpendicular or horizontal tick for a " joined a or an " had been used for many years, but as it was found to clash in rapid writing with the joined tick for the, it was now given up.

1887.—The double consonant sw expressed by a large initial circle introduced, thus, ⌐ sweet, ⌐ swim. The triphthong ⌐ wi re-introduced.

1888.—The signs ⌐ thl, ⌐ thl discontinued.

1889.—The double consonant ⌐ rch, rj discontinued.

APPENDIX III

BIBLIOGRAPHY

I. SHORTHAND WORKS

MANUAL

Stenographic Sound-hand, by Isaac Pitman. London : Samuel Bagster, at his Warehouse for Bibles, Testaments, Prayer Books, Lexicons, &c., in Ancient and Modern Languages, No. 15 Paternoster row. Also sold by the Author, Wotton Underedge ; and by all Booksellers. Price four-pence. [The above is on the cover. The heading to the text is : " Short-hand, founded on ' Walker's Principles of English Pronunci-ation.' " The book consists of 12 pp. and 2 plates. Plate i. Vowel sounds, and single and double consonants ; ii. The " Wheel " diagram of characters, Examples, Lord's Prayer, Psalm 100, and Rules of Life. This was the FIRST EDITION, and consisted of 3,000 copies. (15th Nov., 1837.) 12mo.]

Phonography or Writing by Sound, being also a New and Natural System of Short-Hand. Invented and drawn by I. Pitman, 5 Nelson place, Bath. Price one penny. S. Bagster, 15 Paternoster row, London. [Post 4to, 8 in. by 6½ in., printed from an engraved steel plate, published simultaneously with the introduction of the Penny Postage, 10th Jan., 1840. The first issue had no reading matter down the left and right sides outside the rule. Along the bottom was the statement that " Any person may receive lessons from the Author by post at 1s. each to be paid in advance, etc." The second issue had the notice : " To purchasers of early impressions," etc., down the sides. The third issue had along the bottom the altered statement : " Any person may receive lessons from the Author by post gratuitously." The SECOND EDITION of the system.]

Mounted on canvas and bound in cloth, lettered, with two chapters from the N. T. (Rev. 21 and Mat. 5) as additional exercises [at the back], 1s.   London : S. Bagster, 15 Paternoster row, 1840.   Exercises in Phonography containing the above chapters was issued separately as plate No. 2, price 1d. [Eng. steel plate, 7 in. × 8½ in., folded in six.   Also the Second Edition of the system.]

Phonography, or Writing by Sound ; being a Natural Method of Writing applicable to all Languages, and a complete system of Short Hand.   By Isaac Pitman, 5, Nelson place, Bath. Entered at Stationers' Hall.   London : Samuel Bagster & Sons, 15 Paternoster row.   [Sept.]   1840.   Price 8d. ; cloth 1s.   [Demy 8vo.   24 pp.   This is Part I., consisting of Introduction, System, and Rules.   There was also an issue in Dec.   Part II., when published separately, was called Exercises in Phonography, or Writing by Sound, being a Natural Method of Writing applicable to all Languages, and a Complete System of Short Hand.   By I. Pitman.   London : Samuel Bagster.   1840.   Price 8d.   Demy 8vo.   15 pp. When bound together the second part was paged 25-38. Price 2s.   The Exercises were engraved on wood.   The diagram shown below appeared on the title page and, when bound, on the cloth cover of these books.   Whether single or together, the parts were the THIRD EDITION.]

Title Page and 11 pages of Part I.   Printed on 'a large sheet. Bagster & Sons.   1840. Price 8d.

Twelve Pages of Part II., or the Exercises printed on a large sheet.   Bagster & Sons, 1840.   Price 8d.

Phonography and Shorthand.   A Natural Method of Writing all Languages by Signs that Represent their Sounds.   By Isaac Pitman.   FOURTH EDITION, 50,000 copies [including previous editions.]   Price one penny.   London, Samuel Bagster & Sons, 1841.   [Demy 4to.   Letterpress and woodcuts, printed on both sides.]

Same as above.   Price threepence.   On pink enamelled paper ; a double sheet, printed on one side only.

Phonography, or Writing by Sound, a Natural Method of Writing all Languages by Signs representative of Sounds.   And a Complete System of Shorthand.   By Isaac Pitman, 5 Nelson place, Bath.   London : Bagster & Sons, 15 Paternoster row, 1842.   [Large 8vo.   Introduction, System, and Rules form a first part.   Sold separately.   To this was added a second part.   Examples cut in wood, 37 pp. in all, numbered 1-24 and 3-15.   This was a first issue of the FIFTH EDITION.]

Pocket Edition. Phonography, or Writing by Sound ; a Natural Method, etc. Fifth Edition, improved. Seventieth thousand. London : Samuel Bagster & Sons, 15 Paternoster row. 1842. [Royal 32mo. 64 pp., bound, price 2s. The cover bore the design illustrated on p. 71. The same work was also issued as a " People's Edition," in royal 8vo. (four of the small pages in one), price 1s. ; and as a " School Edition," royal 32mo., 24 pp., price 3d. See next two entries.]

A Manual of Phonography or Writing by Sound ; a Natural Method of Writing all Languages by one Alphabet, composed of Signs that represent the Sounds of the Human Voice : adapted also to the English Language as a complete system of Short Hand, briefer than any other system, and by which a speaker can be followed verbatim, without the use of any arbitrary marks, beyond the Letters of the Alphabet. By Isaac Pitman. Fifth Edition, improved. London : Samuel Bagster & Sons, 15, Paternoster row. 1842. [Royal 8vo. 16 pp. The same as the last entry, four pages in one. It is called the " People's Edition " on the paper cover. In some copies the title commences " Phonography, or writing by sound."]

(School Edition.) Abridged from the " Pocket Edition," for the use of British, National, and Charity schools. Phonography, or Writing by Sound, etc. Fifth Edition, improved. Eightieth thousand. London : Samuel Bagster & Sons, 15 Paternoster row. 1843. [Royal 32mo. 24 pp. 3d.]

Phonetic Writing. By Isaac Pitman. Price 1d., mounted 6d. Pitman, Bath ; Bagster, London. December, 1843. 5th Edition, 90,000 copies.

Phonography, or Phonetic Short Hand. Price, on plain paper, 1d. ; on card folded up as a book, 6d. Fifth Edition. Total number of copies, 90,000. [4to lith. sheet.]

Phonography, by Isaac Pitman. 5th Edition, 100,000 copies. [4to lith. sheet. Dec. 1843. Price 1d.]

A Penny Sheet of the First and Second Styles of Phonography. June, 1844. [4to sheet. Type and wood cuts.]

A Table of the Third Style of Phonography. SIXTH EDITION. London, June, 1844. 6d. [Royal 4to sheet, introducing the improvements of the Seventh Edition while the book was in preparation.]

A Table of the Second Style of Phonography. SEVENTH EDITION, March, 1845. Pitman, Bath. Bagster, London. [Royal 4to. Type and wood cuts. 3d.]

A Penny Sheet of the First Style of Phonography. Seventh Edition. April, 1845. Price 3d. Bagster & Sons, London.

A Manual of Phonography ; or Writing by Sound : a natural Method of Writing by Signs that represent the sounds of language, and adapted to the English language as a complete System of Phonetic Shorthand. By Isaac Pitman. Seventh Edition. Published by Isaac Pitman at the Phonographic Institution, 5 Nelson place, Bath ; and at the Phonographic and Phonotypic depot, 1 Queen's Head passage, Paternoster row, London. Edinburgh, John Johnstone, Hunter square ; Dublin, S. B. Oldham, 8 Suffolk street ; Paris, M. Degetau et Cie, 12 Place de la Bourse ; Boston, Andrews & Boyle, 339, Washington street. Sept. 1845. A " People's Edition," London and Bath, bore the date 1845. [Fcap. 8vo. This size was from this time adopted for the text-books. 64 pp. 1s.]

A Manual of Phonography, etc. By Isaac Pitman. With an Appendix on the application of Phonography to foreign languages. By A. J. Ellis, B.A. (Seventh Edition.) London : Samuel Bagster & Sons, 15 Paternoster row, Bath : Isaac Pitman, Phonetic Institution, 5 Nelson place. 1845. [64 pp. ; Appendix, 36 pp. 2s. The Appendix was also published separately, price 6d.]

Phonography, or Writing by Sound. By Isaac Pitman. Price 3d. Feb., 1847. Another issue, May, 1847. [Royal 4to sheet.]

Additions to Phonography supplementary to the Eighth Edition. 4 pp. letterpress and engraved shorthand. Price 1d. 5th March, 1852.

Rough draft of the Eighth Edition. 14 pp. of lithographed Phonography. 5th April, 1847.

EIGHTH EDITION. [Quotation from the *English Review* on title page, as given on p. 186 *ante.* This was continued down to 1894.] London : Fred. Pitman, Phonetic Depot, 1 Queen's Head Passage, Paternoster Row. Bath : Isaac Pitman, Phonetic Institution, 5 Nelson place. 1847. [72 pp., including 8 steel plates. 1s. 6d. The Appendix is discontinued.]

Seventh thousand of the Eighth Edition.
Ninth thousand of the Eighth Edition. 1848.
Eleventh thousand of the Eighth Edition. 1848.
Twelfth thousand of the Eighth Edition. 1848.
Fifteenth thousand of the Eighth Edition. 1848.
Twentieth thousand of the Eighth Edition. 1849.
Twenty-fifth thousand of the Eighth Edition. 1849.
Thirtieth thousand of the Eighth Edition. 1849.
Thirty-third thousand of the Eighth Edition. 1851.
Fifty-sixth thousand of the Eighth Edition. London : Fred Pitman, Phonetic Depot, 20 Paternoster Row. 1851.

NINTH EDITION.   One hundred and twenty-fifth thousand.   1852.
One hundred and thirtieth thousand.   1853.
One hundred and thirty-fifth thousand.   1853.
One hundred and fortieth thousand.   1855.

Circular letter on the Changes proposed to be introduced into the Tenth Edition.   [Small 8vo, 8 pp. in litho. shorthand. 7th Nov.   1857.]

TENTH EDITION.   One hundred and fiftieth thousand.   1857.

One hundred and fifty-fourth thousand.   1858.
One hundred and fifty-fifth thousand.   1860.
One hundred and sixtieth thousand.   1860.
One hundred and sixty-sixth thousand.   1861.

Supplement to the Ninth Edition.   [Fcap. 8vo, 4 pp. letterpress and shorthand.]   " Purchasers of the Ninth Edition of the Manual of Phonography are requested to paste these four pages in their copies after page 64."   March, 1861.

Rough proof of a new Edition of the supplement to the Tenth Edition, containing a new downward *r*.   4 pp. letterpress and shorthand.   Six editions (Nos. 1 to 6) issued in Sept., 1862.

ELEVENTH EDITION.   One hundred and seventieth thousand. 1862.

One hundred and seventy-seventh thousand.   1863.

Supplement to the Tenth Edition of the Manual of Phonography. [Fcap. 8vo, 4 pp. letterpress and shorthand.]   20th January, 1863.

One hundred and eightieth thousand.   1864.

One hundred and eighty-sixth thousand.   1865.   [The monogram given below appeared on the title page from this edition down to 1873.]

One hundred and ninetieth thousand.   1866.

TWELFTH EDITION.   Two hundredth thousand.   1867.

Two hundred and tenth thousand.   1868.

Two hundred and twentieth thousand.   1868. [Editions discontinued, this being the last bearing the words " Twelfth Edition " on the title page.]

Two hundred and thirtieth thousand.   1870.
Two hundred and thirty-fifth thousand.   1871.
Two hundred and fortieth thousand.   1871.
Two hundred and fiftieth thousand.   1872.

Two hundred and fifty-fifth thousand.   1873.   [Shorthand reading matter at end first printed from engraved type, in place of steel plates.]

Two hundred and sixtieth thousand.   1873.
Two hundred and sixty-fifth thousand.   1873.

Two hundred and seventy-fifth thousand. 1874. [The mono-
gram given below appeared on the title page from this edition
down to 1886.]
Two hundred and ninetieth thousand. 1875.
Three hundredth thousand. 1876. [64 pp.]
Three hundred and tenth thousand. 1877.
Three hundred and twentieth thousand. 1877.
Three hundred and twenty-eighth thousand. 1879.
Three hundred and thirty-sixth thousand. 1880.
Three hundred and sixtieth thousand. 1881.
Three hundred and seventy-sixth thousand. 1882.
Three hundred and ninety-fourth thousand. 1883.
Four hundred and tenth thousand. 1883.
Four hundred and twenty-fifth thousand. 1884.
Four hundred and thirty-eighth thousand. 1885.
Four hundred and fiftieth thousand. 1885.
Four hundred and seventieth thousand. 1886.
Four hundred and eighty-fifth thousand. 1886.
Four hundred and ninety-eighth thousand. Isaac Pitman and
Sons, 1 Amen Corner, London ; Bath : Phonetic Institute.
1887.
Five hundred and sixth thousand. 1887.
Five hundred and twentieth thousand. Proof of the Jubilee
Edition of the Manual of Phonography. 88 pp. 1887.
Five hundred and twentieth thousand. New Edition. 89 pp.
1888.
Five hundred and seventieth thousand. 1888.
Six hundred and fiftieth thousand. 1889.
Seven hundred and fiftieth thousand. Rough Proof. 87 pp.
London, Bath, and 3 East Fourteenth Street, New York.
1890.
Seven hundred and fiftieth thousand. 1890.
Eight hundredth thousand. 1892.
Eight hundred and fiftieth thousand. 1893.
Nine hundredth thousand. 1894.

[From the date last given Sir Isaac Pitman discontinued the
personal supervision of the issue of his works, and the present
Bibliography is throughout brought down to this point.]

Questions on the Manual.

Questions on Isaac Pitman's Manual of Phonography. Adapted
to the Ninth Edition. 1854. 3d. [16 pp.]
Questions. Tenth Edition. 1858 and 1860.
Questions. Eleventh Edition. 1863. 1864.
Questions. 1873. 1875. 1877. 1879. 1883. 1884. 1885.
Questions. New Edition. 1888. 1889. 1891. 1894.

Exercises on the Manual.

Exercises in Phonography : a series of Graduated Writing Exercises, illustrative of the principles of the art, as developed in the " Manual of Phonography." Adapted to the latest edition. [Compiled by William Silver, with introduction by Isaac Pitman. 1871. 1d. 16 pp.]
Thirty-sixth thousand. 1874.
Fifty-fifth thousand. 1876.
One hundred and sixth thousand. 1879.
One hundred and fourteenth thousand. 1880.
One hundred and fifty-sixth thousand. 1882.
One hundred and sixty-fifth thousand. 1882.
One hundred and eighty-first thousand. 1883.
Two hundredth thousand. 1884.
Two hundred and tenth thousand. 1884.
Two hundred and thirtieth thousand. 1885.
Two hundred and fiftieth thousand. 1886.
Two hundred and sixtieth thousand. 1887.
Two hundred and eightieth thousand. 1888.

Key to the Manual.

Key to Exercises in the Manual of Phonography. By Isaac Pitman. [Key to exercises in the New Edition of the Manual, chiefly in engraved shorthand. 31 pp.] 1888. 1889. 1890. 1891. 1892. 1894.

REPORTER.

The Reporter's Book, or Phonography adapted to verbatim reporting. [First edition.] Isaac Pitman, Bath. S. Bagster & Sons, London. 1843. [12mo. 36 printed and lith. pp.] 2s.
The Reporter ; or Phonography adapted to verbatim reporting. By Isaac Pitman. Published by Isaac Pitman, Bath and London. Sold by all booksellers, phonographic lecturers, and teachers. 1845. [Demy 8vo. 79 pp., partly lith.] 2s.
The Reporter. Second edition, 1846.
The Reporter's Companion : an adaptation of Phonography (as developed in the EIGHTH EDITION of the " Manual " of the system,) to verbatim reporting. By Isaac Pitman. Third edition. London: Fred. Pitman. 1849. [Fcap. 8vo. 88 pp. 2s. 6d.]
In the above edition the following quotation appeared for the first time on the title page (and was continued till 1894) :—
" Shorthand, on account of its great and general utility, merits a much higher rank among the arts and sciences than is commonly allotted to it. Its usefulness is not confined to any particular science or profession, but is universal ; it is therefore by no means unworthy the attention and study of men of genius and erudition."—*Dr. Samuel Johnson.*

The Reporter's Companion, etc. (as developed in the NINTH EDITION of the " Manual " of the system) etc. 1853. [8vo. 96 pp.]

Eighteenth thousand. Fourth edition. 1854.

Nineteenth thousand. 1858.

Twenty-first thousand. (As developed in the TENTH EDITION of the " Manual " of the system.) 1859.

Twenty-third thousand. 1860.

Twenty-fifth thousand. ELEVENTH EDITION. 1862.

Twenty-ninth thousand. 1863.

Thirty-fourth thousand. 1866.

Thirty-sixth thousand. TWELFTH EDITION. 1869.

The Phonographic Reporter, or Reporter's Companion : an Adaptation of Phonography to Verbatim Reporting. By Isaac Pitman. Thirty-sixth thousand. London and Bath. 1896.

Thirty-eighth thousand. 1869.

Forty-third thousand. 1870.

Forty-fifth thousand. 1871.

Fiftieth thousand. 1872.

Fifty-third thousand. 1873. [94 pp.]

Fifty-eighth thousand. 1874.

Sixty-third thousand. 1875. [96 pp.]

Sixty-ninth thousand. 1876.

Seventy-seventh thousand. 1877.

Eighty-fifth thousand. 1878.

Ninety-third thousand. 1880.

One hundred and second thousand. 1882.

One hundred and tenth thousand. 1882.

One hundred and eighteenth thousand. 1884.

One hundred and twenty-eighth thousand. 1884.

One hundred and thirty-third thousand. 1885.

One hundred and thirty-sixth thousand. 1886.

One hundred and forty-second thousand. 1886.

One hundred and fifty-third thousand. 1887.

One hundred and fifty-third thousand. 1887. Isaac Pitman & Sons, 1 Amen Corner, London, and Bath.

One hundred and fifty-ninth thousand. 1888.

One hundred and sixty-ninth thousand. 1888. [Enlarged edition. 112 pp.]

One hundred and seventy-second thousand. 1889. 2s.

One hundred and eighty-sixth thousand. 1890. London, Bath, and 3 East Fourteenth Street, New York.

One hundred and ninety-sixth thousand. 1892.

Two hundred and first thousand. 1893.

Two hundred and eleventh thousand. 1894.

Two hundred and twenty-first thousand. 1894.

Grammalogues and Contractions for use in classes. 1876. [8 pp. Frequently re-issued in subsequent years.]

Reporting Exercises.

Reporting Exercises : intended as a companion to the Phonographic Reporter, or Reporter's Companion. London and
Bath. 1872. [30 pp. in letterpress. Preface by Isaac
Pitman, who states that the exercises were compiled by
William Silver and that T. G. Johnson contributed the exercise
on the law phrases : " The publisher has inserted the ' Rules
for Writing *l* and *r*, added a short praxis on Intersected Words,
and made some other improvements."]

Reporting Exercises : A Praxis on the Phonographic Reporter,
or Reporter's Companion. Enlarged to 32 pp. Editions
appeared in 1877 and 1879. Enlarged to 36 pp. Editions
appeared in 1881, 1883, 1884, 1885, 1887, 1888, 1889, 1890,
1891, 1894.

Key to Reporting Exercises. In Pitman's Phonography. 1879.
[62 pp. Contains at the end an article on the extension of
the double length principle to straight letters—the first
appearance of the method in the text-books. In the issues
for 1883, 1884, 1886, 1887 and 1888 this article also appeared,
but was discontinued in succeeding editions.

Key to Reporting Exercises. In Pitman's Phonography. New
Edition. 1889. [64 pp.]

Other editions appeared in 1891, 1894.

Reporter's Assistant.

Reporter's Assistant (The) ; a key to the reading of the Reporting
Style of Phonography. 1867. [8vo. 86 pp. lith.]

Reporter's Assistant and the Learner's Guide to a knowledge of
Phonography (The) ; a key to the reading of the Reporting
Style of Phonography, and a Course of Lessons for learners
in Shorthand outlines. By Isaac Pitman. Second edition.
1883. [8vo. 79 pp., letterpress and engraved characters.]

Third edition. 1885.

Fourth edition. 1890, 1892. [80 pp.]

Phrase Books.

Phonographic Phrase Book (The), with the Grammalogues of the
Reporting Style of Phonography. By Isaac Pitman. 1858.
[Fcap. 8vo. 48 pp. The phrases were indicated in stenotypy.
This work succeeded two editions issued by T. A. Reed with
the permission and approval of Isaac Pitman.]

Subsequent editions in 1859, 1860, 1862, 1864, and 1866.

New edition. 1866. [100 pp., partly letterpress, partly lith.]

Also in 1868 and 1871. [96 pp., partly letterpress, partly lith.]

Phonographic Phrase Book (The). By Isaac Pitman. 1873.
[Fcap. 8vo. 48 pp. Phrases entirely in lithographed
shorthand.]

Phonographic Phrase Book (The), with the Grammalogues of the Reporting Style of Phonography. By Isaac Pitman. 1874. [48 pp. engraved shorthand characters.]
Subsequent editions in 1875, 1877, 1881, 1883, 1885, 1887, 1889, 1890, and 1893, the last named edition having an exercise on the phrases in letterpress, compiled by George Andrews.

Phonographic Railway Phrase Book (The). 1869. [20 pp. lithographed. In the preface Isaac Pitman expressed indebtedness to Edward Johnson and others in the preparation of the work.]
Phonographic Railway Phrase Book (The) ; an adaptation of Phonography to the requirements of Railway Business and correspondence. By Isaac Pitman. Second edition. 1872. [20 pp.]
Third edition. 1874.
Other editions, 1880 and 1884, 1889, 1892 (all litho.).

Phonographic Legal Phrase Book (The). An adaptation of Phonography to the requirements of Legal Business and Correspondence. 1882. [20 pp. Frequently re-issued in subsequent years.]

TEACHER SERIES.

Class-Book.

The Phonographic Class-Book. Pitman, Bath. Bagster, London. [Fcap. 8vo. 24 lith. pp. 1843. 6d.]
The Phonographic Class-Book. By Isaac Pitman. 1844. [24 pp. letterpress with shorthand characters engraved on wood.]
The Phonographic Class-Book. An improved edition, adapted to the FIFTH EDITION of Phonography. Bath : published by Isaac Pitman, at the Phonographic Institution, 5 Nelson place. London : S. Bagster & Sons, 15 Paternoster row. Sold by all booksellers, and by phonographic lecturers and teachers. 1844. [24 pp. similar to previous edition.]
The Phonographic Class-Book, adapted to the SIXTH EDITION of Phonography. 1844. [24 lith. pp.]
The Phonographic Class-Book. 1845. [24 pp. letterpress and wood engraved shorthand.]
The Phonographic Class-Book. 1846. [24 pp. similar to previous edition.]
The Phonographic Class-Book. 1847. [24 lith. pp.]

Exercises.

Exercises in Phonography. By Isaac Pitman. London : Bagster & Sons, 15, Paternoster row. Sold also by the author, 5 Nelson place, Bath, and by all booksellers. 1842. [12mo. 24 pp. lith. shorthand reading matter only.]

Exercises in Phonography. 1842. [8 pp. lith. shorthand reading matter only. Another work.]

Exercises in Phonography. 6d. 1843. [24 pp. lith. shorthand reading matter only.]

Exercises in Phonography. Designed to conduct the pupil to a practical acquaintance with the art. (Formerly called " The Phonographic Class-Book.") By Isaac Pitman. *English Review* quotation on title page ; see p. 186. London and Bath. 1847. Price 6d. [32 pp. letterpress rules with shorthand characters and reading matter engraved on wood.]

Eleventh thousand of the EIGHTH EDITION. London. 1848.

Fourteenth thousand of the Eighth Edition. 1848.

Sixteenth thousand of Eighth Edition, 1848.

Twentieth thousand of the Eighth Edition. 1848.

Twenty-fourth thousand of the Eighth Edition. 1848.

Twenty-fifth thousand of the Eighth Edition. 1848.

Thirtieth thousand of the Eighth Edition. 1849.

Fortieth thousand of the Eighth Edition. 1849.

Fiftieth thousand of the Eighth Edition. London and Bath. 1850.

Fifty-sixth thousand of the Eighth Edition. 1851.

Instructor.

The Phonographic Instructor. A new and improved edition of " Exercises in Phonography," designed to conduct the pupil to a practical acquaintance with the art. By Isaac Pitman. NINTH EDITION. Two hundred and third thousand. London and Bath. 1852. [Fcap. 8vo. 32 pp. The passage from Henry Sutton's " Evangel of Love," which forms the plate facing p. 287, is first quoted in this edition.]

Ninth edition. Two hundred and sixth thousand. 1852.

Ninth edition. Two hundred and fifteenth thousand. 1853.

Ninth edition. Two hundred and twentieth thousand. 1853.

Ninth edition. Two hundred and twenty-fifth thousand. 1854.

Exercises in Phonography. A course of Reading Lessons in Phonetic Shorthand. By Isaac Pitman. In accordance with the Ninth Edition of Phonography. 1853-4. [48 pp. wood engraved shorthand with letterpress key at foot, " supplementary to the Phonographic Instructor."]

The Phonographic Instructor : a Course of Lessons in Phonetic Shorthand. By Isaac Pitman. Ninth edition. Two hundred and thirtieth thousand. 1856.

TENTH EDITION. Two hundred and thirty-fifth thousand. 1857.

Tenth edition. Two hundred and fiftieth thousand. 1857.

Teacher.

New Edition of the "Phonographic Instructor." The Phonographic Teacher : a Course of Lessons in Phonetic Shorthand. By Isaac Pitman. Tenth Edition. Two hundred and fiftieth thousand. 1858. 6d.

Tenth Edition. Two hundred and sixtieth thousand. 1859.

The Phonographic Teacher. Tenth Edition. Two hundred and sixty-fifth thousand. 1860.

Tenth Edition. Two hundred and seventy-fifth thousand. 1861.

Tenth edition. Two hundred and eightieth thousand. 1861.

ELEVENTH EDITION. Two hundred and eighty-fifth thousand. 1862.

Eleventh Edition. Two hundred and ninety-fifth thousand. 1862.

Eleventh Edition. Three hundredth thousand. 1863.

Eleventh Edition. Three hundred and fifth thousand. 1863.

Eleventh Edition. Three hundred and tenth thousand. 1863.

Eleventh Edition. Three hundred and twenty-fourth thousand. 1864.

Eleventh Edition. Three hundred and twenty-fifth thousand. 1864.

Eleventh Edition. Three hundred and forty-fifth thousand. 1865.

Eleventh Edition. Three hundred and fifty-fifth thousand. 1866.

Eleventh Edition. Three hundred and sixty-fifth thousand. 1867.

TWELFTH EDITION. Three hundred and seventy-fifth thousand. 1868.

Twelfth Edition. Three hundred and eighty-fifth thousand. 1868.

Twelfth Edition. Four hundred and tenth thousand. 1869.

[Editions discontinued.]

Four hundred and twenty-fifth thousand. 1870.

Four hundred and thirtieth thousand. 1870.

Four hundred and thirty-fifth thousand. 1871.

Four hundred and forty-fifth thousand. 1872.

Four hundred and sixty-fifth thousand. 1873.

Revised Edition. Four hundred and sixty-ninth thousand. 1873.

Four hundred and ninetieth thousand. 1874.

Five hundredth thousand. 1874.

Five hundred and tenth thousand. 1874.

Five hundred and twentieth thousand. 1875.

Five hundred and thirtieth thousand. 1875.

Five hundred and fortieth thousand. 1875.

Five hundred and fiftieth thousand. 1876.

Five hundred and sixtieth thousand. 1876.

Five hundred and seventieth thousand. 1876.

Five hundred and eightieth thousand. 1877.

Five hundred and eighty-fifth thousand. 1877.
Six hundred and eighty-sixth thousand. 1879.
Seven hundred and fortieth thousand. 1881.
Seven hundred and seventy-eighth thousand. 1882.
Seven hundred and ninety-fourth thousand. 1882.
Eight hundred and tenth thousand. 1882.
Eight hundred and thirty-sixth thousand. 1883.
Eight hundred and fifty-third thousand. 1883.
Eight hundred and sixty-ninth thousand. 1884.
Nine hundred and fourth thousand. 1884. [Quotation from Henry Sutton discontinued after this edition.]
Nine hundred and twenty-fourth thousand. 1884.
Nine hundred and forty-fourth thousand. 1885.
Nine hundred and seventieth thousand. 1885.
Nine hundred and ninetieth thousand. 1885.
One million and thirtieth thousand. 1886.
One million and seventieth thousand. 1886.
Proof of Jubilee Edition. 1886, 1887. [Three editions.]
Jubilee Edition. The Phonographic Teacher : a Guide to a Practical Acquaintance with the Art of Phonography or Phonetic Shorthand. By Isaac Pitman. One million and one hundred thousand. Isaac Pitman & Sons, 1 Amen Corner, London, and Bath. 1887. [46 pp.]
One million one hundred and thirtieth thousand. 1887.
One million one hundred and seventieth thousand. 1887.
One million two hundredth thousand. 1888.
One million two hundred and twentieth thousand. 1888.
One million two hundred and seventieth thousand. 1888.
One million three hundred and seventieth thousand. 1889.
One million five hundred and twentieth thousand. 1890.
One million six hundredth thousand. 1891.
One million seven hundred and fiftieth thousand. 1891.
One million eight hundred and fiftieth thousand. 1892-3.
One million nine hundred and fiftieth thousand. 1894.
Second million. 1894.

Key to the Teacher.

Key to the " Phonographic " Teacher and to the " Exercises in Phonography." By Isaac Pitman. 1874. 6d. [32 pp. of lithographed shorthand and letterpress forming a key to the " Teacher " exercises and to the " Exercises " on the " Manual."]
Key to " Teacher " and " Exercises." 1879. [40 pp. of engraved shorthand and letterpress.] 1880. 1881. 1882. 1883. 1884. 1885.
Key to the " Phonographic Teacher." By Isaac Pitman. Jubilee Edition. 1887. 6d. [28 pp. of engraved shorthand and letterpress.] 1888. 1889. 1891. 1892. 1895.

Teacher Exercises, Etc.

Exercises in Phonography : A Series of Graduated Sentence Exercises, illustrating the Principles of the Art, as Developed in the " Phonographic Teacher." 1890. 1d. [15 pp. in letterpress. Compiled by G. H. Gunston, with introduction by Isaac Pitman. Also on cards. Numerous subsequent editions.]

Progressive Studies in Phonography. · A Simple and Extended Exposition of the Principles of the Art of Phonetic Shorthand as set forth in " The Phonographic Teacher," " The Manual of Phonography " and " The Reporter," intended for the use, principally, of self-taught students. [Fcap. 8vo. 104 pp. Edited by Isaac Pitman, who contributed a preface ; the compiler of the " Studies " was T. A. Turner. 1884.]

Subsequent editions in 1887, 1888, 1890, 1893.

Copy Books.

Phonographic Copy-book (The) : designed to conduct the learner, in three lessons, to an acquaintance with the principles and practice of Phonography, or writing by sound ; a new system of shorthand. By Isaac Pitman. Second thousand. 1842. Price 6d. [Fcap. 8vo. 16 pp., interleaved with ruled paper ; engraved characters and letterpress.]

Phonographic Copy-book (The). [With the phonographic alphabet on the cover.] London and Bath. (1849.)

Compends.

Summary of Phonography (A). By Isaac Pitman. Abstracted from the " Manual of Phonography." Small 8vo. 16 pp. 3d. 1868.

Compend of Phonography. 1862.

Compendium of Phonography (A), or Phonetic Shorthand, containing the alphabet, grammalogues, and principal rules for writing. By I. Pitman. 1864. One penny. [A folding card of 6 pp.]

Penny edition. For use in schools and as a pocket companion. A Compendium of Phonography, or phonetic shorthand ; containing the alphabet, grammalogues, and principal rules of writing. By Isaac Pitman. 1865. [4 pp.]

Compendium. 1866. [6 pp. folding card.]

Summary of Phonography (A), with the grammalogues and principal rules for writing. 1868.

Compend of Phonography (A). Fiftieth thousand. 1871.

Compend of Phonography (A).   Hundredth thousand.   1874.

Compend of Phonography (A), or Phonetic Shorthand ; containing the alphabet, grammalogues, and principal rules for writing. By Isaac Pitman.   Hundred and thirty-eighth thousand. 1880.

One hundred and seventy-fourth thousand.   1885.

One hundred and ninetieth thousand.   1887.

Two hundred thousand.   1890.

Two hundred and eighteenth thousand.   1891.

Two hundred and twenty-eighth thousand.   1893.

DICTIONARIES.

Phonographic Dictionary of the English Language.   Issued in the *Ipswich Phono-Press*, Aug., 1845, to Dec., 1846.   [Demy 8vo. 136 pp.]

Rough Draft of a Phonographic Vocabulary of the most Common Words in the English Language.   10 May, 1848.   [Fcap. 8vo.   40 pp.]

Phonographic and Pronouncing Vocabulary of the English Language (A).   By Isaac Pitman.   1850.   [iv. and 295 pp. Fcap. 8vo., alternately lith. and letterpress.   Written in accordance with the EIGHTH EDITION of Phonography.]

Second edition.   London.   1852.   [8vo.   iv. and 295 pp. Written in accordance with the NINTH EDITION.]

Third Edition.   By Isaac Pitman, Inventor of Phonography, or Phonetic Shorthand.   1867.   [Demy 16mo.   336 pp. lith.]

Draft of the Phonographic Dictionary.   By Isaac Pitman. Printed for private circulation.   1869.   [Crown 4to, 32 pp.]

Phonetic Shorthand and Pronouncing Dictionary of the English Language (A).   By Isaac Pitman, inventor of Phonography, a system of Phonetic Shorthand, based on the Sounds of Speech and the Science of Phonetics.   [Fourth Edition.] 1878.   [Crown 8vo.   vi. and 344 pp.   Engraved characters and letterpress, pronunciation in phonotypy and meanings in ordinary spelling.]

Phonetic Shorthand and Pronouncing Dictionary of the English Language (A).   By Isaac Pitman, inventor of Phonography, a system of Phonetic Shorthand, based on the Sounds of Speech and the science of Phonetics.   Fifth edition.   1883. [iv. and 277 pp., giving only shorthand forms with longhand spelling.]

Also in 1884

Sixth Edition.   1889.   [iv and 299 pp.]   1890, 1891, 1894.

HISTORY.

History of Shorthand. In the *Phonotypic Journal*, vol. vi., 1847, pp. 53-58, 213-218, 269-274, 282-292, 317-343, 349-382, 389-428 : including·16 lith. pp. of stenographic and phonographic alphabets.

History of Shorthand (A). By Isaac Pitman. Written in Phonography. 1852. [8vo. 167 pp. litho. shorthand.]

History of Shorthand (A). By Isaac Pitman. Reprinted from the *Phonotypic Journal*, 1847. Second edition. (Corresponding Style.) 1868. [8vo. 192 pp. litho. shorthand.]

History of Shorthand. *Phonetic Journal*, 1884, pp. 97, 109, 122, 134, 145, 158, 178, 181, 194, 206, 238, 250, 262, 265, 279, 292, 304, and 313.

History of Shorthand (A), by Isaac Pitman. Reprinted from the *Phonetic Journal*, 1884. Third edition. [193 pp. in letterpress, with litho. specimens and alphabets, and preceded by " A Brief Presentation of Pitman's Phonetic Shorthand," xvi pp.]

Also in 1891.

AMERICAN PHONOGRAPHIC TREATISES.—The following are the principal American authors who published Isaac Pitman's Phonography in treatises bearing their names : S. P. Andrews and A. F. Boyle (1845). J. C. Booth (1849). E Longley (1849). H. M. Parkhurst (1849). E. Webster (1852). A. J. Graham (1854). Benn Pitman (1855). J. E. Munson (1867). Eliza B. Burnz (1870). C. Haven (1875). W. W. Osgoodby (1877). D. L. Scott-Browne (1882). In 1893 the United States Bureau of Education published a Circular of Information on Shorthand which contained a large amount of information as to systems used, etc. The preface was contributed by Dr. W. T. Harris, Commissioner of Education, who wrote : " It will be seen in the chapter giving the statistics of instruction in shorthand in the United States, that the system mainly followed is that of Isaac Pitman. Few inventors within the last two hundred years have been so happy as he in discovering devices that have proved useful in practice and at the same time called forth universal admiration for their theoretic perfection. . . . It will be seen by the chronological lists of English and American authors of textbooks that very many systems have been published that are but slight modifications upon the system of Phonography."

FOREIGN ADAPTATIONS OF PHONOGRAPHY.—The following published adaptations of Phonography to the languages mentioned were made by the authors named during the lifetime of Isaac Pitman, to which period the list is limited : Bengalee, D. N. Shinghaw (1892). Dutch, F. de Haan (1886). French, P. Barrué (1881) ; T.A. Reed. (1882) ; J. R. Bruce (1888) ; T. Van den Bergh (1892). German, C. L. Driesslein (1886). Italian, G. Francini (1883). Japanese, Minamoto Taunanori. Malagasy, A. Tacchi (1888). Spanish, G. Parody (1879). Welsh, Rev. R. H. Morgan (1878).

II. BOOKS IN SHORTHAND CHARACTER.

The works mentioned below were produced from Isaac Pitman's lithographic transfers, except where described as engraved.

1844 Phonographic Reading Book (The), written in the Third [Learner's] Style. [Crown 8vo., 24 pp. See 1857.]

1844 Key to the Phonographic Reading Book [in letterpress].

1846 Sermon on the Mount. In Phonography written in an Easy Style for Learners. [16 pp.]

1847 Prize Essay. Phonographic Teacher (The). An Essay on the Best Method of Teaching Pitman's Phonography. By Sunergos (Corresponding Style).
Also " Written in Accordance with the 9th Edition " (1853). Third Edition (1867). Fourth Edition (1871). Subsequent editions were in letterpress.

1848 Laura ; Edward's Dream. By Miss A. A. Gray. [Small 8vo. 48 pp. Corresponding Style.]

1849 New Testament (The), and Book of Psalms (The). [Royal 32 mo. Corresponding Style. Issued together and separately.]
Other editions of the New Testament were issued by Isaac Pitman in 1853 (Corresponding Style) in 1865 (Corresponding Style) and 1869 (Easy Reporting Style). The first edition of the New Testament from engraved shorthand type, 368 pp. (Easy Reporting Style), appeared in 1886.

1850 Hart's Orthography, 1569. [Produced from a copy in the British Museum in shorthand and phonotypy. Litho. 78 pp. Corresponding Style.]

1853 Book of Psalms (The). [Fcap. 8vo, 143 pp. See 1876.]

1857   Phonographic Reader (The), a series of Lessons in Phonetic
Shorthand, TENTH EDITION. [Fcap. 8vo, 32 pp. engraved
shorthand, Learner's Style ; see 1877.]
    Also in 1858, 1860, 1862, 1864, 1865, 1867, 1869, 1870,
and 1871.

1865   Pentateuch (The), or five books of Moses. In Learner's,
Business, Corresponding, and Reporting Styles, each
opening of the book displaying one style. [Demy 8vo,
159 pp.]
    Another edition appeared in 1872.

1867   Bible (The Holy). In Corresponding Style. [Demy 8vo.
812 pp.]
    In 1872 The Old Testament was lithographed from
Genesis i to 2 Kings xviii, 25, and also the New Testament,
but this edition was never completed, and remained
unpublished.

1867   Book of Common Prayer (The). [Small 8vo. 250 pp.
Corresponding Style.]
    In 1869 a second edition appeared (Fcap. 8vo.). In
1887 the Book was printed in engraved shorthand type,
Easy Reporting Style [Fcap. 8vo. 296 pp.]

1867   Dairyman's Daughter (The). By Legh Richmond, M.A·
[Small 8vo. 96 pp. Corresponding Style.]

1867   Rasselas. By Dr. Johnson. Fcap. 8vo, 101 pp. (Reporting Style.)

1868   Macaulay's Biographies. [Small 8vo. 199 pp. Reporting Style. 126 pp., key in phonotypy.]
    In 1870 a Second Edition appeared. [Demy 16mo.
187 pp. Reporting Style. No key.]

1869   Debate on the Irish Church Bill in the House of Lords
(The), June, 1869. [Fcap. 8vo. 173 pp. Reporting
Style, with letterpress key to the introductory speeches.]

1869   Diet, by Dr. Lambe ; with a Preface and Notes by Edward
Hare, C.S.I. [Small 8vo. 176 pp. Corresponding Style.]

1869   Church Services (The). [Fcap. 8vo. 592 pp. Easy
Reporting Style.]
    In 1893 an edition from engraved characters was issued.
Fcap. 8vo. 935 pp.

1869   The Vicar of Wakefield : An Exercise in Phonography, in
the several styles of the Art, from the Learner's to the
Reporting Style ; to be written by the pupil in shorthand
from a typic representation of the shorthand form for each
word, by Isaac Pitman. [Fcap. 8vo. With a preface
containing the Rev. W. J. Ball's appreciation of stenotypy]
    In 1891 The Vicar of Wakefield was produced from
engraved shorthand, Corresponding Style. [Fcap. 8vo.
280 pp.]

1870 Macaulay's Essays. [Demy 8vo. 462 pp. Corresponding Style.]

1871 Pilgrim's Progress, Narrative only of the. [Small 8vo. 84 pp. Corresponding Style.]
   In 1876 an engraved edition was issued. [Fcap. 8vo. 176 pp. Corresponding Style.]

1871 Sexes Here and Hereafter (The). By W. H. Holcombe, M.D. [Demy 16mo. 155 pp. Corresponding Style.]

1871 Milton's " Paradise Lost." [Small 8vo. 280 pp. Corresponding Style.]

1872 Heaven and its Wonders. By Emanuel Swedenborg. [Demy 16mo. xlviii and 272 pp.   Corresponding Style.]

1873 Æsop's Fables, in words of one syllable printed in the Learner's Style of Phonography. [Fcap. 8vo. 48 pp. engraved.] Many subsequent issues.

1875 Self-Culture. By J. S. Blackie. [Fcap. 8vo. 92 pp. engraved.] 1882, 1892.

1876 Book of Psalms (The). [Fcap. 8vo. 160 pp. Corresponding Style. Engraved.]

1876 Selections No. 1 by Isaac Pitman in the Reporting Style of Phonography with Key. [48 pp. Engraved. There were succeeding issues in 1885, 1891, etc.]

1876 Selections No. 2. [48 pp. Engraved. No Key. Also in 1881, 1891, etc.]

1876 Extracts No. 1. In the Corresponding Style of Phonography by Isaac Pitman. Engraved. [48 pp.]

1876 Extracts No. 2. [48 pp.] Also subsequent issues.

1876 Extracts No. 3. [52 pp.] Also subsequent issues.

1877 Phonographic Reader (The). A Course of Reading Lessons in Phonetic Shorthand in the Corresponding Style with a Key. [Fcap. 8vo. New edition, with longhand key facing the engraved shorthand.]
   Many subsequent issues.

1881 Select Poetry in the Corresponding Style by Isaac Pitman. [47 pp. Engraved.]

1883 Selections No. 3.

1888 Easy Readings in Phonography. Printed in the Learner's Style of Phonography by Isaac Pitman. Selected from " Evenings at Home in Words of One Syllable." [48 pp.] Also issued in 1890 and subsequently. Engraved.
   Various other reprints were made from the engraved shorthand of the *Phonetic Journal.*

III.   PERIODICALS.

Phonographic Journal (The).   No. 1.   January, 1842.   Price 2d., or 3d. post-paid.   Editor, Isaac Pitman, 5 Nelson Place, Bath ; Publisher, Bagster, 15 Paternoster Row, London.   Fcap. 8vo. 8 pp. lithographed shorthand.   The first number of this monthly was printed at Manchester from the transfers of Isaac Pitman.   It was the first shorthand periodical ever published in the character of any system in this country.   In Vol. 2, beginning January, 1843, the size was increased to crown 8vo., and the number of lithographed shorthand pages to 12.   In Vol. 3, 1844, the size was increased to demy 8vo, 8 pp., and at the end of this year the periodical was discontinued under the above title and combined with the *Phonographic Correspondent*.

Phonotypic Journal (The).   Conducted by I. Pitman, Phono-graphic Institution, 5 Nelson Place, Bath.   Vol. 2, No. 13, January, 1843.   Crown 8vo.   24 pp.   This was a companion monthly periodical to the *Phonographic Journal*, was num-bered to correspond, and printed in the ordinary type.   The first article, which began as follows, explained its scope : " The title of this Journal has been chosen prospectively.   We have reason to hope that the time is not very distant, when it will be printed with phonotypes.   As the primary aim of the *Phonographic Journal* will be to attempt to introduce a quicker and briefer manner of writing than the one in common use ; so, the object of the *Phonotypic Journal* will be to attempt a similar beneficial change in the usual mode of printing." This periodical was enlarged to 16 pp., demy 8vo. in Vol. 3, beginning January, 1844, and from this date onwards a portion of the contents consisted of phonotypy, Vol. 6 being printed entirely in phonetic spelling, and subsequent vols. partially. In December, 1847, Isaac Pitman relinquished the editing and publishing to Alexander John Ellis.

Phonetic Journal (The), No. 1 January, 1848.   Price 1d.   Mr. Ellis announced this as " The successor to the *Phonotypic Journal*.   It is the same in size and price, but it is conducted by a different editor on a somewhat different plan and for a somewhat different purpose."   Mr. Ellis conducted the *Journal* throughout the year, and discontinued it in December, on the appearance of his *Phonetic News*.

Phonotypic Journal (The), Vol. 8, March to Dec., 1849.   Isaac Pitman re-started a new series of the same size as Mr. Ellis's late monthly, with the object of providing an organ for the Phonetic Society.

Phonetic Journal (The), Vol. 9, January, 1850.   From this time Isaac Pitman changed the title to the above as " more con-venient and progressive " than the old name.   The periodical was from this date issued fortnightly. On 3rd January, 1852, the *Journal* was enlarged and issued weekly at 1d. under the style of

Phonetic Journal (The), " To read and write comes by nature."— *Shakspere.* London : Fred. Pitman, Phonetic depot, 20 Paternoster row. [4to. 8 pp.] To Vol. xii., 1853 was added : " Conducted by Isaac Pitman, Phonetic Institution, Bath," and the Shaksperean motto was left out. With Vol. xiv., 1855, each number was increased to 12 pp. 1½d. A series of full-paged lithographed specimens of Phonography commenced with the number for 5th January, 1861 (Vol. xx.), and 16 pp. were given per number. 2d. The lith. specimens ceased soon after, but shorthand supplements were given instead, and in 1866 the price was increased to 3d. On 4th January, 1873, a new series was started, entitled

Phonetic Journal (The) : Published weekly. Devoted to the Propagation of Phonetic Shorthand, and Phonetic Writing, Reading, and Printing. No. 1, Vol. xxxii. New series, 1d. [4to. 8 pp.] Two pages were given of specimens of Phonography from engraved type. In 1875 (Vol. xxxiv.), the size was increased to 12 pp., and 4 pp. cover, four pages being occupied with engraved shorthand. At the commencement of 1887 (Vol. xlvi.), the magazine had the following title and description :—

Phonetic Journal (The). Published weekly. Devoted to the propagation of Pitman's Shorthand (Phonography), and Phonetic Reading, Writing, and Printing. Printed by Isaac Pitman & Sons, at the Phonetic Institute, Kingston buildings, Bath ; and published at their Phonetic depot, 1 Amen Corner, Paternoster row, London. [4to. 16 pp., including cover.] In January, 1888, the number of shorthand pages was increased to five. At the commencement of 1891 the size of the *Journal* was increased to 24 pp., and soon afterwards six pages of shorthand were given weekly. The whole of the above series of periodicals were edited by Isaac Pitman, with the exception of Vol. vii. (1848), the first which was called the *Phonetic Journal,* his editorship extending for a period of fifty-two years down to his retirement in 1894.

Phonographic Correspondent (The), No. 1, January, 1844. 3d. monthly, demy 8vo. 8 pp. of lithographed shorthand. From April, 1844, this periodical bore the title of the *Phonographic Correspondent and Reporter.* During 1845 it was the *Phonographic Correspondent ;* in 1846 *and Reporter* was added. In January, 1847, the title was altered to the *Phonographic Correspondent* only, and the size reduced to a small 8vo of 16 pp. At this date the portion entitled *Reporter* became *The Reporters' Magazine,* called " Vol. 4, No. 37," and at the same time there was started a new series of

Phonographic Correspondent (The). Edited by Isaac Pitman, and written in the First or Corresponding Style (also called Vol. iv., No. 37.) Price 2d. F. Pitman, London. [16 mo. 16 pp.]. This gradually became illustrated. The periodical was discontinued at the end of 1858.

Phonographic Correspondent (The). A supplement to the *Phonetic Journal*, edited and lithographed by Isaac Pitman. No. 1, January 7, 1871, 16 mo. 16 pp. In an introductory notice Isaac Pitman mentioned that "During the last seven years the shorthand supplement to the *Phonetic Journal* has with one exception consisted of a sheet of some book. . . . Our reasons for issuing these books thus at the rate of a sheet per week, instead of a shorthand periodical of miscellaneous subjects, was that some standard books in shorthand for reading practice were much wanted, and we could not lithograph both the books and the periodical. We have now secured the assistance of a shorthand lithographic writer who will renew most of these books (many of which are already out of print), and execute others, thus leaving us at liberty to write a weekly sheet of miscellaneous matter under the revived title of the *Phonographic Correspondent.*" This periodical was discontinued at the end of June, 1871.

Reporters' Magazine (The). Conducted by Isaac Pitman, Bath. Vol. 4, No. 37, January, 1847. 3d. Small 8vo. 16 pp. lithographed shorthand. This was a new series of the *Reporter* portion of the *Correspondent*, and was continued by Isaac Pitman down to the end of 1848. It was "intended only for the perusal of advanced phonographers." At the beginning of 1849 the title was altered to that of the *Phonographic Reporter*, and the periodical was edited and lithographed for the future by Thomas Allen Reed.

Ipswich Phono-Press (The). No. 1. August, 1845. 3d. Demy 8vo. 8 pp. of lithographed shorthand and 8 pp. of shorthand dictionary in each number. Edited by John King to Dec., 1845, when Isaac Pitman (who wrote the transfers throughout), took up the editorship. The last number appeared in December, 1846. With it was issued a notice that a new series of monthly phonographic periodicals would commence in the following year, namely, the *Phonographic Star* (Learner's Style), *Phonographic Correspondent* (Corresponding Style), and *Reporters' Magazine* (Reporting Style).

Phonographic Star (The). Conducted by John Newby, Friends' School, Ackworth, Wakefield. [A large phonographic star is here displayed.] Published by C. Gilpin, 5 Bishopsgate street Without, London ; afterwards by Isaac Pitman, 5 Nelson place, Bath, and Queen's Head passage, London. Price 2d. No. 1, March, 1844. [Small 8vo. 8 pp. monthly.] In the number issued December, 1846, the Editor announced that " He bequeaths its name to a new periodical about to be commenced by Isaac Pitman."

Phonographic Star (The), New Series, demy 16 mo. January, 1847. 16 pp. Conducted by Isaac Pitman, and written in the First Style of Phonography. At the end of the issue for December, 1851, appeared a notice stating that " With this number closes the *Phonographic Star*. So many duties devolve upon the Editor, who is also the lithographer, that he finds it necessary to relinquish this for some other engagement which would be of greater service to the cause of the Writing and Printing Reform.

Phonographic Magazine (The). No. 1, January, 1849. Small 8vo. Price 2d. Conducted by Isaac Pitman, Bath. Written in an Easy Reporting Style " at the rate of 100 words a minute." The last number appeared December, 1851. Isaac Pitman announced that he " is compelled to decline the work solely on account of his increasing labours in connection with the extension of Phonetic Writing and Printing, and inability to procure an assistant who combines the requisites of a good phonographer and a good lithographer."

Precursor (The). Published by Isaac Pitman for private circulation among members of the Phonetic Council. Demy 8vo. 8 pp. lithographed shorthand. Issued at irregular intervals from 7th October, 1844. The copy, No. 12, October 22, 1846, is described as " the last number of the present issue." Revived in 1850 and 1851 and later.

Phonographer (The). January, 1851. Demy 16 mo. 16 pp. " Devoted to the solution of the problem—to find the easiest way of writing legibly every word of the English language on the basis of the phonetic alphabet." It was printed for private circulation and sold at cost price, 2s. per annum. Issued irregularly. Discontinued in December, 1860.

Reporting Magazine (The). Vol. 1, Jan. to April, 1864. 16 mo., lithographed shorthand. The work terminated with the number for December, 1864, which closed Vol. 2.

Speler (The). Conducted by Sir Isaac Pitman, Bath. Vol. 1, No. 1, January, 1895. Monthly, ½d. Crown 8vo. 8 pp. Printed in the First Stage of the Spelling Reform. Engraved shorthand reading matter introduced in No. 10, October, 1895. Vol. 1 was completed with the issue for December, 1896. The last number was that for January, 1897.

IV. SPELLING REFORM TRACTS.

The orthographic reform, to the advocacy of which Isaac Pitman devoted so large a portion of his life, was chiefly promoted by means of leaflets and pamphlets ; a great variety appeared, and these were circulated in millions. They were known as " Spelling Reform tracts," and usually exhibited the phonetic alphabet with some explanatory matter, as an introduction to the essay or article advocating the reform. No attempt is here made to give a list of such publications.

In association with the above should be noted a volume entitled : " A Defence of Phonetic Spelling, drawn from the history of the English Alphabet and Orthography, with a remedy for their defects." By R. G. Latham, M.A., M.D., F.R.S. This was published in 1872, and Dr. Latham during its production stayed at Bath.

V. BOOKS IN REFORMED SPELLING.

Arranged according to date of publication. Except where otherwise stated the books were printed in full phonotypy.

1846   Milton's " Paradise Lost."
1849   The Book of Psalms (Authorized Version).
1849   Book of Proverbs (A.V.).
1850   The Holy Bible (A.V.). [Demy 8vo. O.T. 580 pp.,
        N.T. 164 pp.]
1850   The Psalms of David in Metre (allowed by the authority
        of the General Assembly of the Church of Scotland).
1850   A Thousand Gems of Thought.
1850   Longfellow's " Evangeline."
1850   The Bath Fables, by the Rev. Sheridan Wilson.
1853   Daily Bread from the Word of God.
1853   St. Luke's Gospel. Also a smaller edition in 1856.
1855   Lucy's Temptation.
1855   Outlines of Astronomy.
1856   An English Grammar printed phonetically.
1856   St. Luke's Gospel in Mikmak.
1856   The Acts of the Apostles in Mikmak.
1857   Tomi Plouman.
1857   The Book of Genesis in Mikmak.
1859   The Book of Psalms in Mikmak.
1860   A Triple (twelve gross) Gems of Wisdom on Moral and
        Spiritual subjects.
1868   The Trial of William Rodger.
1870   A Rhymed Harmony of the Gospels, by Francis Barham
        and Isaac Pitman (second edition published subsequently).
1870   The Writings of Solomon, etc., translated by Francis
        Barham.
1871   The Other Life, by William H. Holcombe, M.D.

1871   Our Children in Heaven, by William H. Holcombe, M.D.
1871   Conversations on the Parables of the New Testament, by Edward, Lord Stanley.
1871   The Wonderful Pocket and Other Stories, by Chauncey Giles.
1872   The Game of the Chesse (Second Edition).
1873   A Memorial of Francis Barham, edited by Isaac Pitman. Plea for Spelling Reform (A), Volume of tracts edited by Isaac Pitman.
1878   Emanuel Swedenborg, the Spiritual Columbus. (First Stage.)
1879   A Comprehensive Grammar of the English Language.
1879   Boys of Other Countries, by Bayard Taylor. Susan's Return to Her Old Home, by Katherine M. A. Cooper.
1880   Literary Ladder (The). By A. A. Reade. (First Stage.)
1880   The Vale of Brukli. (First Stage.)
1881   Gospel Epic (The), by Francis Barham and Isaac Pitman. Second edition.
1882   Life and Correspondence of Rev. J. Clowes. (First Stage.)
1883   Gladys, or The Story of Penbirth. (First Stage.)
1884   The Squire of Ingleburn, and what he did with the Lawson Arms, by R. Bailey Walker. (First Stage.)
1884   The Testimony of Jesus, by David Bailey. (First Stage.)
1887–8 Phonetic Readers. First, Second, Third, Fourth, Fifth.
1892   Elokiushon. A Paper red at the Litereri and Filosofical Institiushon, Bath, 18th November, 1892, bei Eizak Pitman. (First Stage.)
1892   The New Testament (Revised Version) with the readings recommended by the American Revision Company incorporated in the text. [This edition contains a preface by Isaac Pitman which states that " Bishop Taylor, of the American Methodist Episcopal Church, superintends above a dozen mission stations, with schools, on the Congo, and teaches the natives the English language by means of Phonetic Reading Books. A very large supply of this edition of the New Testament has been sent to him for use in the schools." This was the last book printed in full phonotypy. The type was set at Bath by an American missionary under the supervision of Isaac Pitman. Crown 8vo. 436 pp.]
1895   Contrasts and Parallels between the First and Second Christian Churches during the First Century of their Existence (First Stage.)
1895   Wesley and Swedenborg. Two Essays by Two Clergymen, American and English, on the two greatest religious men of the last century, with an introduction by Sir Isaac Pitman. [Fcap. 8vo. Printed in First Stage.]

1895 Reminiscences of the Early Life of Sir Isaac Pitman. [This work consists of a reprint of the correspondence in the *Intellectual Repository* of 1836 relating to the author's acceptance of the doctrines of Swedenborg. It has a preface by Sir Isaac Pitman dated Bath, October, 1895. Fcap. 8vo. Printed in First Stage.]

————

(It has not been found possible to include in the above Bibliography notices of an almost innumerable number of small productions and contributions by Sir Isaac Pitman to books and periodicals.)

INDEX

THE END

Printed by Sir Isaac Pitman & Sons, Ltd., Bath.

(2284)